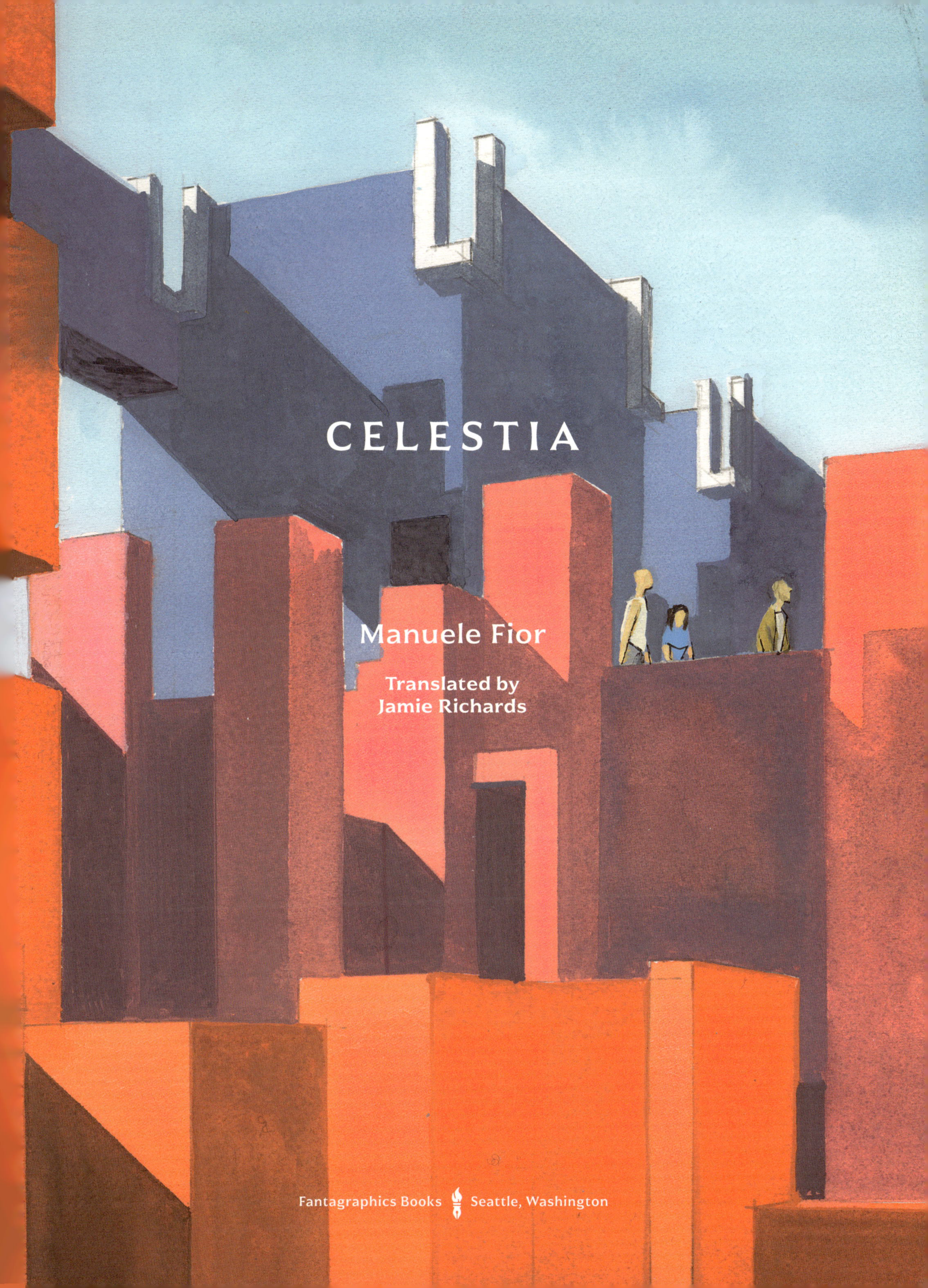

CELESTIA

Manuele Fior

Translated by
Jamie Richards

Fantagraphics Books · Seattle, Washington

"The boat's slow progress through the night was like the passage of a coherent thought through the subconscious."

—*Joseph Brodsky,* Watermark *(1989)*

*" [...] and before coming to Paris
to teach the joy of life,
before coming to London,
to teach being free,
before coming to New York,
to teach brotherhood—
they will destroy Rome
and on its ruins
plant the seed
of Ancient History."*

—*Pier Paolo Pasolini,* Prophecy *(1964)*

THE GREAT INVASION
CAME BY SEA.

IT SPREAD NORTH,
UP THE MAINLAND.

MANY FLED.
OTHERS TOOK REFUGE
ON A SMALL ISLAND.

AN ISLAND OF STONE,
BUILT IN THE WATER
OVER A THOUSAND YEARS AGO.

ITS NAME IS CELESTIA.

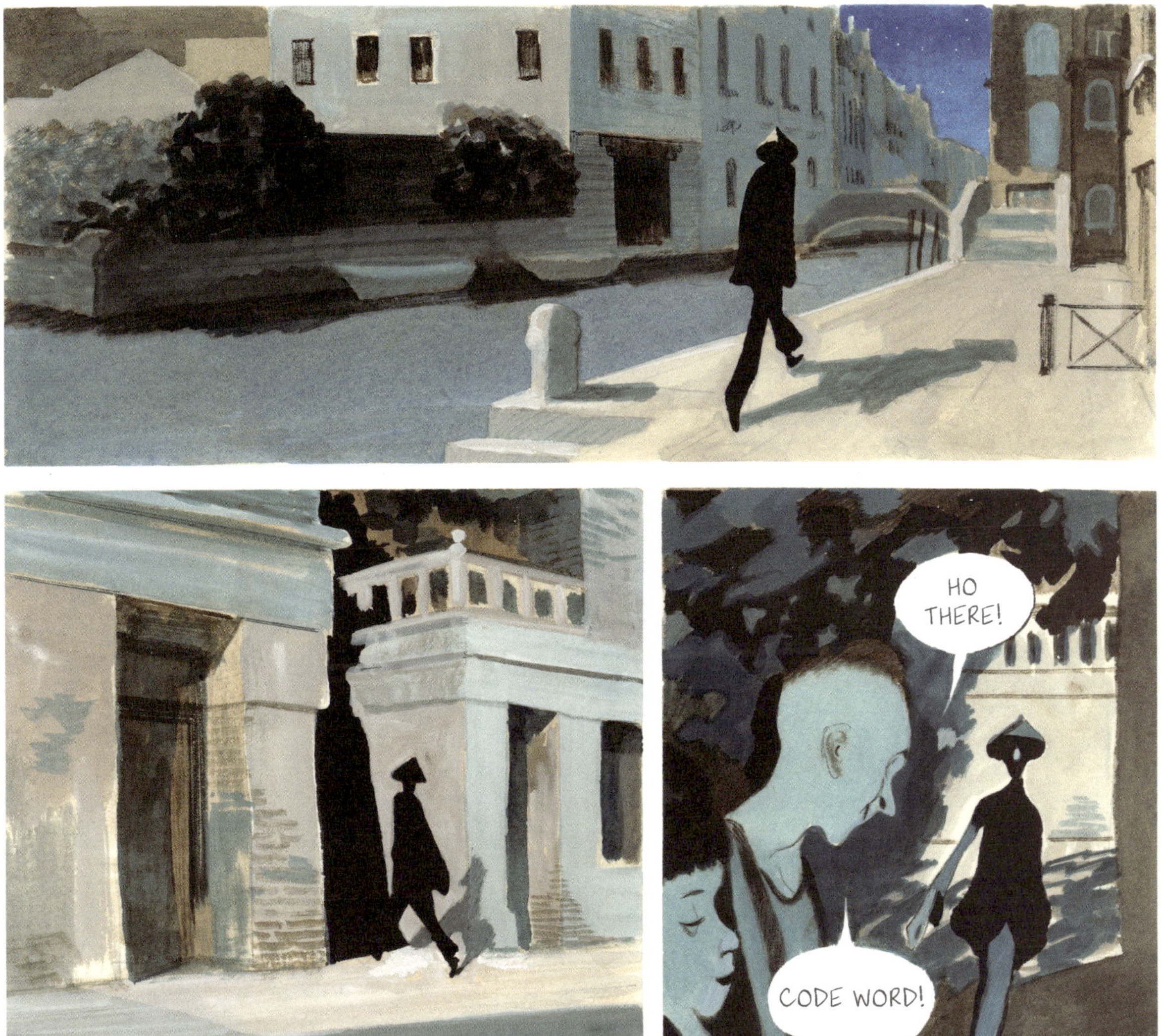
HO THERE!
CODE WORD!

READ IT IN MY MIND!
GO ON, GO ON...
SOMEONE SUMMONED ME.
WE DON'T KNOW ABOUT THAT...
HM.
WE'RE JUST ON LOOK-OUT.
OFF TO A GOOD START.
WE'RE WAITING FOR OUR EVALS...
GOOD FOR YOU.
HEH HEH!
IS ROSSELLA THERE?
YES.
AND DORA?

SHE DIDN'T SHOW UP.
SHE DIDN'T SHOW UP.
SHE KEEPS ODD HOURS, THAT ONE.
IN HIDING.
COY STARLING.
MYSTERIOUS VANISHING.

THE DOG BARKS.

THE CARAVAN PASSES.

GO AHEAD.

THANKS.

KNOCK KNOCK

PALLID FEVERISH FLOWER.

DISTANT FRAGILE FLASH.

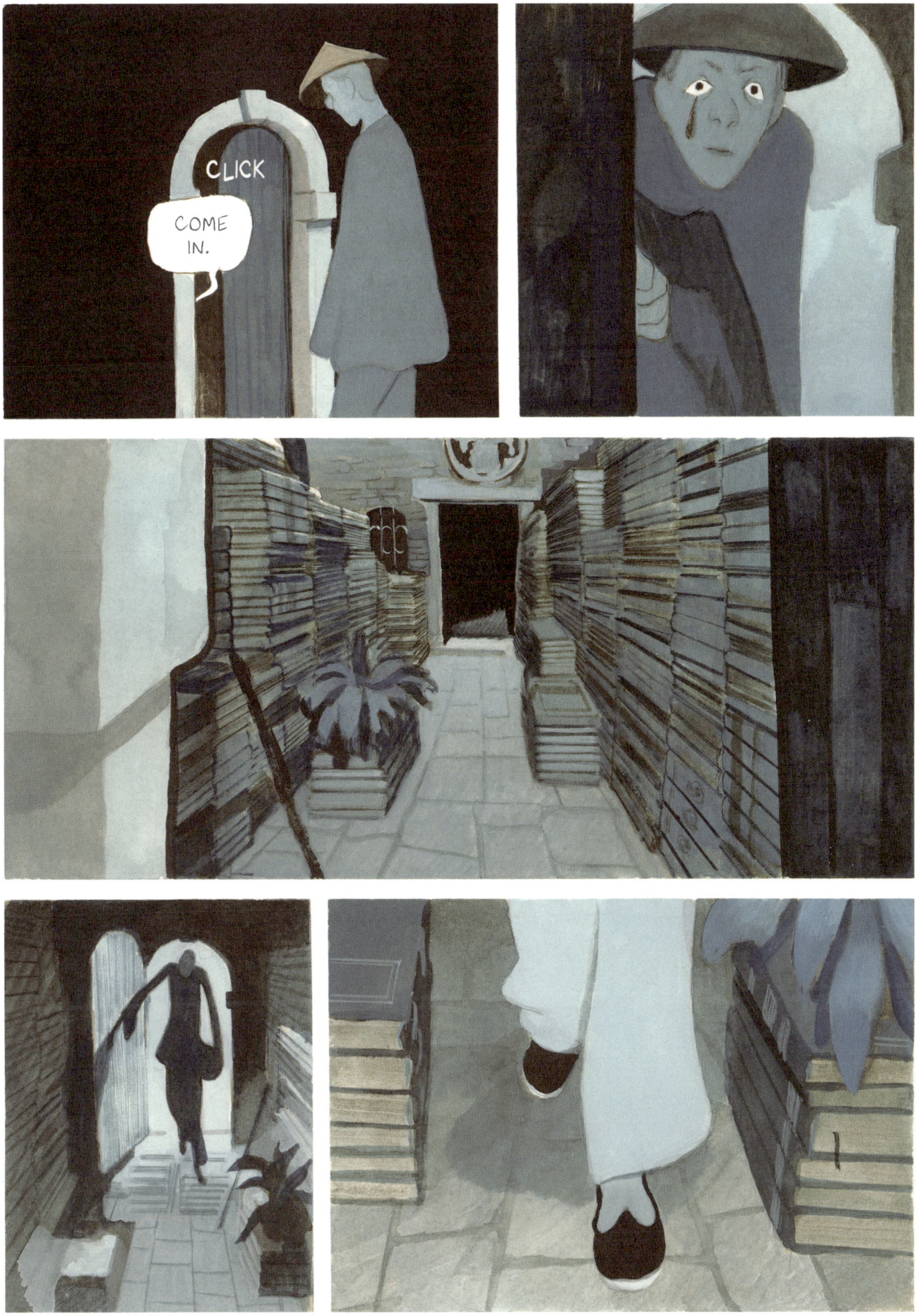
CLICK
COME IN.

LOOK RIGHT.

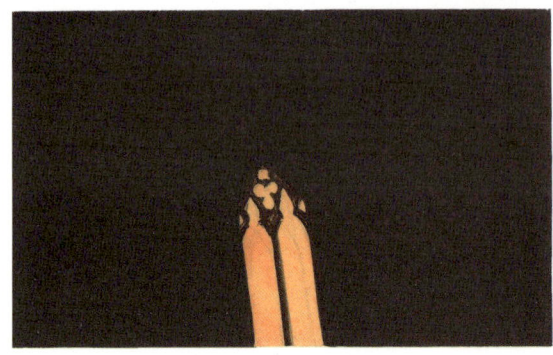

TURN LEFT.

PUSH HARD.

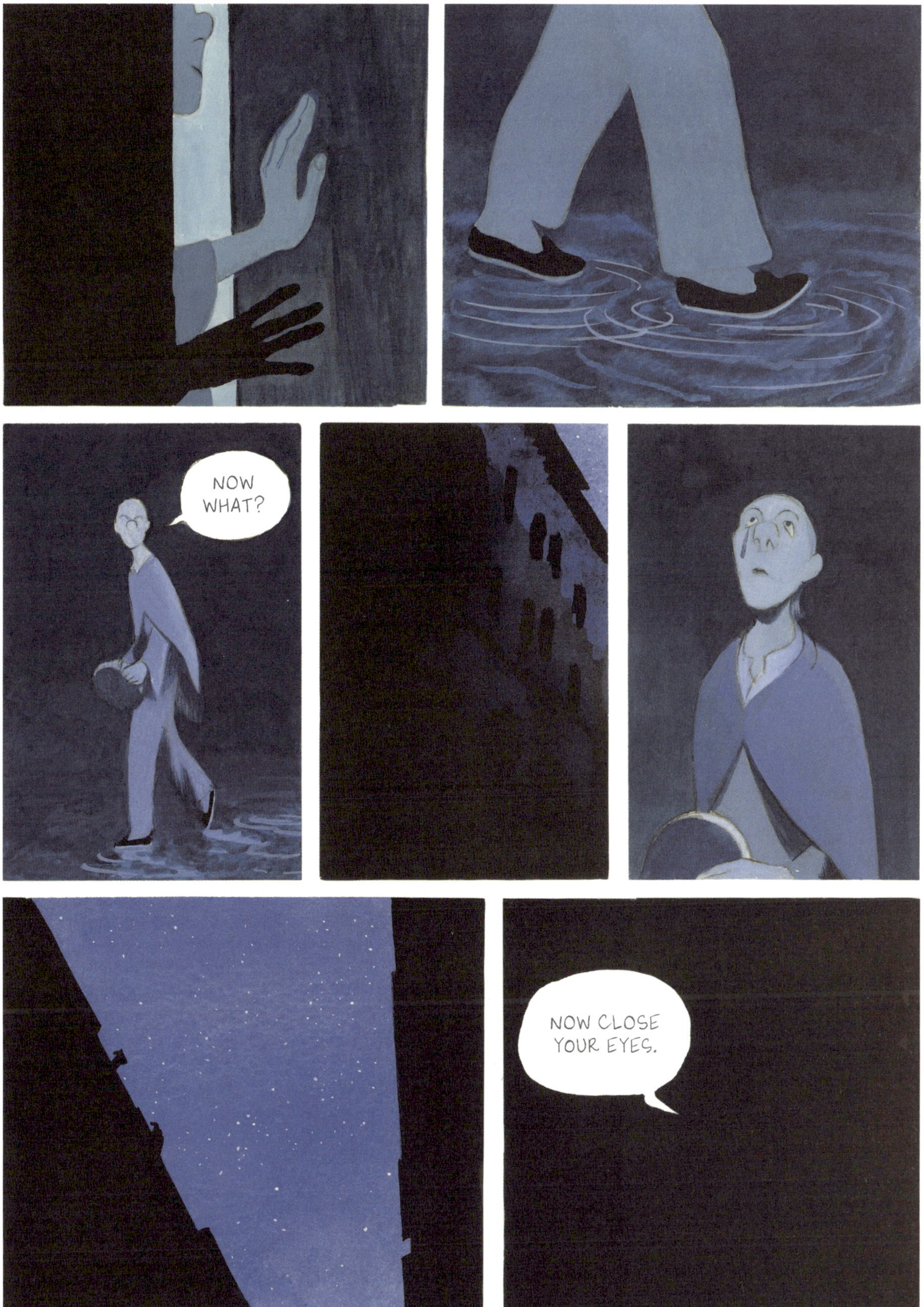
NOW WHAT?
NOW CLOSE YOUR EYES.

NOW OPEN THEM.
MY BOY.
I HAVE A FEELING, LIKE MILD NAUSEA.
DON'T WORRY, IT'LL GO AWAY SOON.
COME IN, PIERROT.
THANKS FOR COMING.
THE IMAGES YOU JUST SAW DON'T REALLY EXIST.
THEY'RE JUST A PRODUCT OF YOUR MIND.
AND THE WATER ON THE GROUND?
DID I DREAM THAT UP, TOO?

YOUR SHOES SEEM DRY TO ME!

ALL I DID WAS OPEN THE DOOR FOR YOU.

IT'S AN APTITUDE TEST WE USE WITH OUR NEW ARRIVALS.

YOU ARE CLEARLY QUITE GIFTED, AS ALWAYS.

CERTAINLY ABOVE AVERAGE. ISN'T THAT RIGHT, ROSSELLA?

Panel 1: ABSOLUTELY, DR. VIVALDI. NICE TO SEE YOU, PIERROT.

Panel 2: HEY THERE, DOLLFACE.

Panel 3: TONI GIANLUCA REBECCA GREETINGS TO ALL.

Panel 4: DORA'S NOT WITH YOU? I HAVEN'T SEEN HER FOR AT LEAST TWO WEEKS.

Panel 5: BUT SHE CAN'T JUST HAVE VANISHED INTO THIN AIR! AH, SO THAT'S THE REASON WHY YOU SUMMONED ME. AND HERE I THOUGHT YOU WANTED TO TAKE ME FOR DRINKS ON THE CANAL.

YOUR FRIENDS IN THE OLD GHETTO! THEY KNOW EVERYTHING THAT HAPPENS ON THE ISLAND!

TRUE.

BUT THEY'RE NOT MY FRIENDS.

THE VIEW'S SO NICE FROM HERE.

THE SAME AS WHEN YOU WERE LITTLE.

EVERYTHING HAS STAYED IN ITS PLACE.

CELESTIA REMAINS UNTOUCHED.

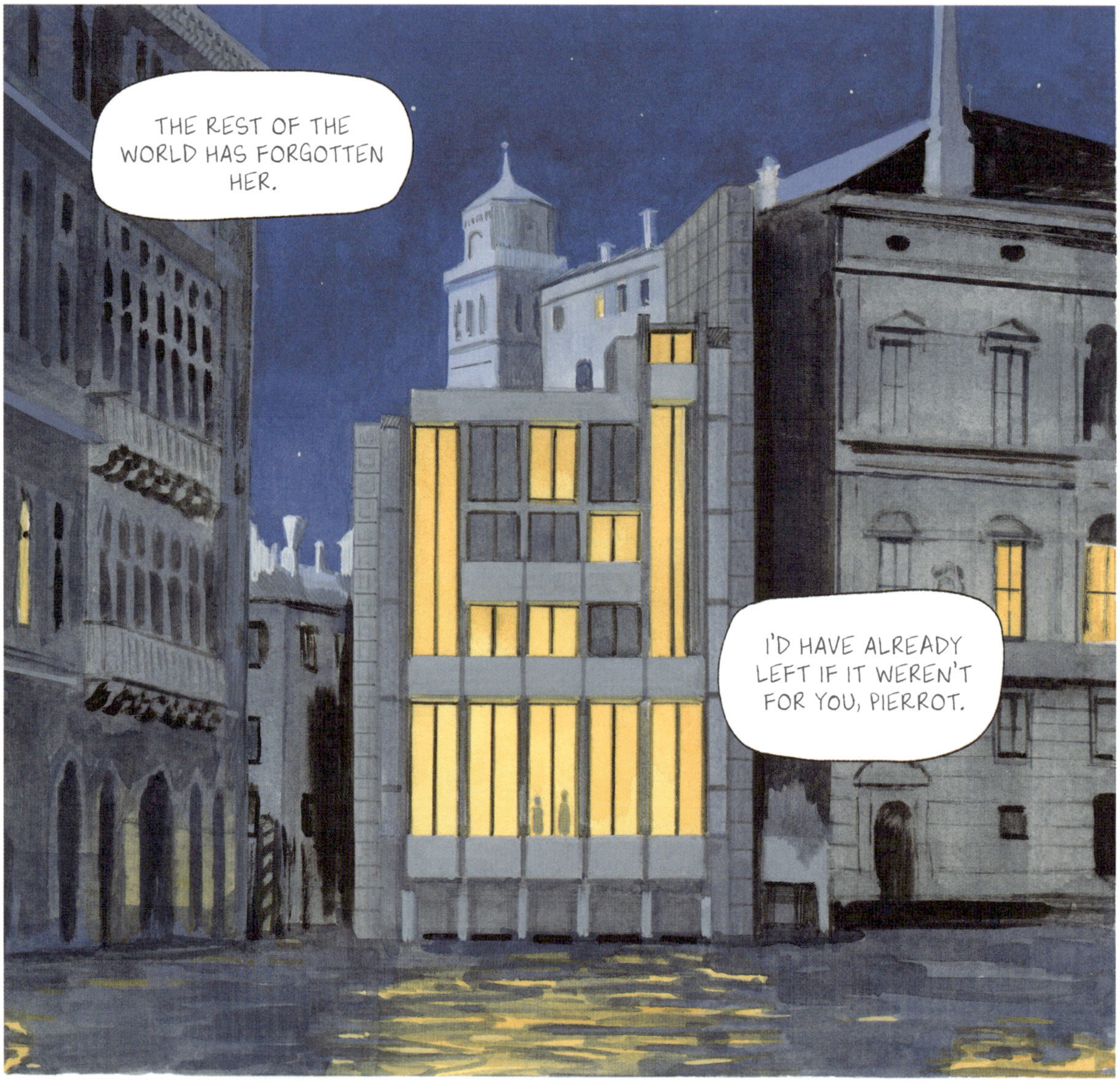
THE REST OF THE WORLD HAS FORGOTTEN HER.
I'D HAVE ALREADY LEFT IF IT WEREN'T FOR YOU, PIERROT.

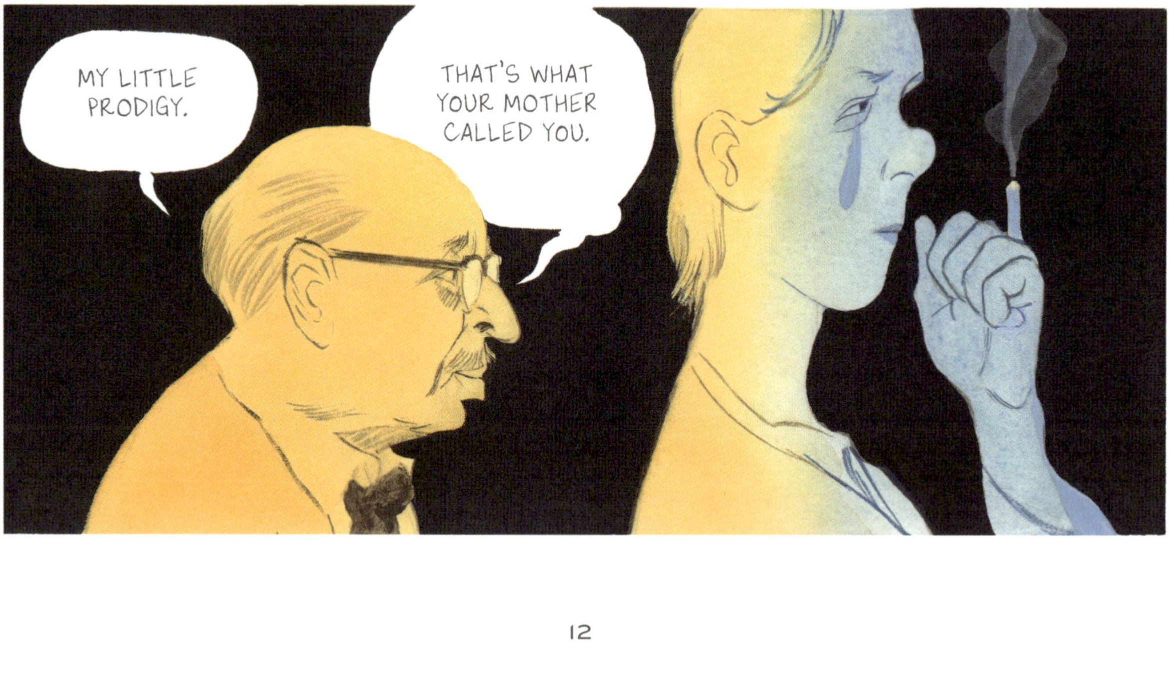
MY LITTLE PRODIGY.
THAT'S WHAT YOUR MOTHER CALLED YOU.

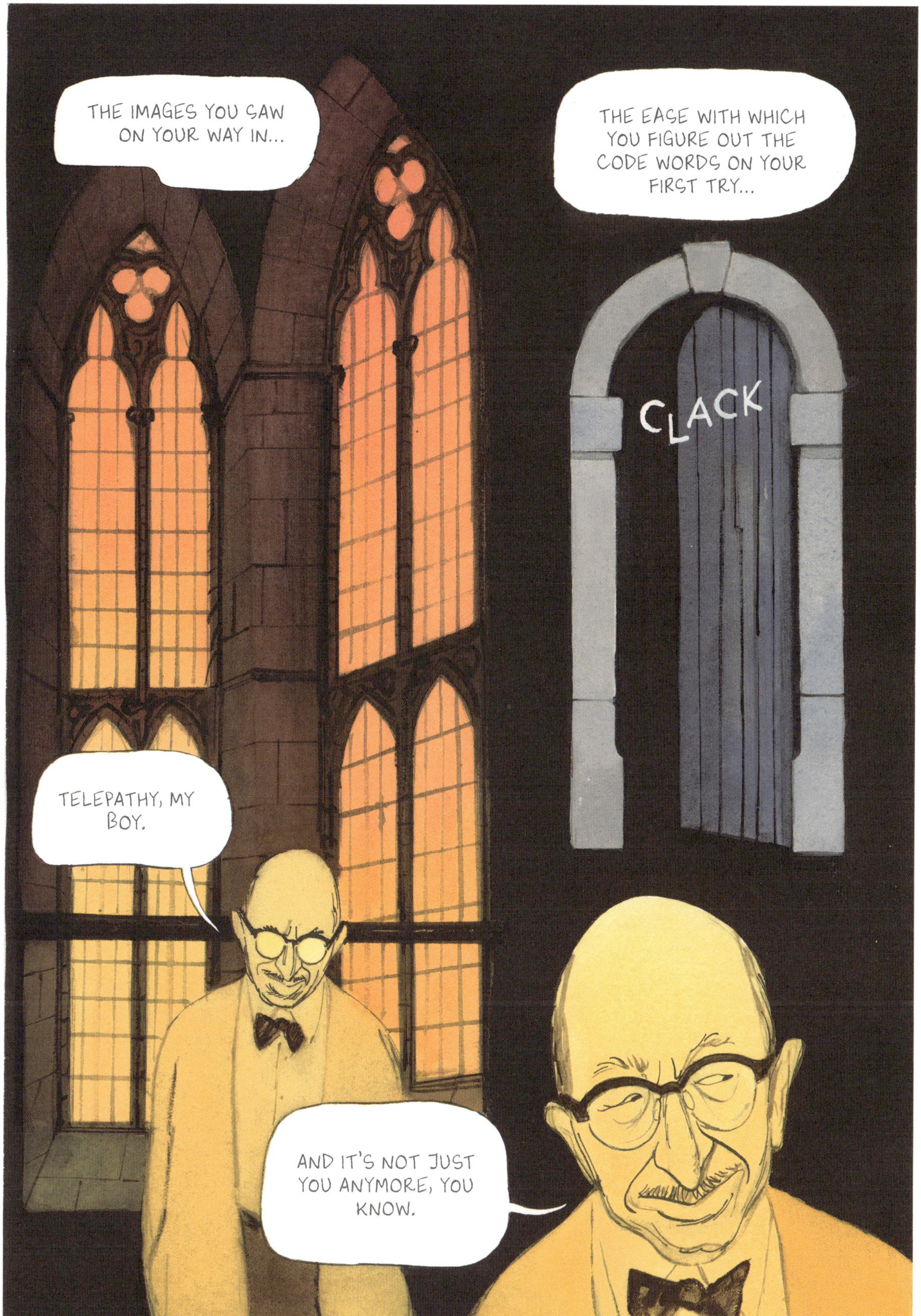
THE IMAGES YOU SAW ON YOUR WAY IN...
THE EASE WITH WHICH YOU FIGURE OUT THE CODE WORDS ON YOUR FIRST TRY...
CLACK
TELEPATHY, MY BOY.
AND IT'S NOT JUST YOU ANYMORE, YOU KNOW.

THESE KIDS ARE LIKE YOU.
YOU COULD LEARN SO MUCH TO-GETHER.
PIERROT.
IGOR!
YOU'RE STILL ALIVE?!
PIERROT.
SEE THAT?
HE STILL REMEMBERS YOU.
HOW ARE YOU, PIERROT?
HE HASN'T MADE MUCH PROGRESS...

WE, HOWEVER, ARE MAKING GREAT PROGRESS.
DR. VIVALDI HAS REALLY DONE SO MUCH FOR US.
WHY DON'T YOU COME BACK, PIERROT?
TRY ASKING THE BLACK-BIRD.
GOOD LUCK, EVERYONE.
THINK ABOUT IT.
I WILL.
BUT FOR NOW, THOSE DRINKS ARE CALLING...
DON'T BE A STRANGER.
AND IF YOU HEAR AT ALL FROM DORA...

"DOUBTFUL."

"I USUALLY KEEP TO MYSELF."

"UNLESS HE'S THE ONE HIDING HER."

"WOULDN'T SURPRISE ME, THAT PSYCHO."

"WHEN DARKNESS FALLS ON THE STREETS,"

"VAMPIRES CREEP TOWARD THE BED,"

"CHOKE YOU AGAINST THE OAK."

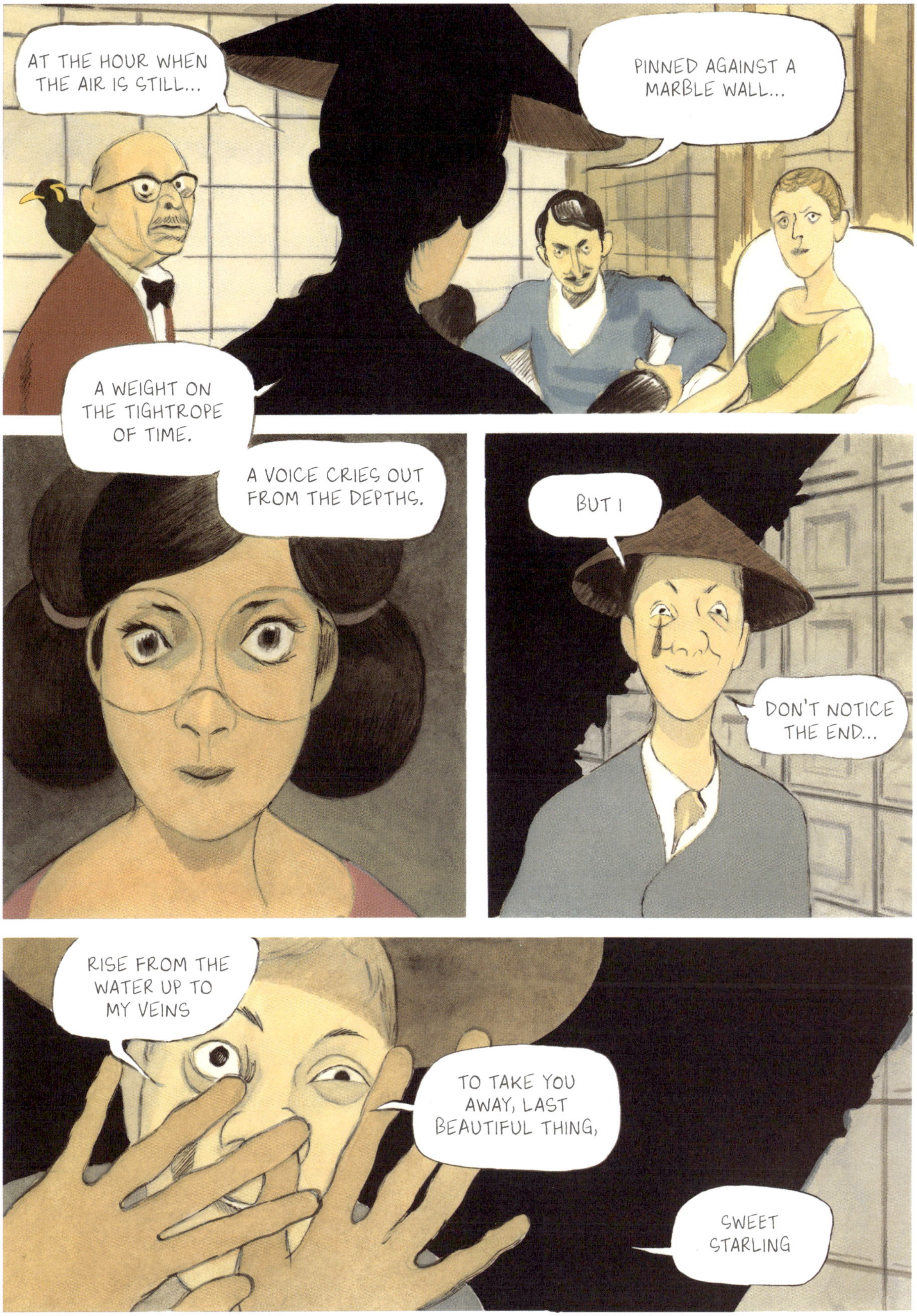
AT THE HOUR WHEN THE AIR IS STILL...
PINNED AGAINST A MARBLE WALL...
A WEIGHT ON THE TIGHTROPE OF TIME.
A VOICE CRIES OUT FROM THE DEPTHS.
BUT I
DON'T NOTICE THE END...
RISE FROM THE WATER UP TO MY VEINS
TO TAKE YOU AWAY, LAST BEAUTIFUL THING,
SWEET STARLING

NOT A WORD ON THE DEAD!

I STAY.

LEST THE SILENCE HELP HIM ALONG.

NICE POEM.

I DIDN'T UNDERSTAND A THING.

IT'S NOT A POEM.

IT'S AN OMEN.

CELESTIA

CELESTIA

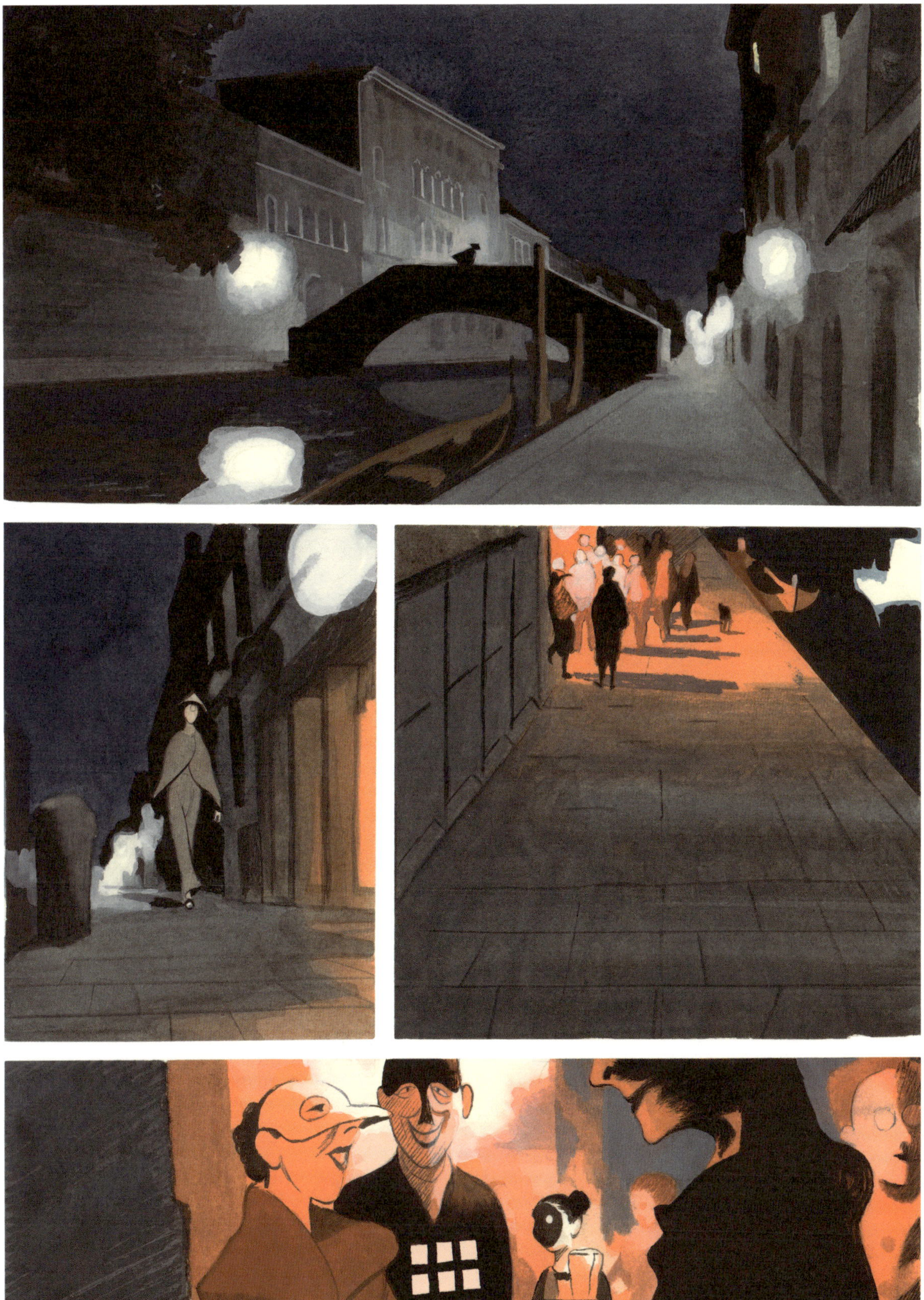

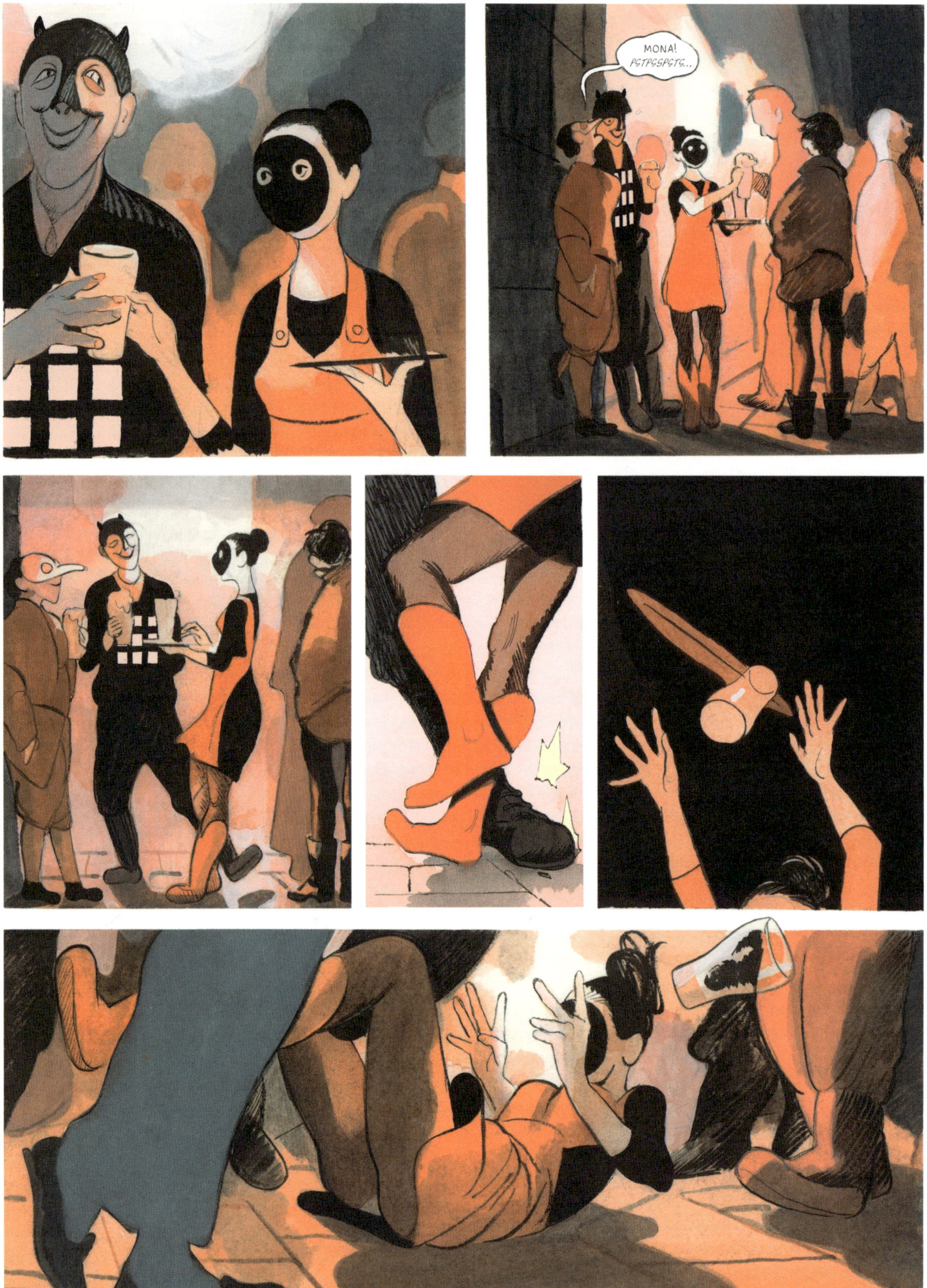
MONA!
PSTPSSPSTS...

"WHAT'S WRONG?"

"WON'T YOU PARTAKE?"

"RAFFAELLA, A BEER FOR THE POET."

"HEY!"

"NO GOODBYES FOR YOUR PALS?"

"WE'LL BE WATCHING YOU, PIERROT!"

"BE CAREFUL!"

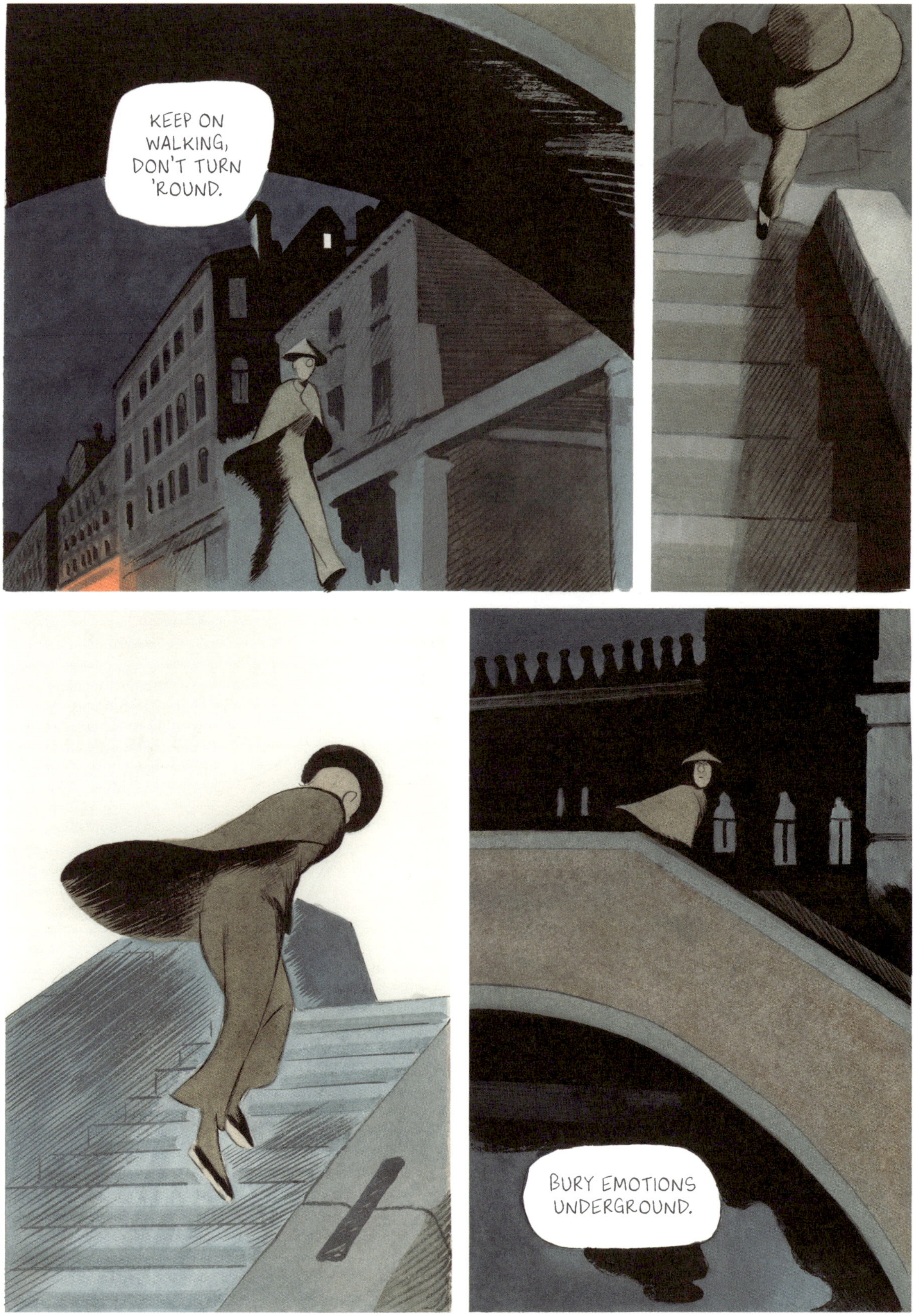
KEEP ON WALKING, DON'T TURN 'ROUND.
BURY EMOTIONS UNDERGROUND.

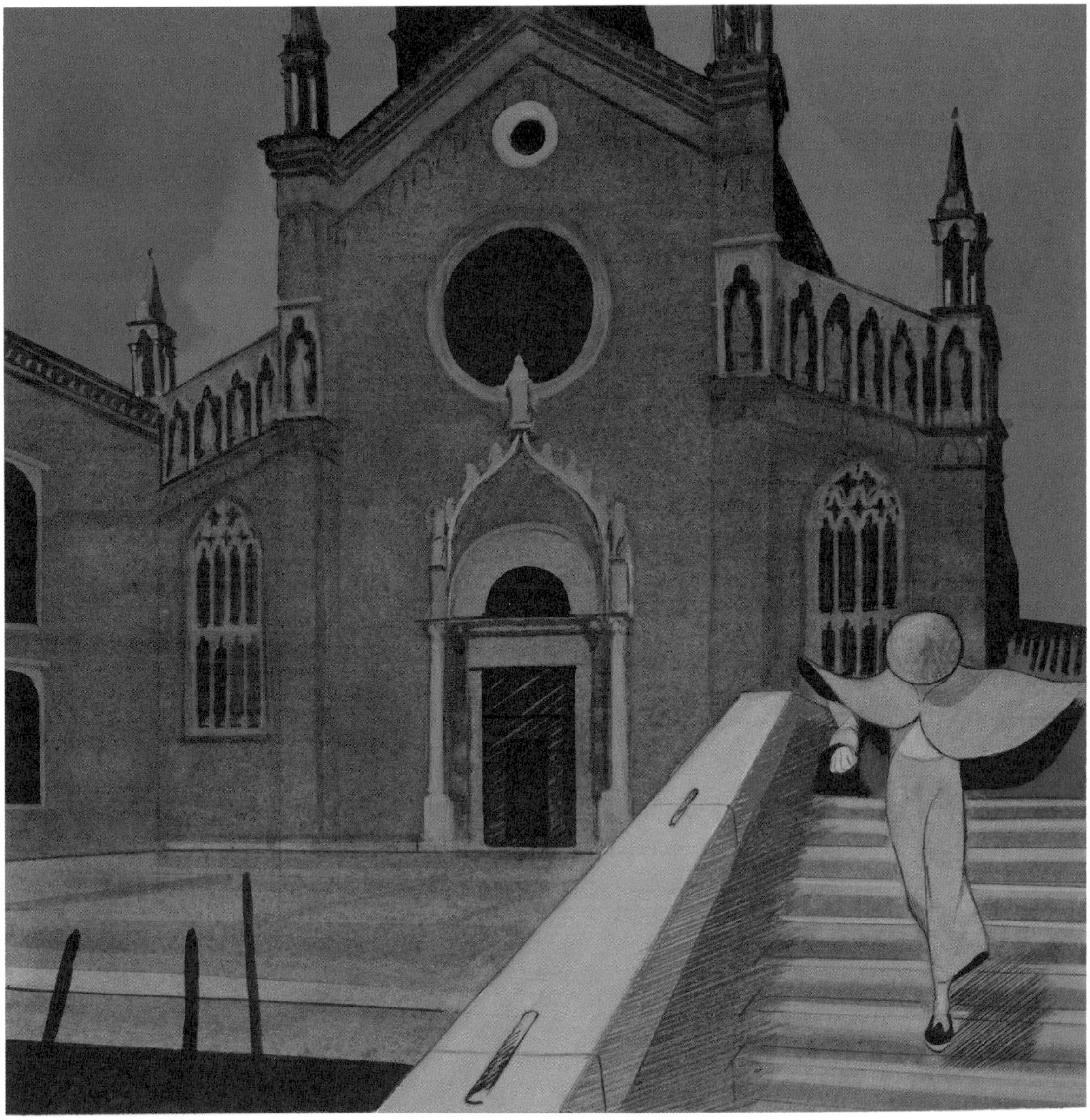

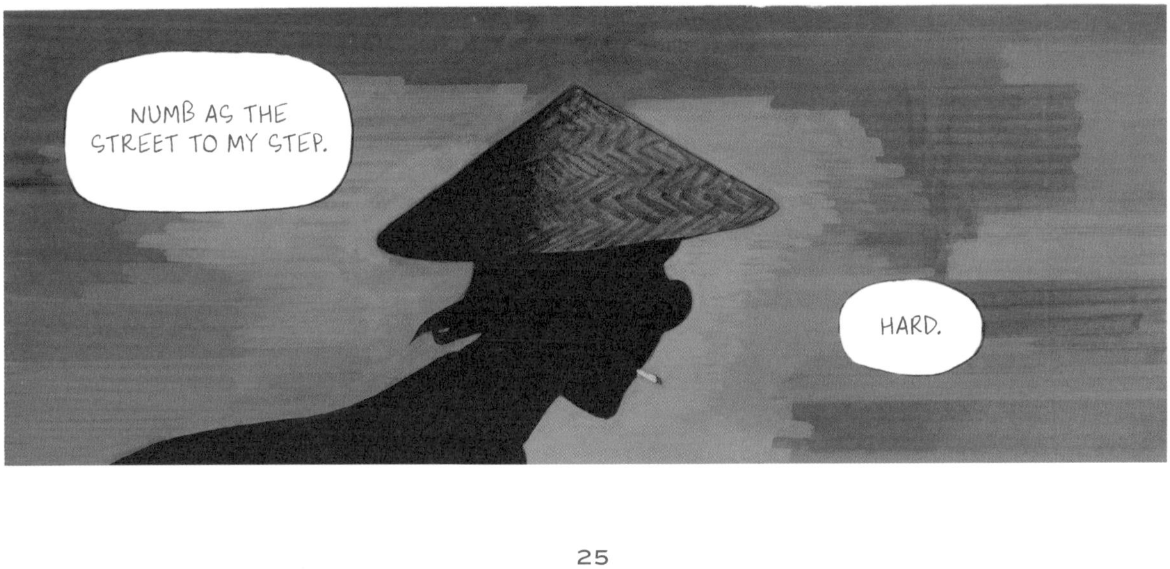
NUMB AS THE STREET TO MY STEP.
HARD.

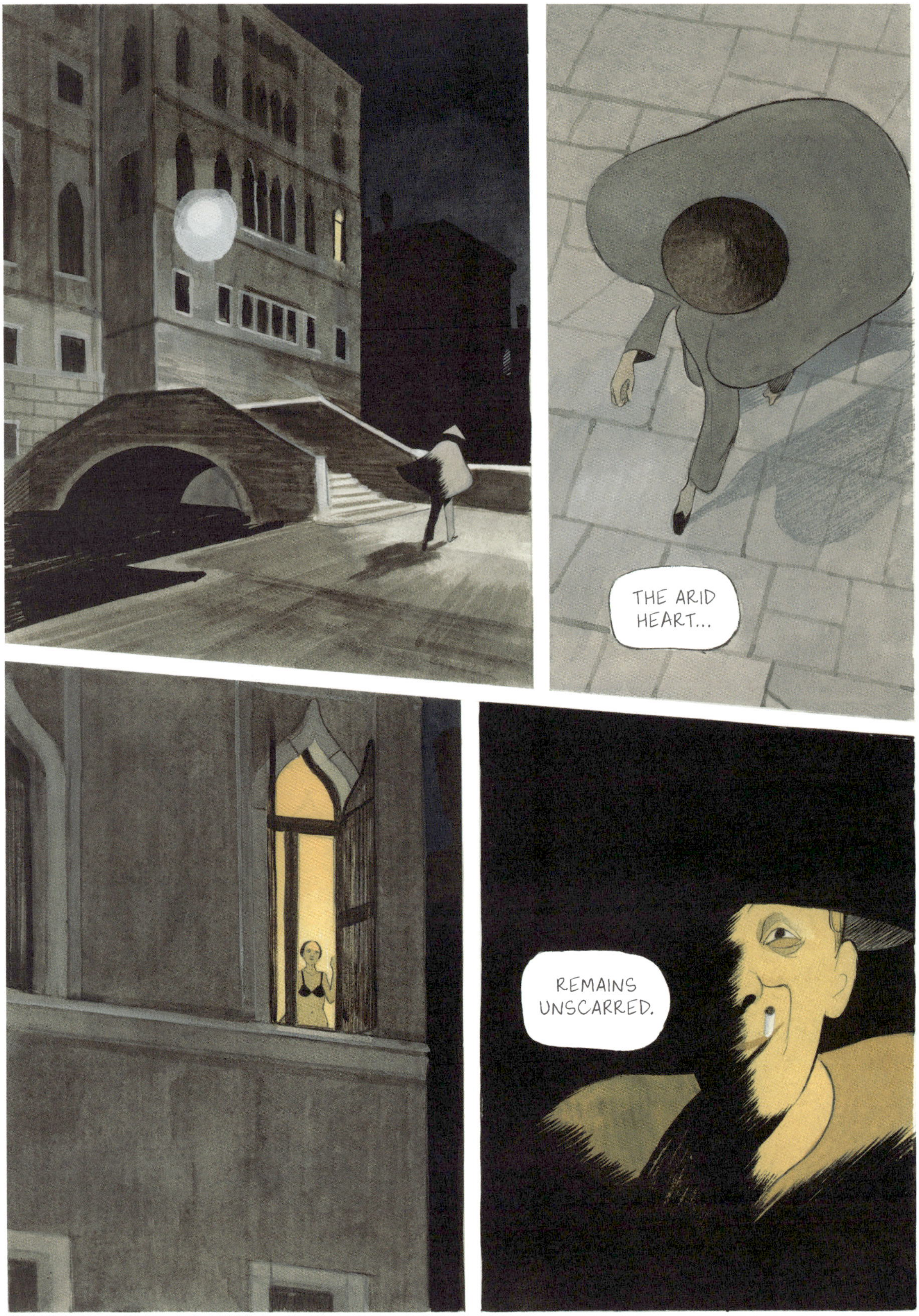
THE ARID HEART...
REMAINS UNSCARRED.

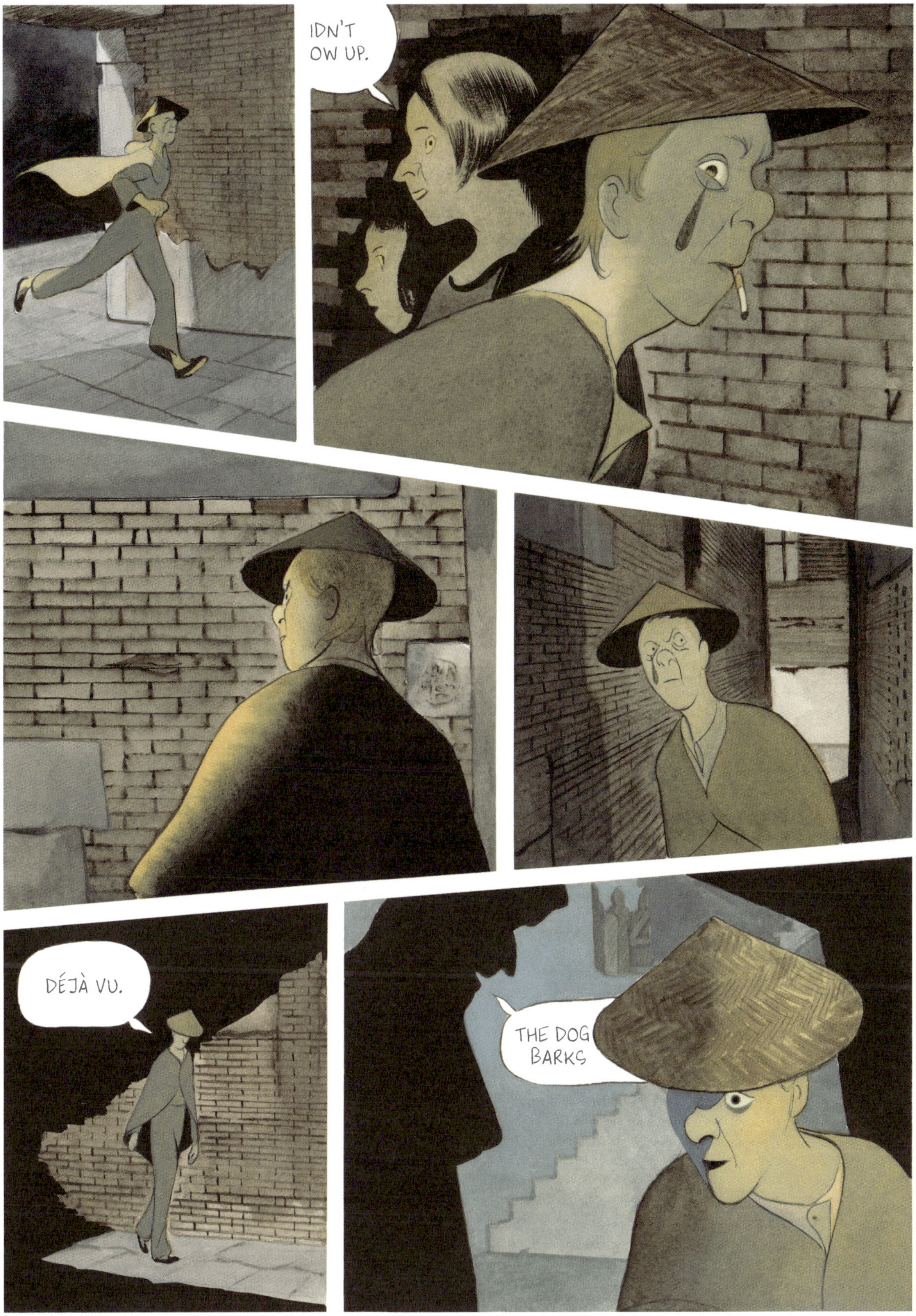
IDN'T
OW UP.
DÉJÀ VU.
THE DOG
BARKS

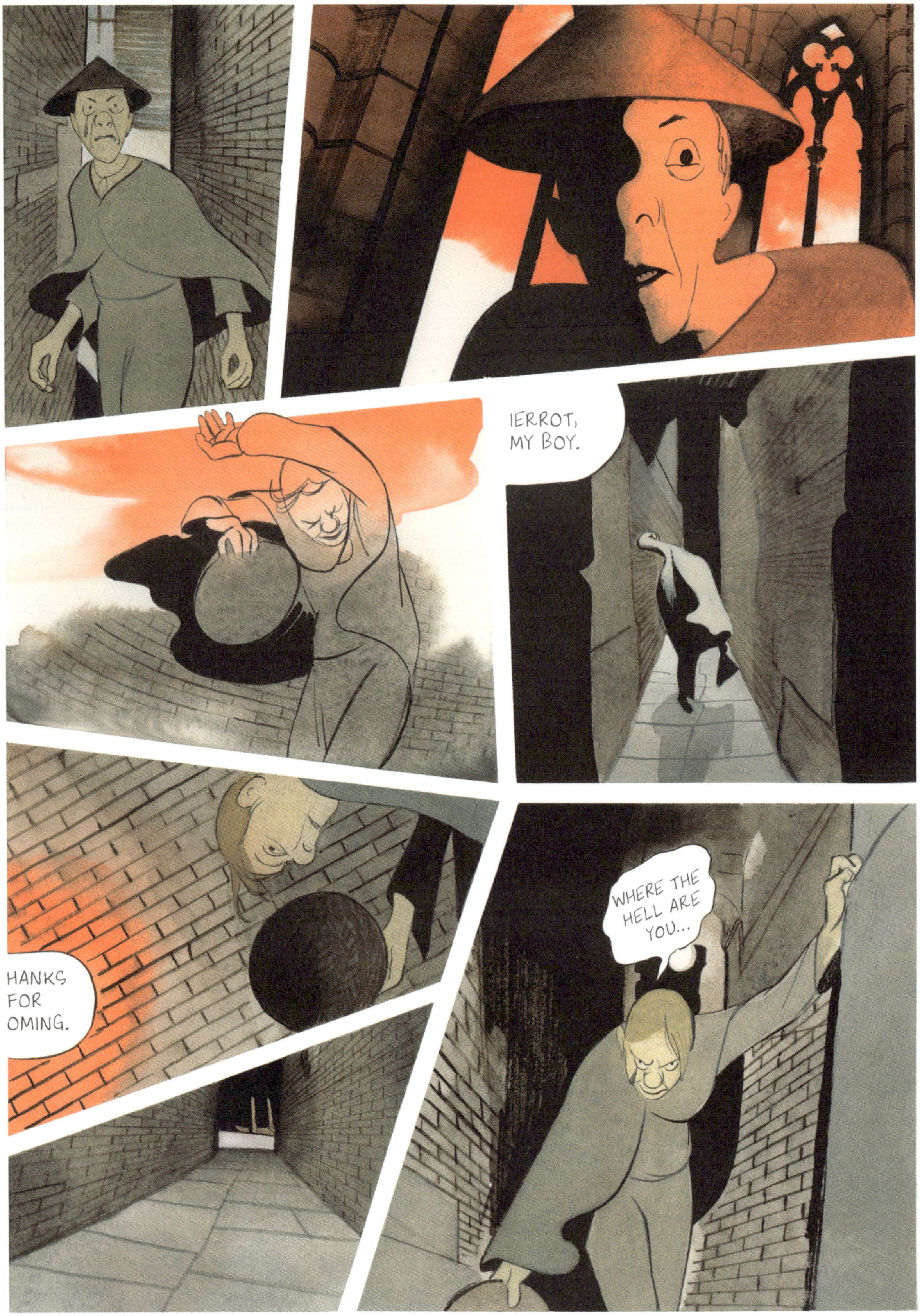
IERROT, MY BOY.
HANKS FOR OMING.
WHERE THE HELL ARE YOU...

MAGES
OU JUST
AW DON'T
EALLY
EXIST.
SHOW YOURSELF!
ABSOLU
DR.
VIVALDI.
GO AWAY!
DON'T COME NEAR ME!

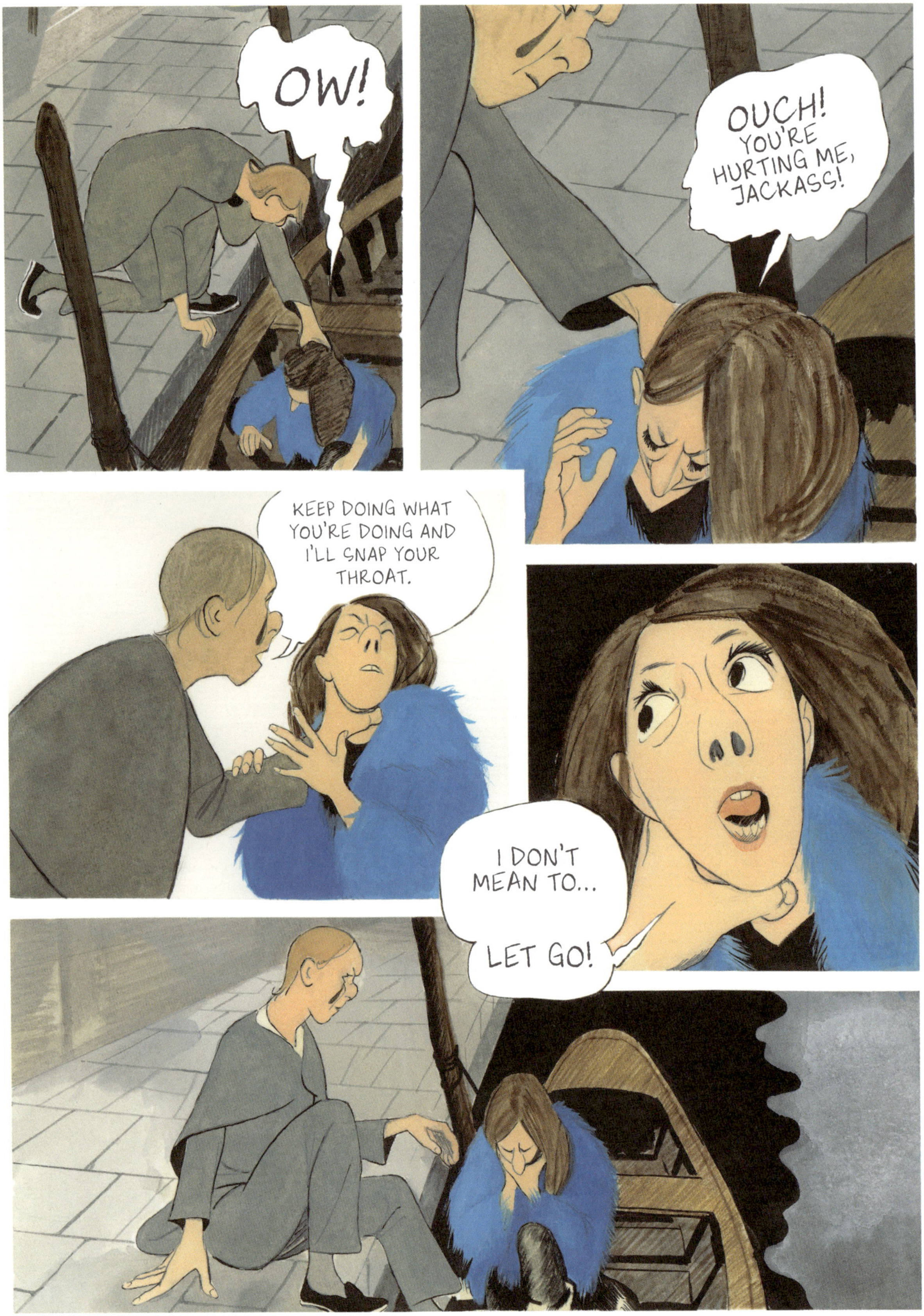
OW!
OUCH! YOU'RE HURTING ME, JACKASS!
KEEP DOING WHAT YOU'RE DOING AND I'LL SNAP YOUR THROAT.
I DON'T MEAN TO...
LET GO!

Panel 1:
- WHY ARE YOU HIDING DOWN THERE?
- I'M AFRAID OF CATS.
- CATS.

Panel 2:
- WHAT CATS?
- BEFORE.
- CATS WERE EVERYWHERE.

Panel 3:
- SNAP!

Panel 4:
- NOW THEY'RE HIDING OUT. BUT THEY'RE STILL THERE.

Panel 5:
- HELP ME, PIERROT.
- I'M GOING TO HAVE A PANIC ATTACK.

DON'T TOUCH ME.
I'M TAKING YOU HOME.
CAN I STAY AT YOUR PLACE?
JUST FOR ONE NIGHT.
THEN TOMORROW I'LL LEAVE YOU IN PEACE, I SWEAR.
WHAT'S IN IT FOR ME?
I DUNNO.
WHAT WOULD YOU LIKE?

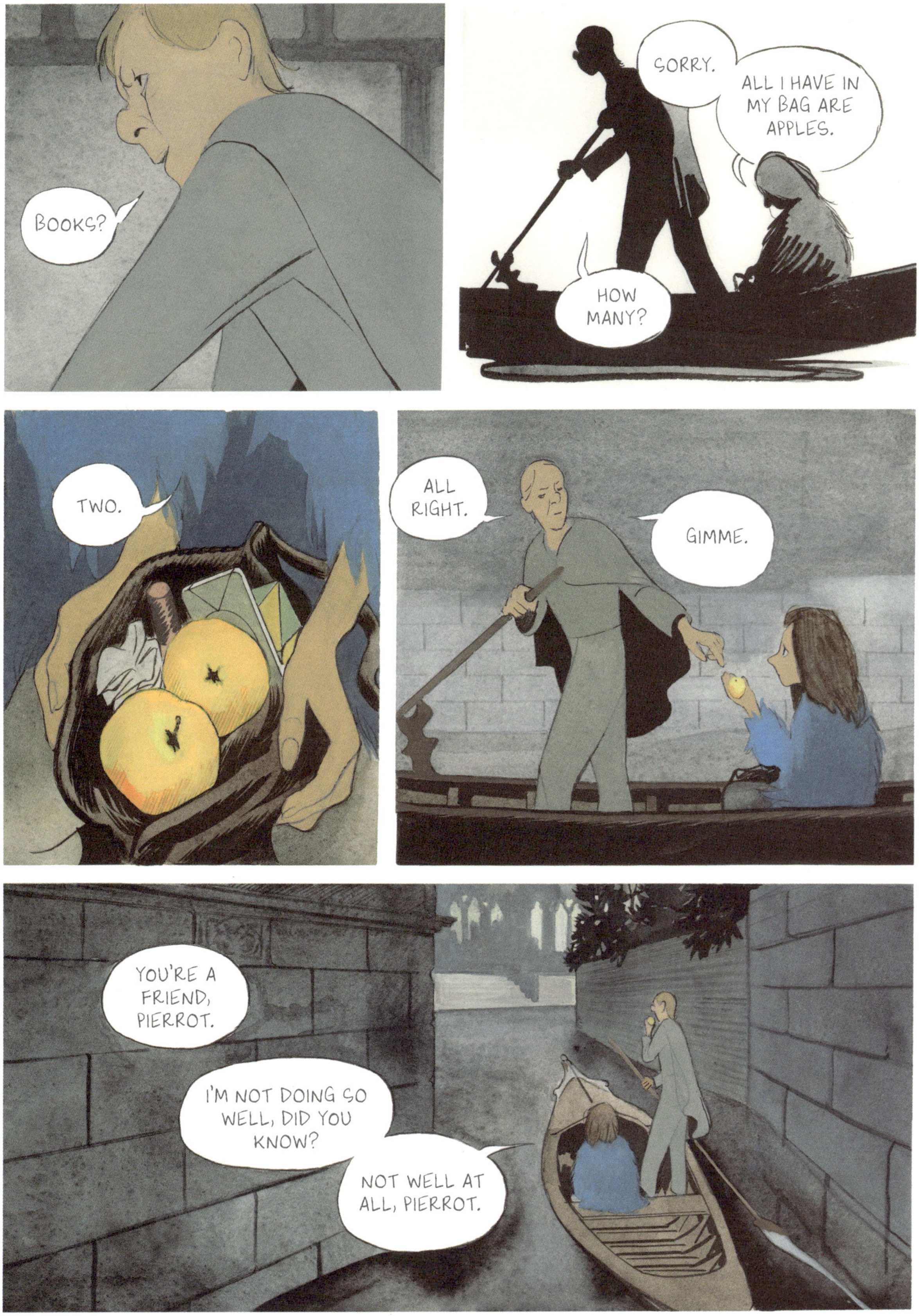
BOOKS?
SORRY.
ALL I HAVE IN MY BAG ARE APPLES.
HOW MANY?
TWO.
ALL RIGHT.
GIMME.
YOU'RE A FRIEND, PIERROT.
I'M NOT DOING SO WELL, DID YOU KNOW?
NOT WELL AT ALL, PIERROT.

"YOU CAN GO TO MY FATHER'S."

"TWO WEEKS, I'VE BEEN WANDERING."

"I'M NOT GOING BACK THERE."

"I REALLY NEED TO SLEEP, YOU KNOW?"

"NO MORE TELEPATHY."

"... SHE SAYS, AFTER RIFLING THROUGH MY BRAIN."

"IT'S WHEN I'M SCARED. I LOSE CONTROL OF MY THOUGHTS."

"I TRIGGER DÉJÀ-VUS. YOU KNOW?"

NO.
WHEN YOU ENTER SOMEONE'S HEAD...
AND YOU SEE AND HEAR THE THINGS THEY JUST DID...
WELL, EVERY SO OFTEN THEY NOTICE...
BECAUSE THEY FEEL LIKE THEY'VE EXPERIENCED THAT MOMENT ALREADY, SO THEY SAY:
HUH!
DÉJÀ VU!

BUT IT'S NOT EVEN TRUE.
THEY HAVEN'T HAD THAT EXPERIENCE.
IT'S JUST THE ECHO OF A THOUGHT IN SOMEONE ELSE'S HEAD.
DO YOU WANT THE OTHER APPLE, TOO?
NO, DORA.
SAVE IT FOR TOMORROW.

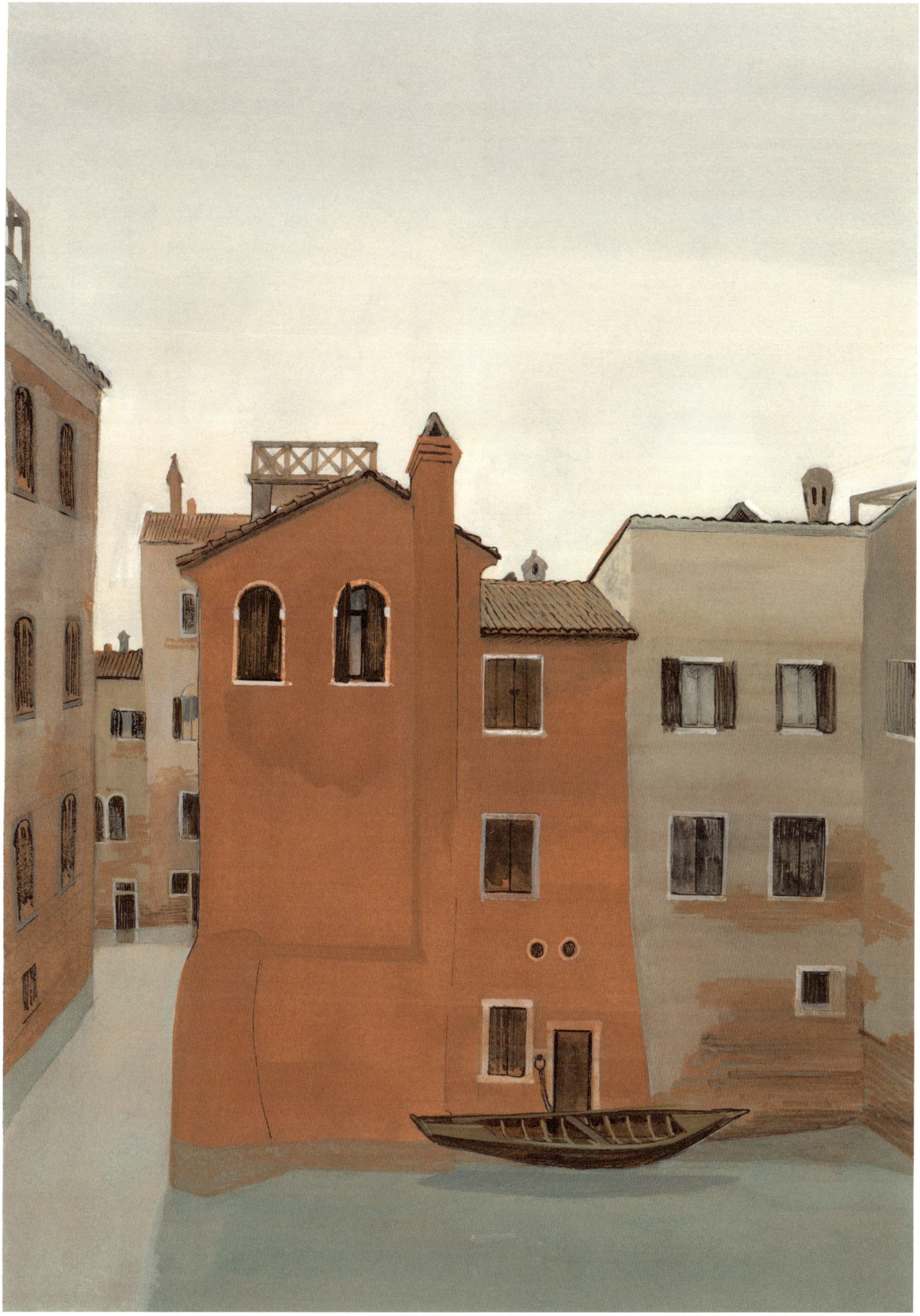

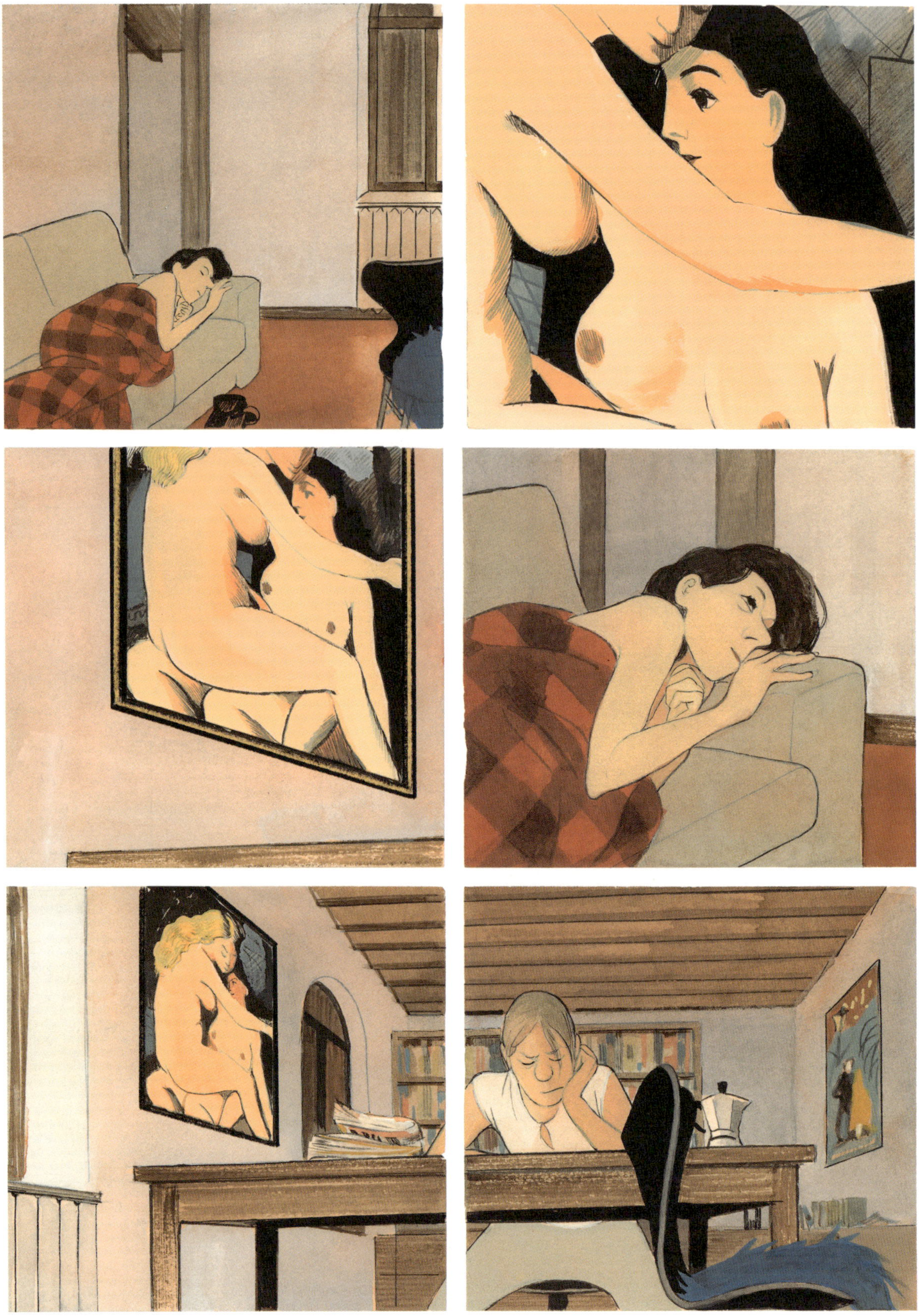

I LOVE THAT PAINTING.
DID YOU DO IT?
YOU PEOPLE. TELEPATHIC, BUT STILL IGNORANT AS GOATS.
SEX BIZARRE
5000 LIRE

PAUL DELVAUX, "LES DEUX AMIES," 1946.
DARLIN 46
GET DRESSED.
RIGHT, OF COURSE!
I THOUGHT YOU... NEVER MIND!
CLIC!

?!?

GURRGGLLLE

SORRY...

I HAVEN'T EATEN FOR THREE DAYS.

THERE'S STILL THAT APPLE.

THAT'S FOR YOU.

WELL, LET'S GO SHOPPING, THEN.

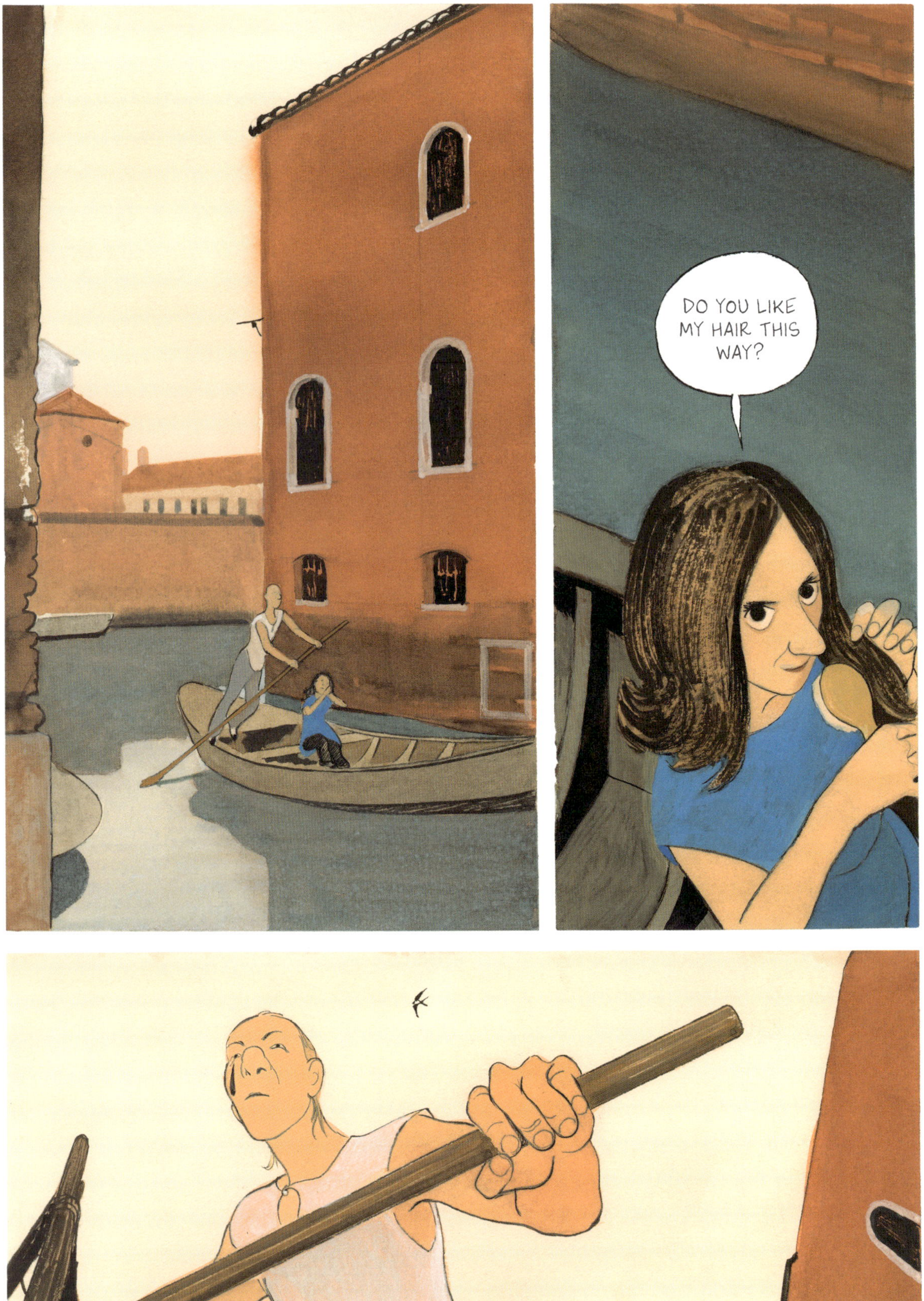
DO YOU LIKE MY HAIR THIS WAY?

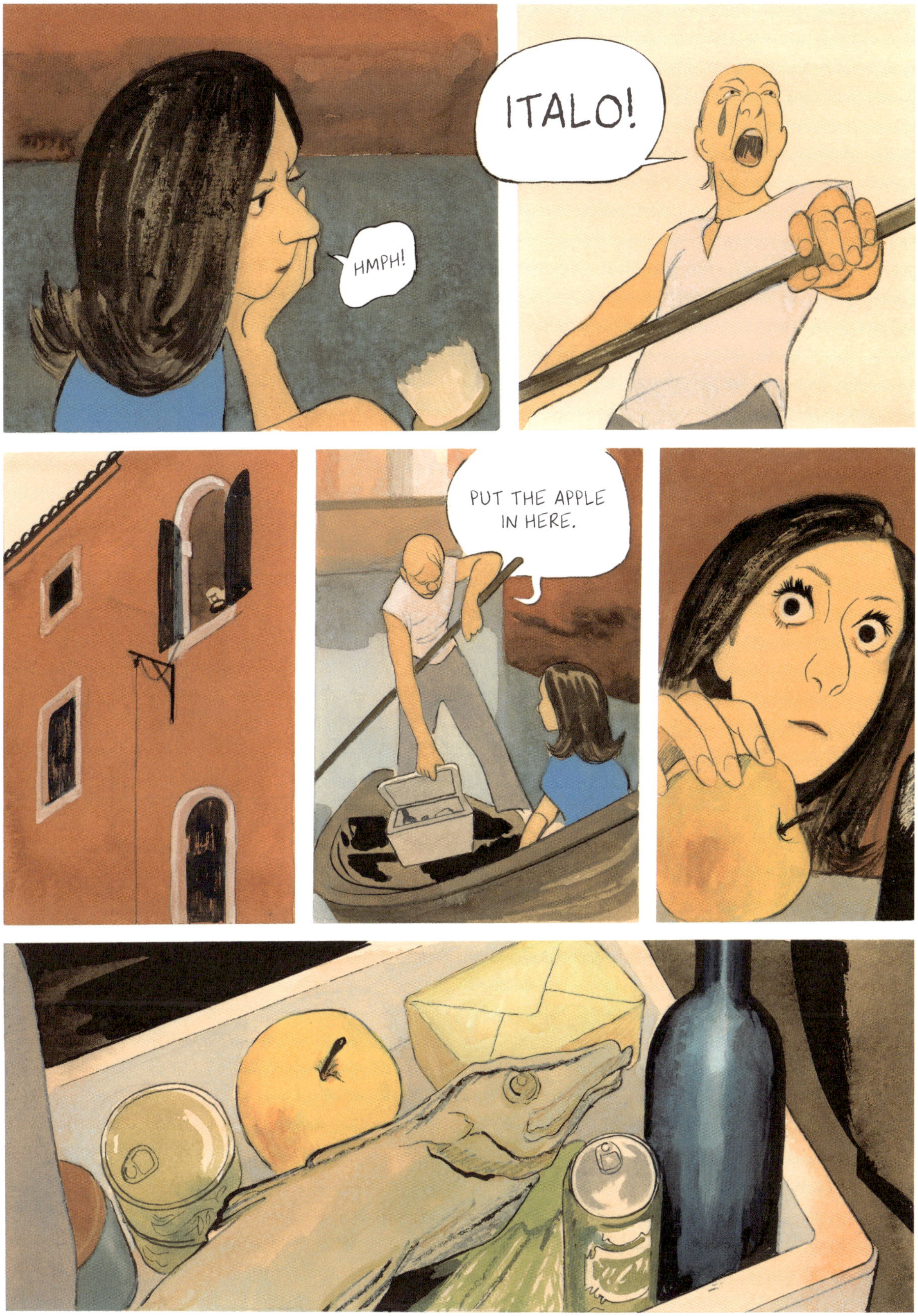
HMPH!
ITALO!
PUT THE APPLE IN HERE.

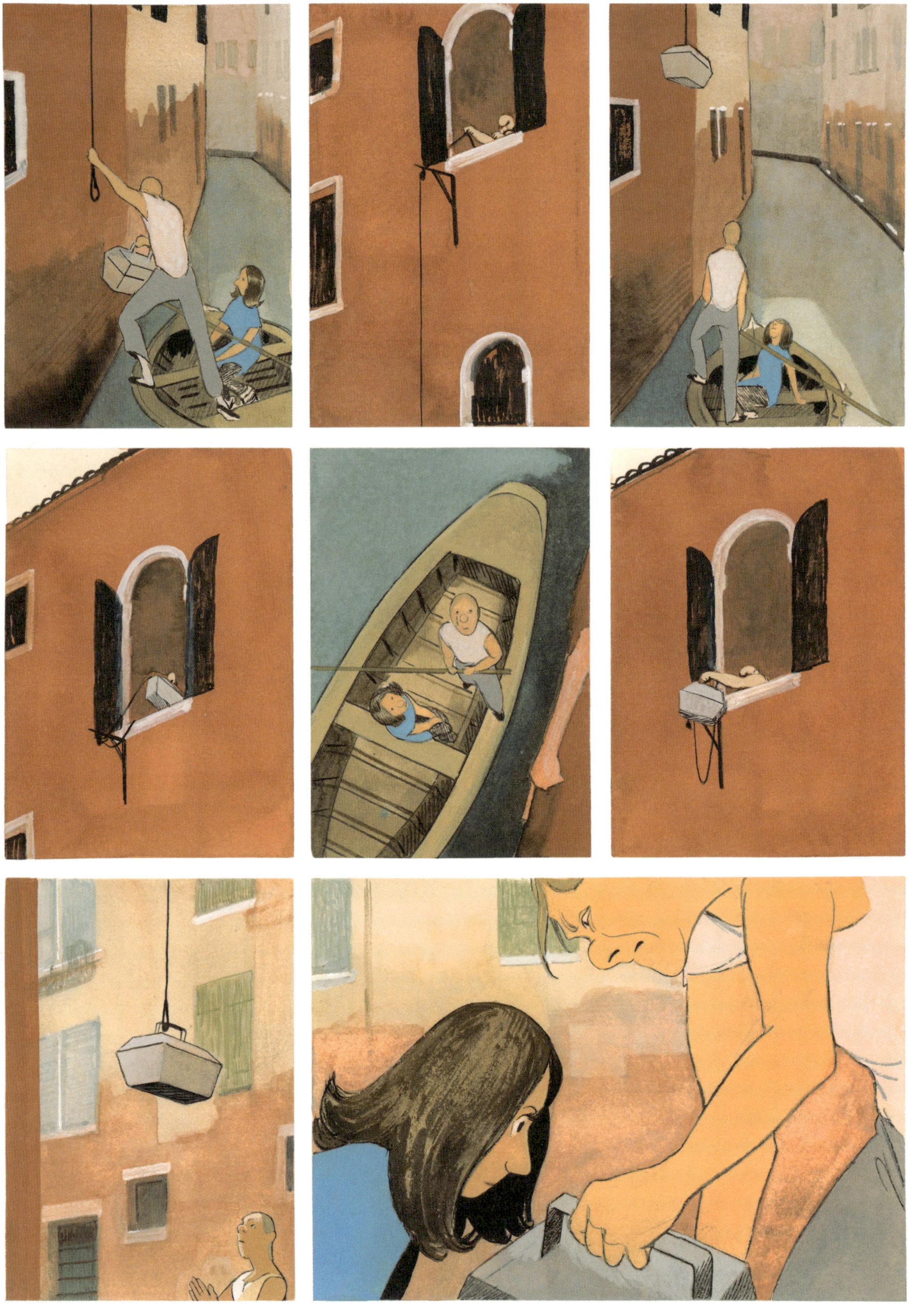

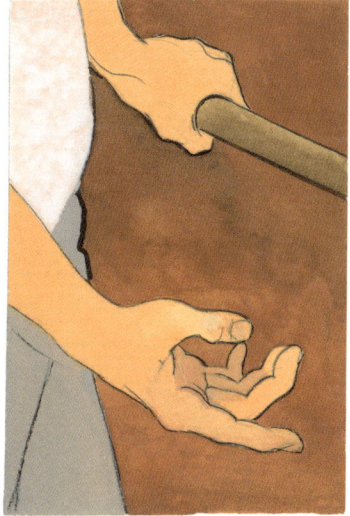

PIERROT, MAYBE YOU DON'T GET IT...

BUT I'M DYING OF HUNGER.

YOU GOT ANYTHING ELSE TO TRADE?

I ALREADY GAVE YOU THE APPLES!

WHAT DO YOU WANT NOW, MY PANTIES?!

NO.

YOUR BRUSH.

WOULD YOU RATHER I TAKE YOU BACK TO YOUR SCHOOLMATES?
SHUT UP.
I SHOULDN'T HAVE COME WITH YOU.
IT WAS A MISTAKE.
THAT'S TRUE.
I CAN'T TRUST ANYONE IN THIS CITY.
EVERYONE WANTS SOMETHING FROM ME.

WHO'S THERE?
ORESTE, IT'S ME.
PIERROT.
I HEARD A WOMAN'S VOICE.
IT'S A FRIEND.
SHE HAS SOMETHING FOR YOU.
FOR ME?
OOOOHHH...

OOOHHHH! IT'S SO SOFT!

THAT'S WORTH AT LEAST A CARTON, ORESTE.

VERY WELL, MY FRIEND, VERY WELL.

NOW TELL ME, WHO'S THIS PRETTY GIRL?

WHAT IS IT YOU NEED, MY DEAR?

DID YOU KNOW THAT OLD ORESTE CAN TAKE GOOD CARE OF YOU?

"WON'T YOU LEAVE HER WITH ME FOR THE NIGHT?"

"I'LL GET YOU SOMETHING EVEN BETTER THAN TOBACCO."

"MAYBE NEXT TIME."

"NEXT TIME, VERY WELL."

"I WISH YOU AN EXCELLENT DAY."

"COME BACK ANYTIME."

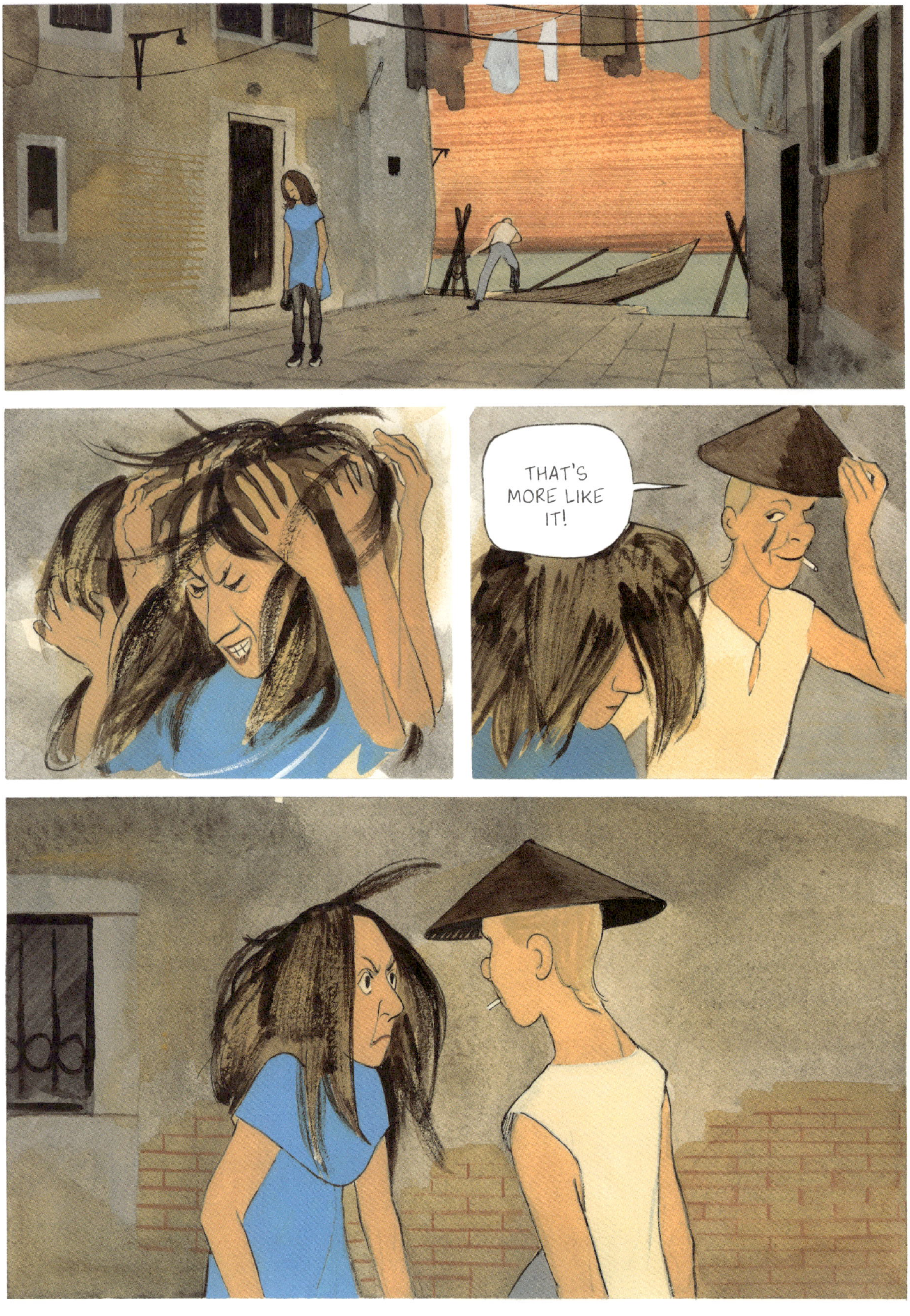
THAT'S MORE LIKE IT!

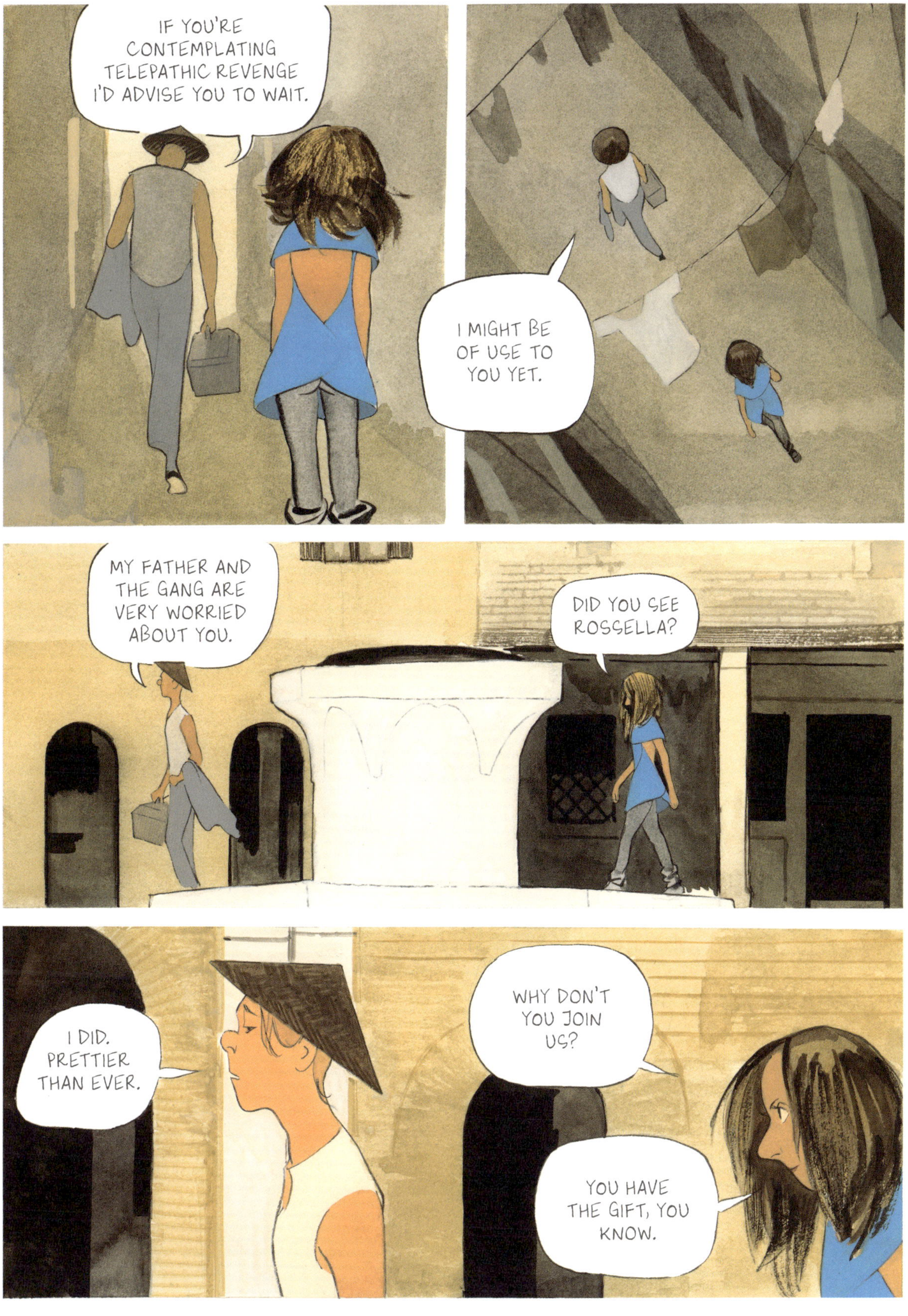
IF YOU'RE CONTEMPLATING TELEPATHIC REVENGE I'D ADVISE YOU TO WAIT.
I MIGHT BE OF USE TO YOU YET.
MY FATHER AND THE GANG ARE VERY WORRIED ABOUT YOU.
DID YOU SEE ROSSELLA?
I DID. PRETTIER THAN EVER.
WHY DON'T YOU JOIN US?
YOU HAVE THE GIFT, YOU KNOW.

NAH, CAN'T STAND THE OLD MAN.
AND I DON'T GIVE A RAT'S ASS ABOUT TELEPATHY.
BUT WHAT I WOULDN'T GIVE TO BANG ROSSELLA.

IT'S THE POET!
AS IF YOU KNOW ANYTHING ABOUT POETRY!
SO WHAT IS THIS PLACE?
A BROTHEL.
AND WHAT ARE WE DOING HERE, EXACTLY?

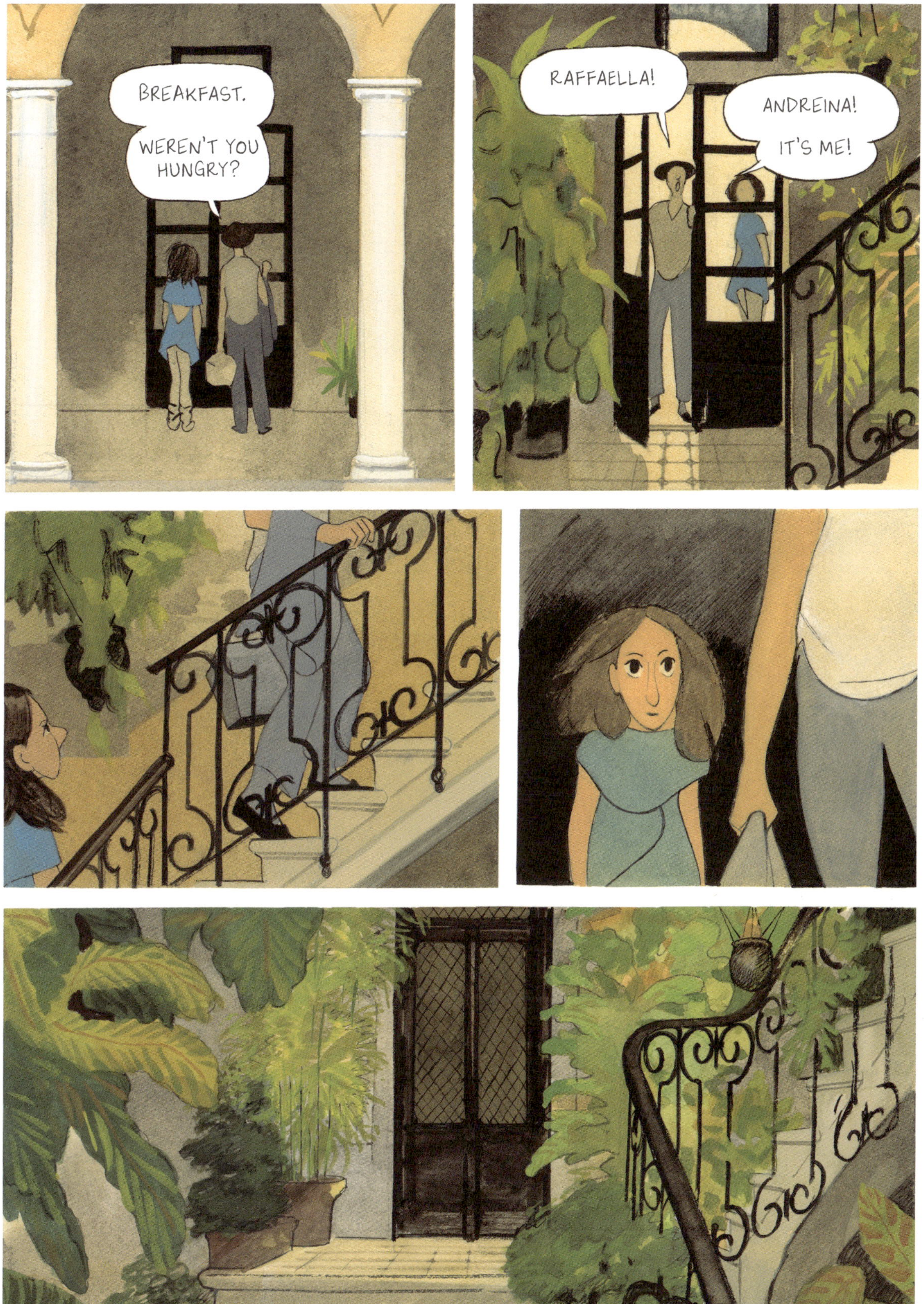
BREAKFAST.
WEREN'T YOU HUNGRY?
RAFFAELLA!
ANDREINA!
IT'S ME!

ANYONE HOME?
PIERROT.
COME.
I'M JUST WAKING UP.
YOU BROUGHT A FRIEND?

SHE'S ONE OF MY FATHER'S.
OH, A TELEPATH...
SHE WON'T BOTHER US.
OH, NO...
NOT WITH A SWEET FACE LIKE THAT...
RAFFAELLA?
SHE'S STILL ASLEEP, SHE WAS AT THE BAR ALL NIGHT WORKING...

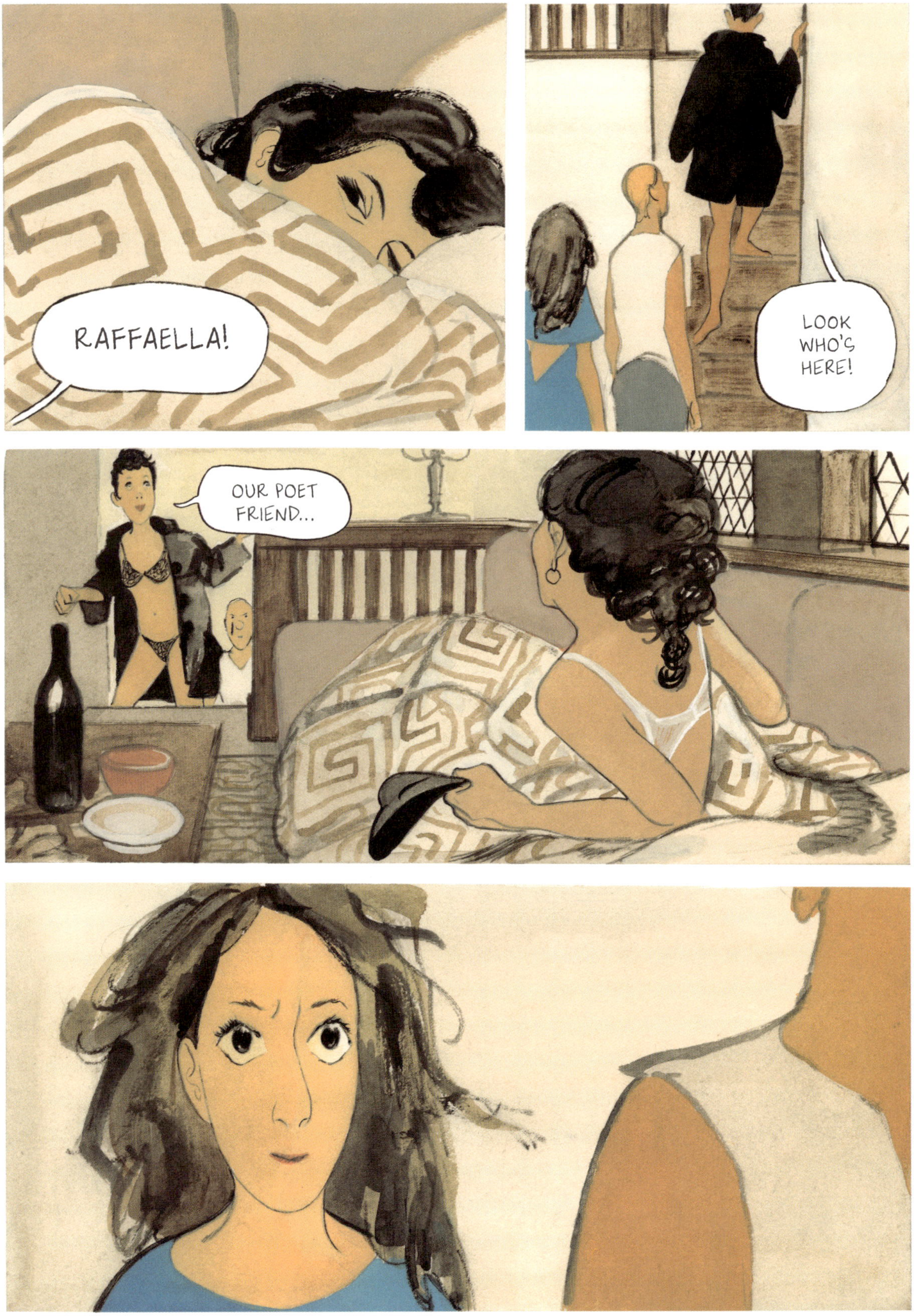
RAFFAELLA!
LOOK WHO'S HERE!
OUR POET FRIEND...

PSSSST!

SHE'S A TELEPATH!

BE CAREFUL WHAT YOU THINK.

HA HA HA HA!!!

WE HAVE LEFTOVERS FROM LAST NIGHT'S PARTY.

SCRUMPTIOUS.

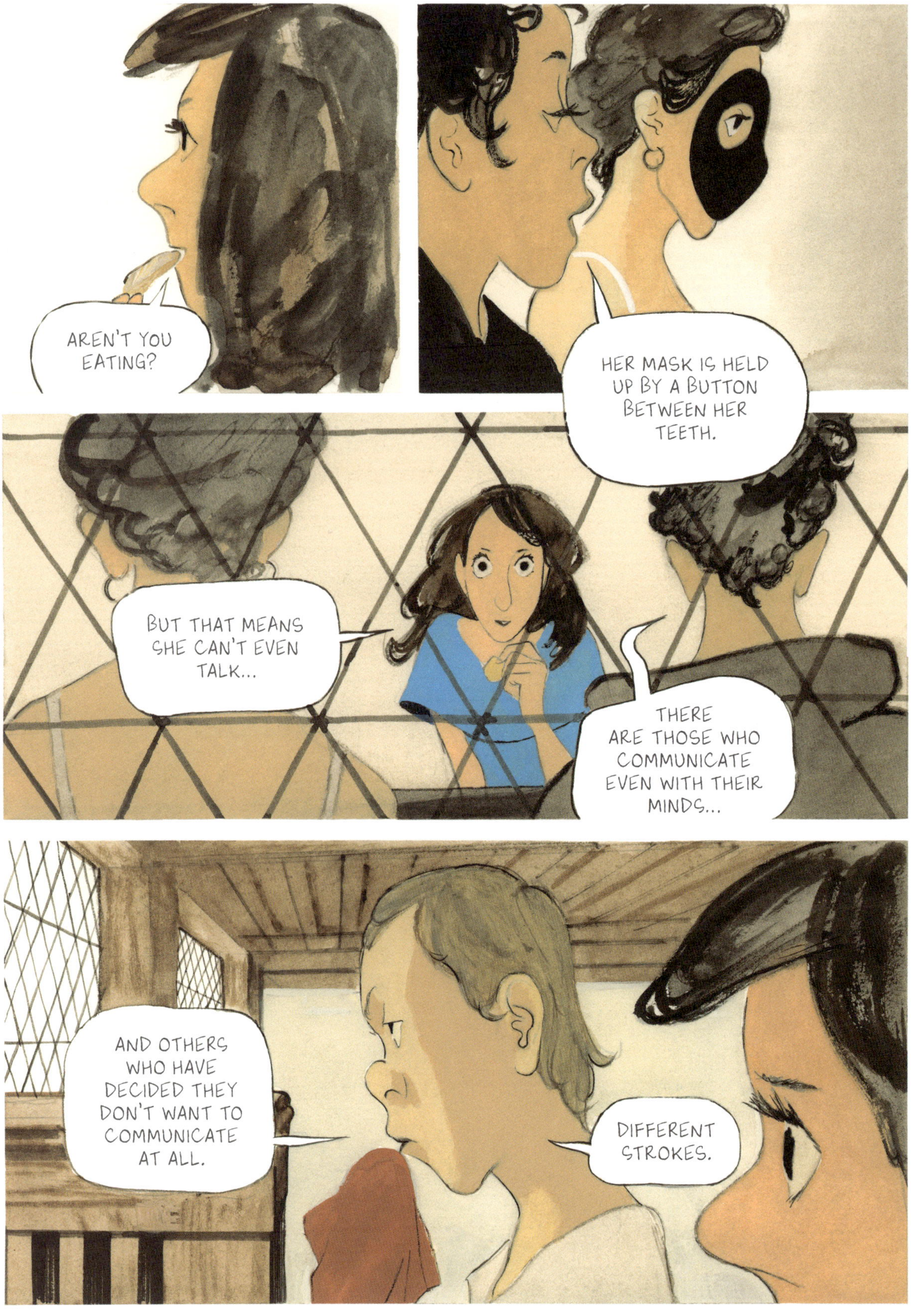
AREN'T YOU EATING?
HER MASK IS HELD UP BY A BUTTON BETWEEN HER TEETH.
BUT THAT MEANS SHE CAN'T EVEN TALK...
THERE ARE THOSE WHO COMMUNICATE EVEN WITH THEIR MINDS...
AND OTHERS WHO HAVE DECIDED THEY DON'T WANT TO COMMUNICATE AT ALL.
DIFFERENT STROKES.

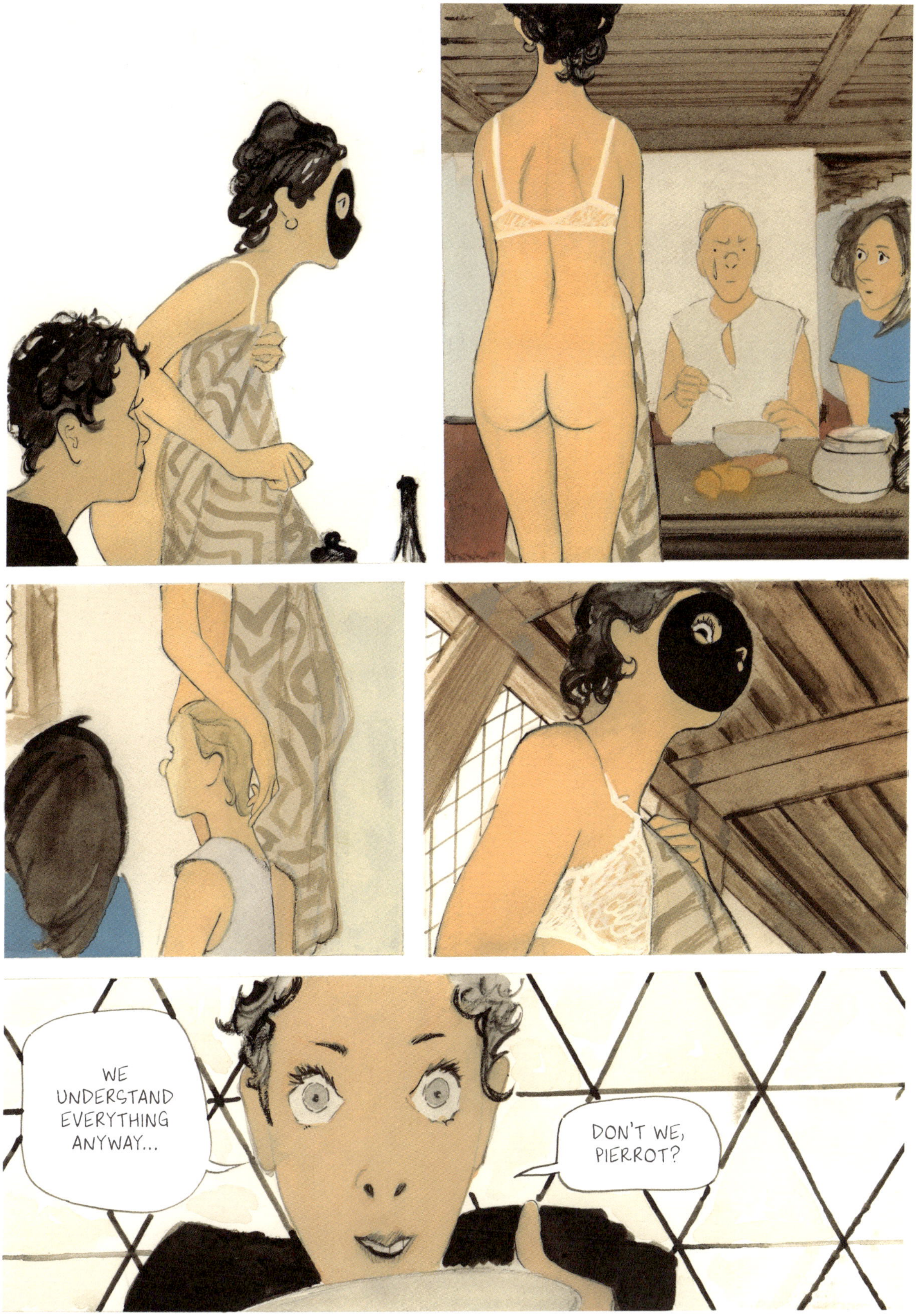
WE UNDERSTAND EVERYTHING ANYWAY...
DON'T WE, PIERROT?

"I'LL BE RIGHT BACK.

YOU GO AHEAD AND EAT."

"LET'S HOPE THIS TIME'S THE CHARM...

BUT HERE WE ARE!

HE JUST COMES HERE TO EAT, WITH THE REST HE'S USELESS...

LET'S DO SOME TELEPATHY, PLEASE!"

WHAT?
OH, NO! IT DOESN'T WORK LIKE THAT.
PLEASE PLEASE PLEASE PLEASE
LOOK...
TELEPATHY ISN'T SOMETHING YOU CAN TURN ON WHENEVER YOU FEEL LIKE IT.
IT'S NOOOT?
BOOOOOOO
WAAAAHHH!
WAIT! SSSSSHH!
SHUT UP FOR A SECOND!
I'LL GIVE IT A TRY, OK?

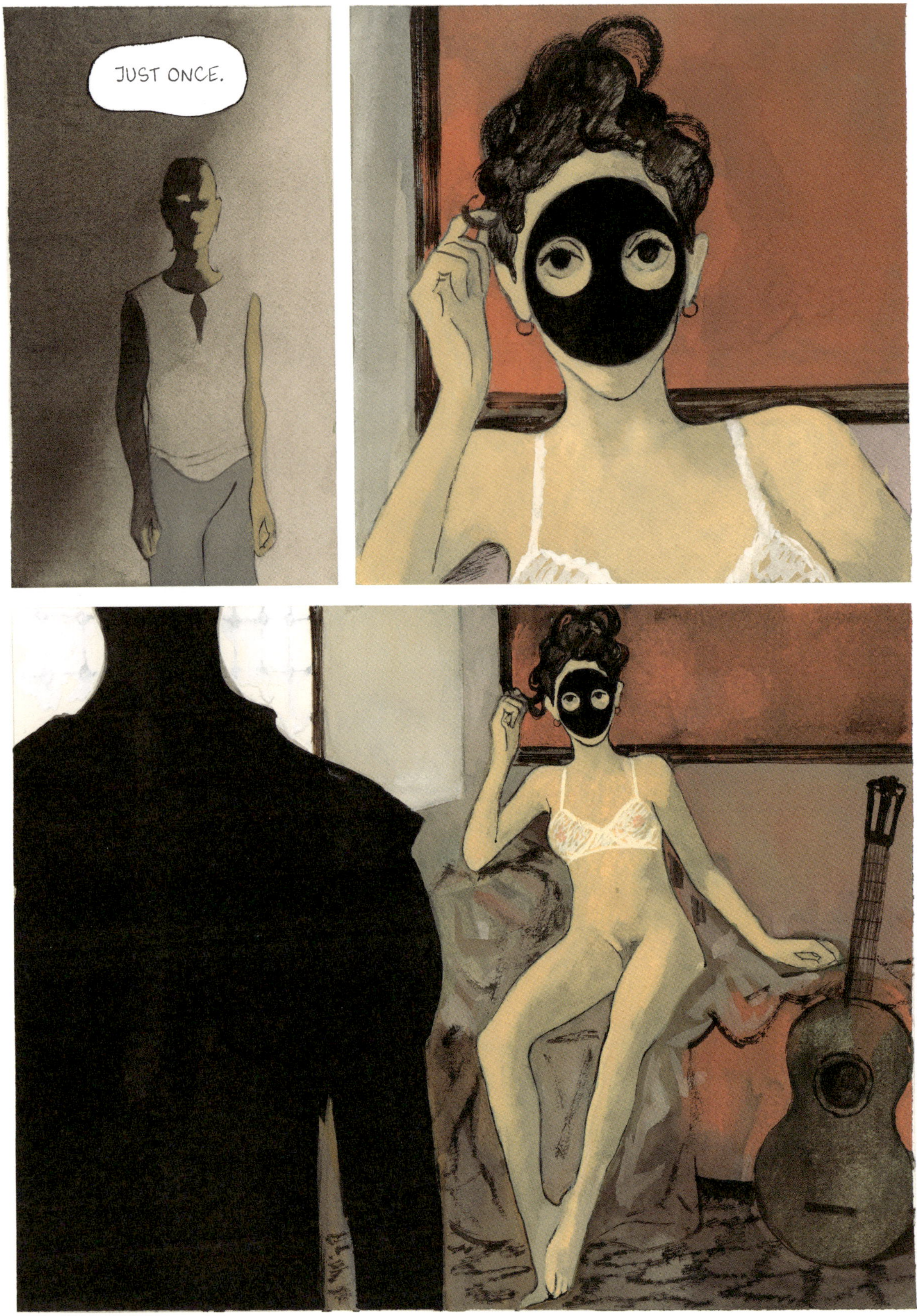
JUST ONCE.

ARE YOU THINKING OF ANYTHING YET?

A BRIDGE.

WHAT BRIDGE?

A BRIDGE.
AND A FLASH.
A BIG EXPLOSION.

Panel 1:
— HMM... I DON'T THINK IT'S WORKING...
YOU SURE YOU'RE NOT READING SOMEONE ELSE'S THOUGHTS?
— MAMMA.

Panel 2:
(no dialogue)

Panel 3:
— MAMMA?
— MAMMA, WHERE ARE YOU?

Panel 4:
— HOW WOULD I KNOW?!
— I'VE NEVER EVEN MET THE WOMAN!

Panel 5:
— MAMMA?

COME ON, TRY AGAIN, MAYBE IT'LL WORK!
WHERE ARE YOU...
WILL IT BE EASIER IF WE LIE DOWN?
LET ME GO, I SAID!
LET'S FOOL AROUND...
THE CATS!
WHAT CATS?!?
GET RID OF THE CATS!
AH HA HA! YOU'RE TOO MUCH!
SHOO, CATS, SHOO!

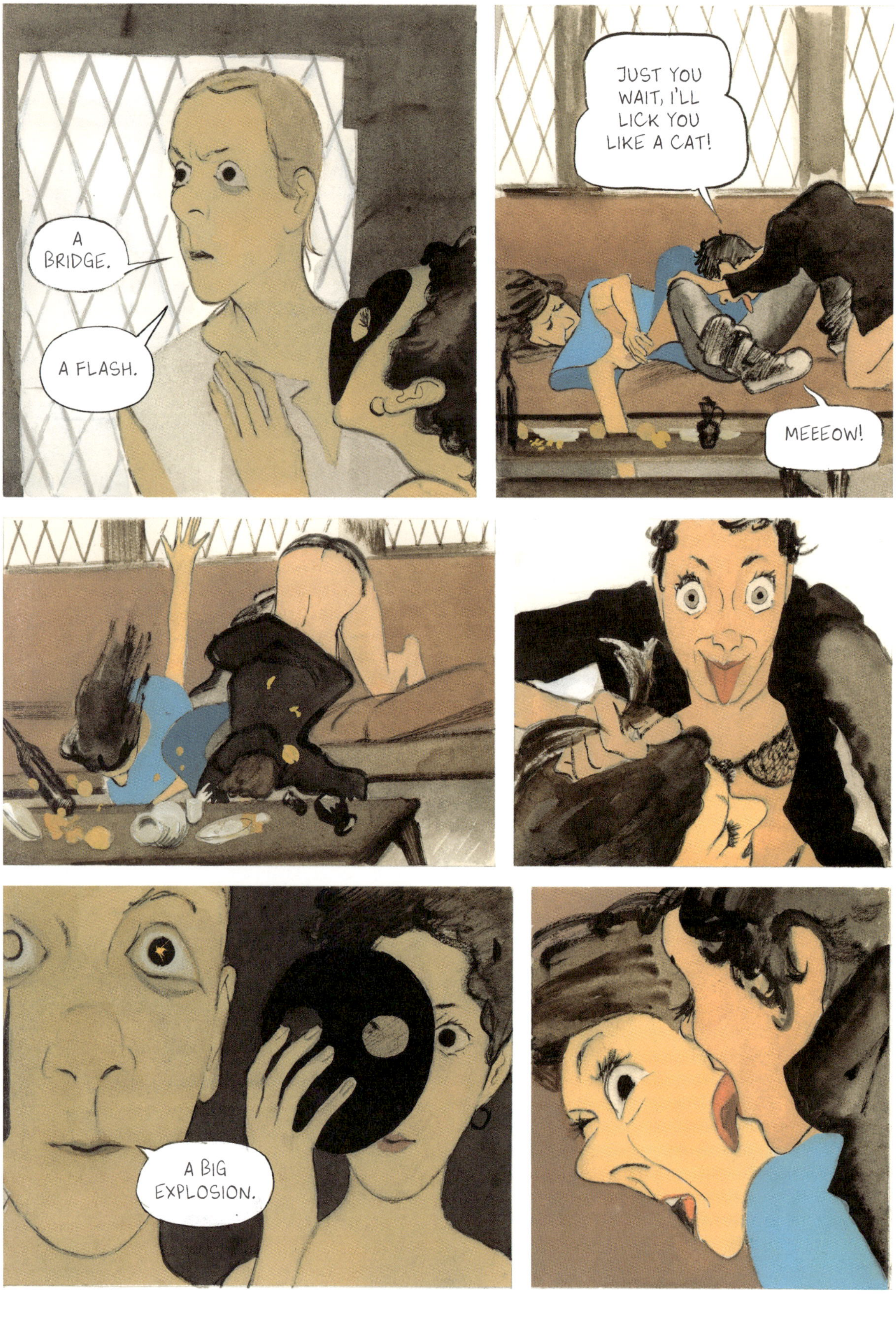
A BRIDGE.
A FLASH.
JUST YOU WAIT, I'LL LICK YOU LIKE A CAT!
MEEEOW!
A BIG EXPLOSION.

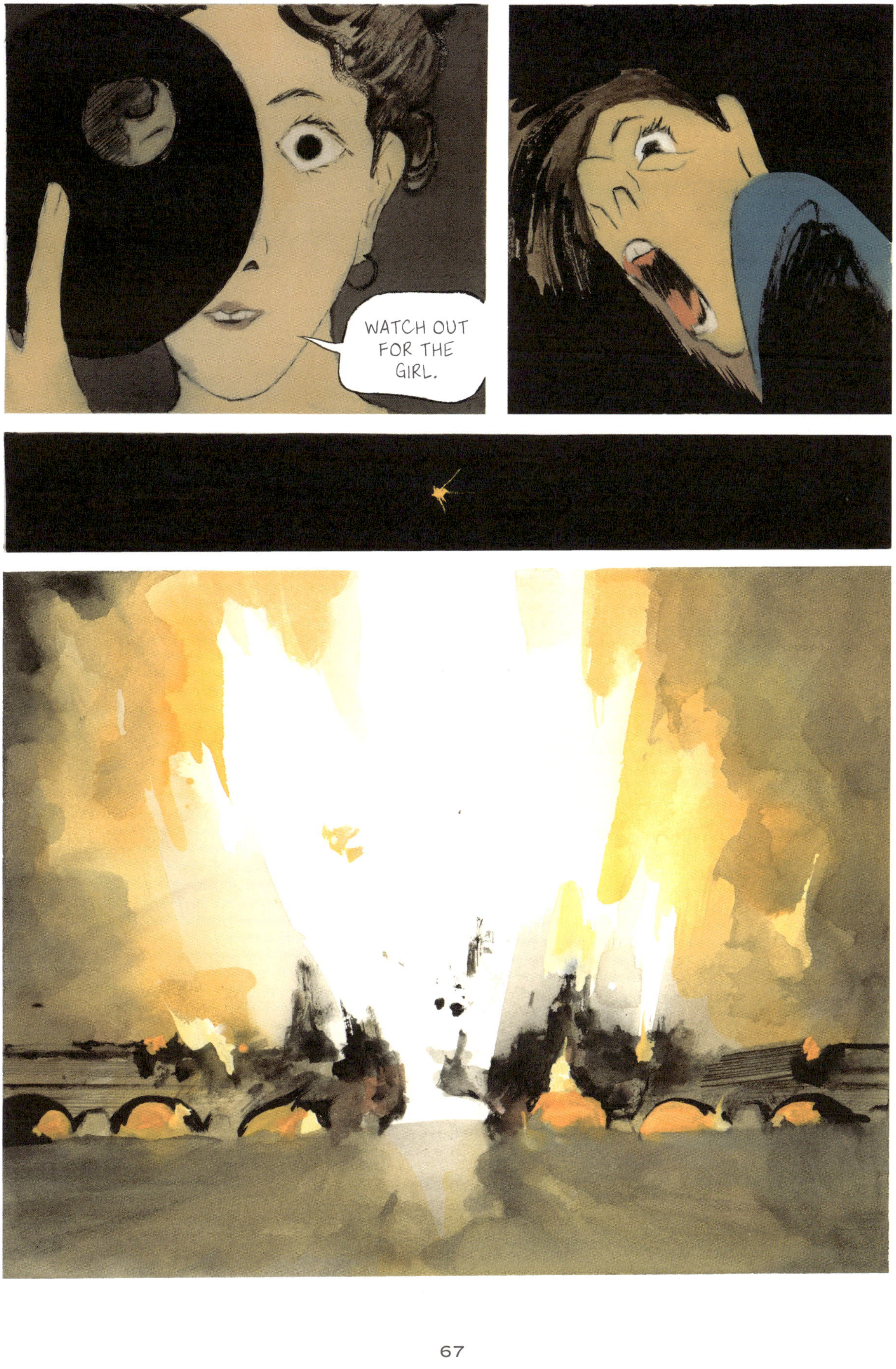
WATCH OUT FOR THE GIRL.

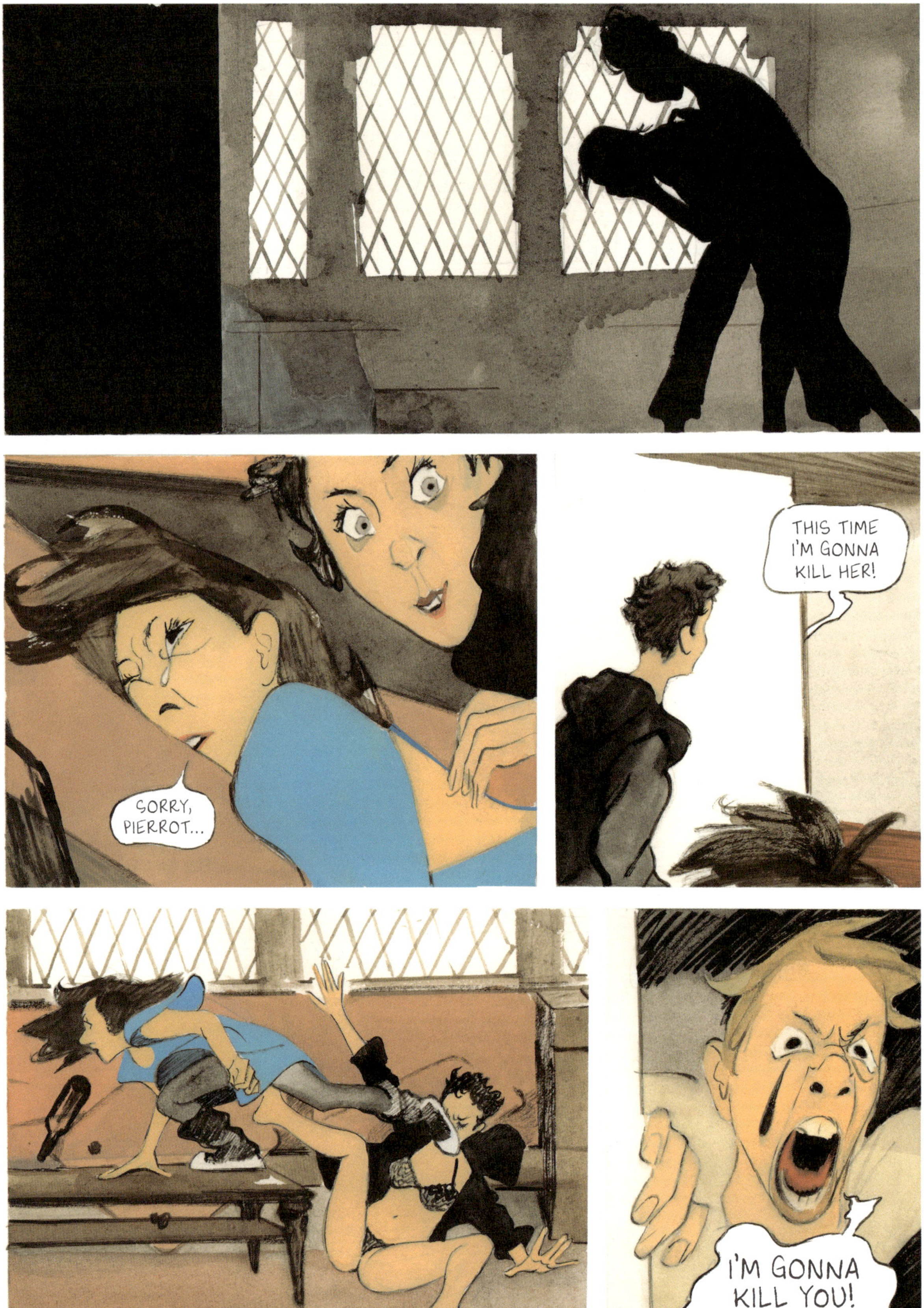
SORRY, PIERROT...
THIS TIME I'M GONNA KILL HER!
I'M GONNA KILL YOU!

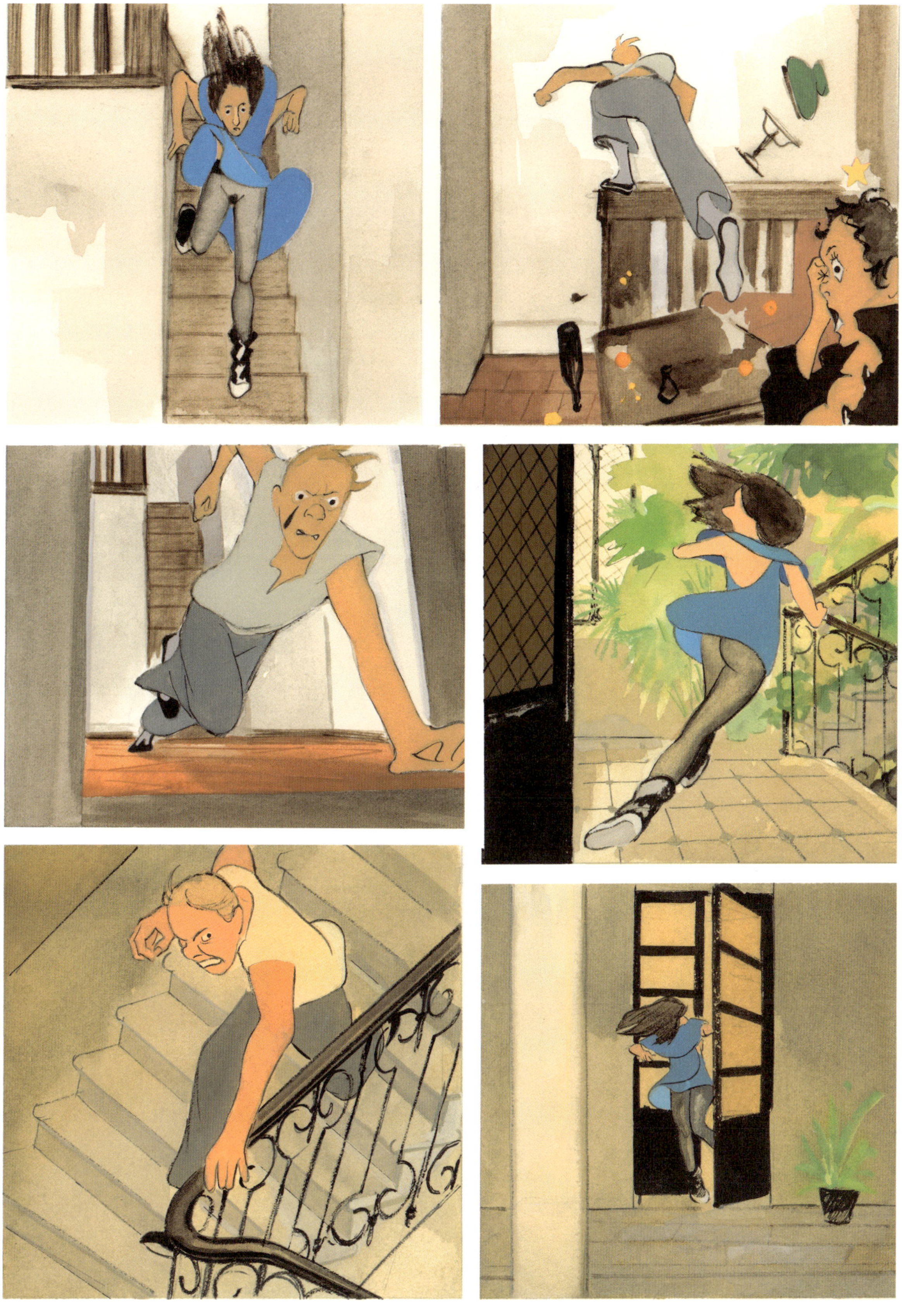

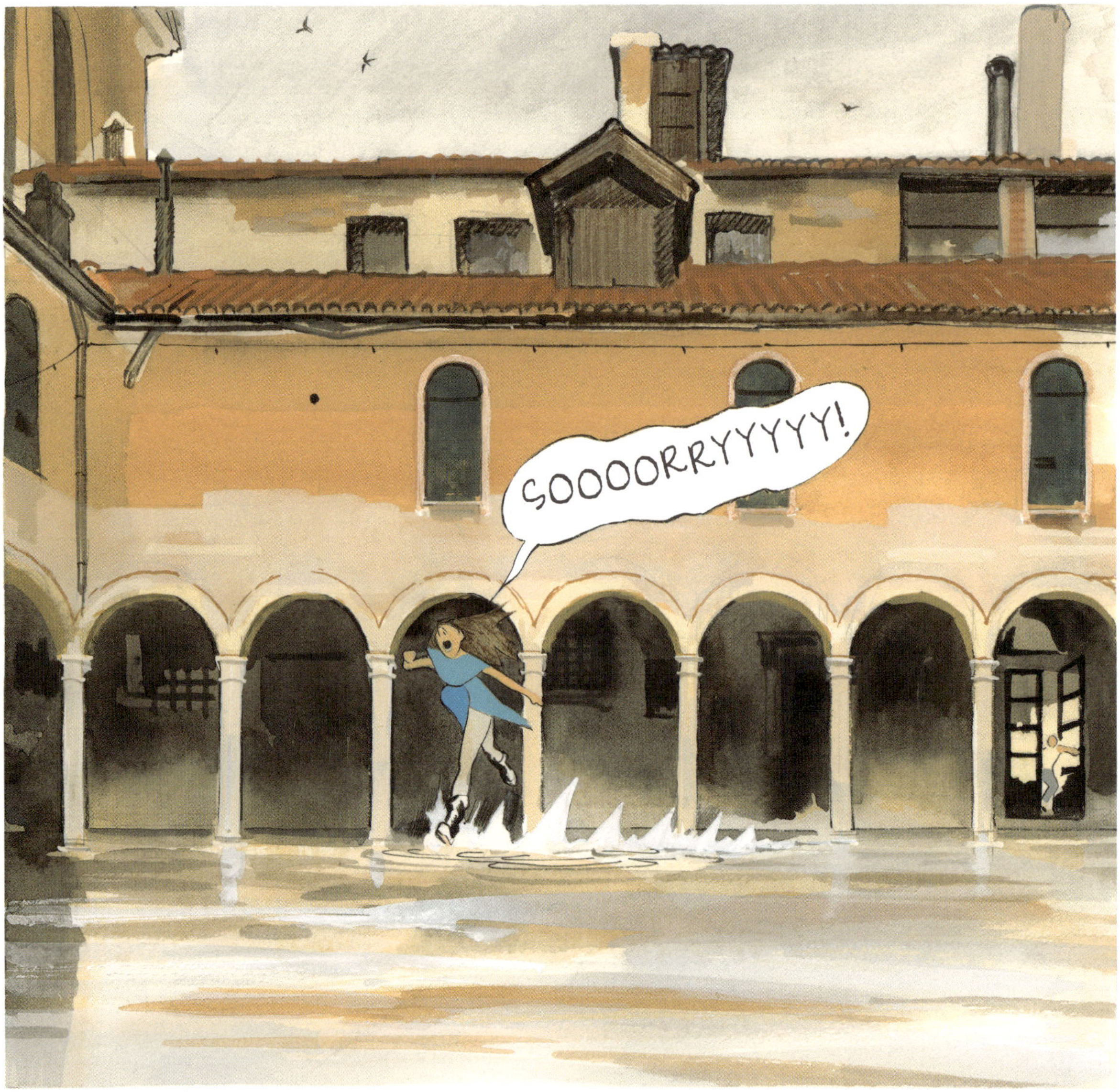
SOOOORRYYYYY!

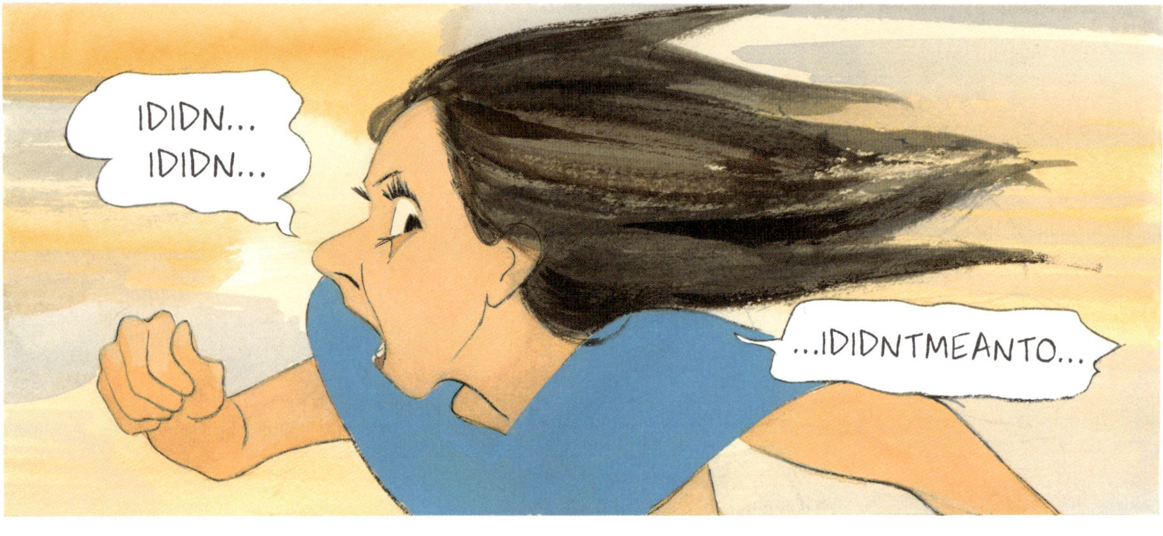
IDIDN...
IDIDN...
...IDIDNTMEANTO...

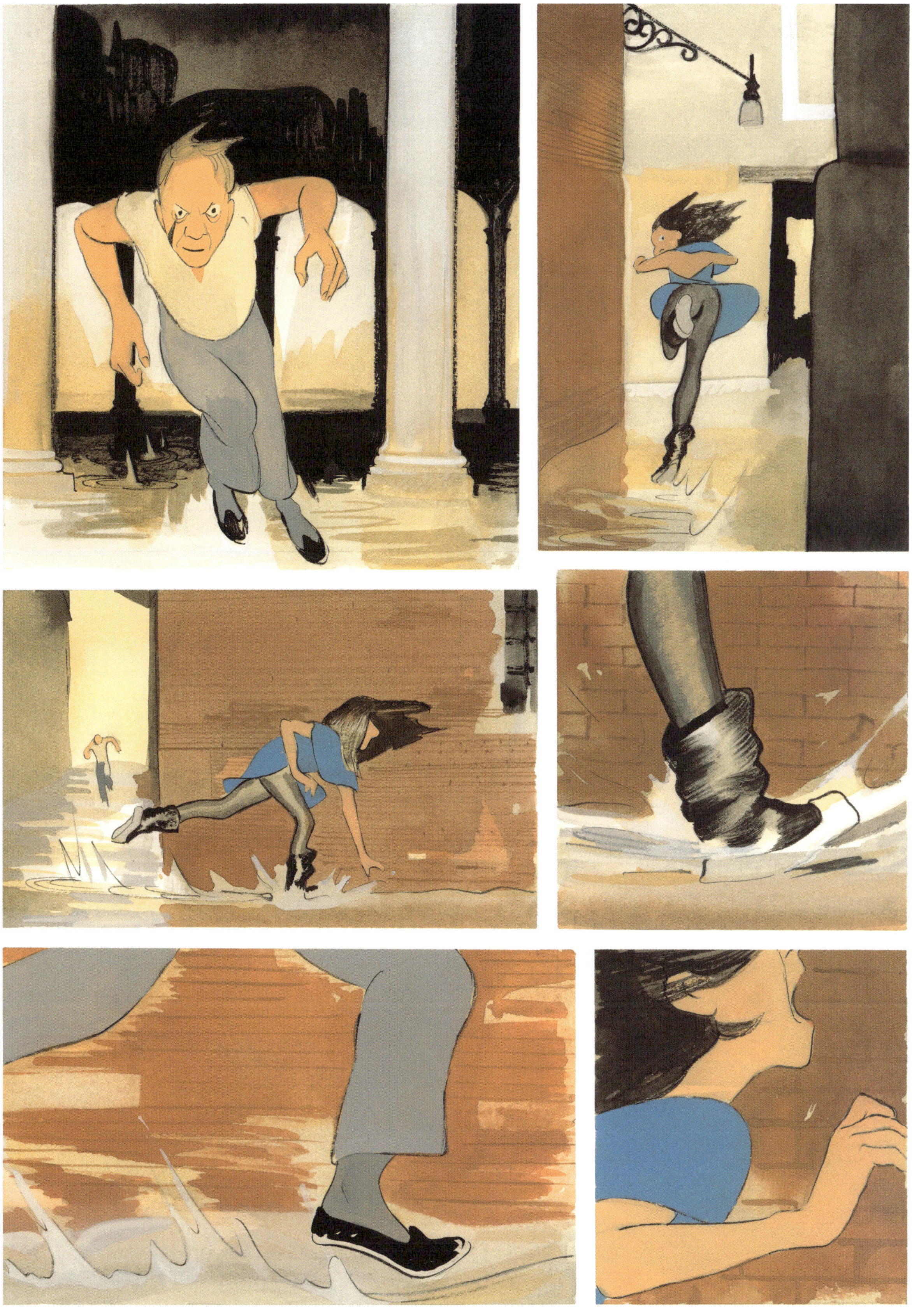

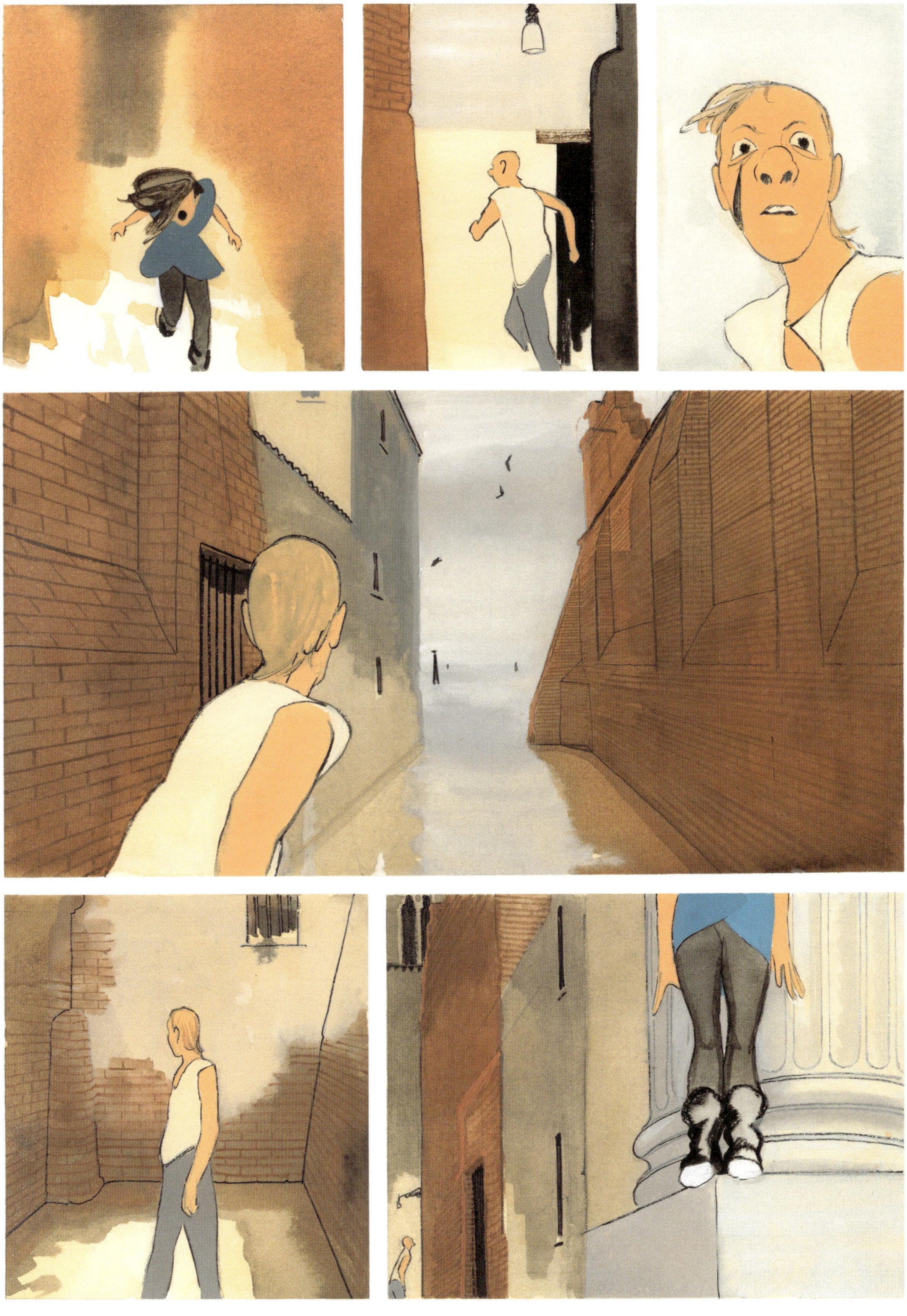

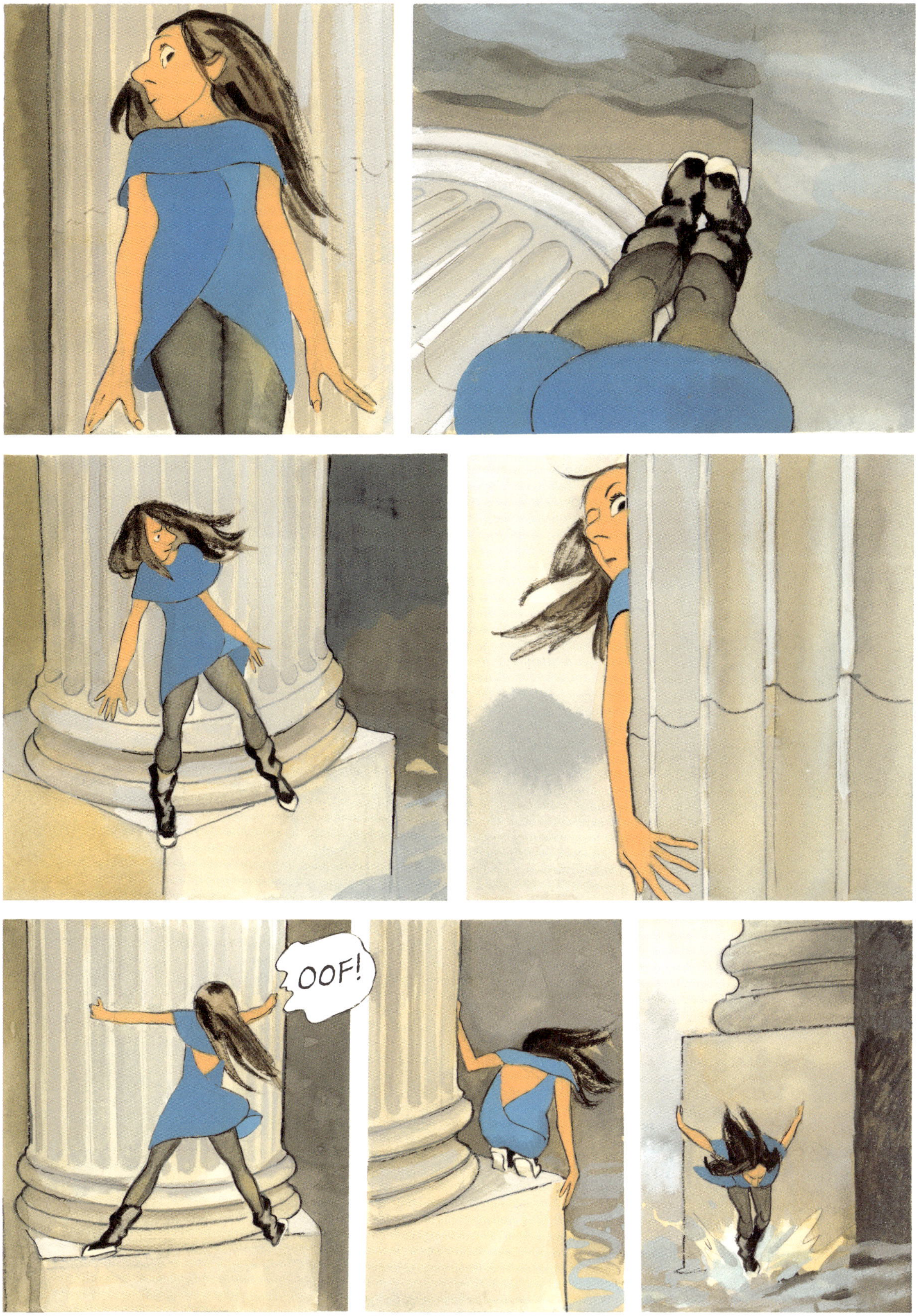
OOF!

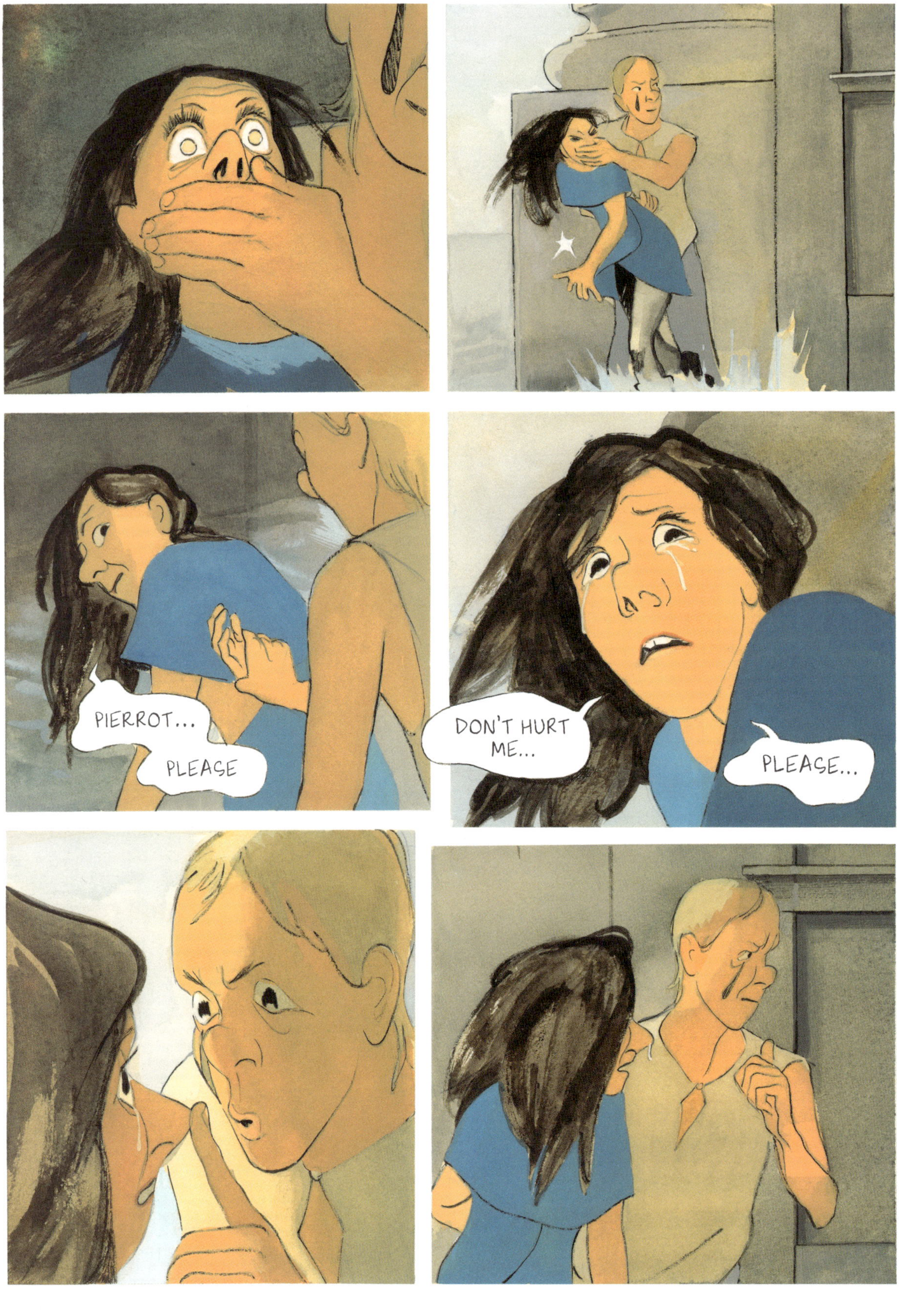
PIERROT...
PLEASE
DON'T HURT ME...
PLEASE...

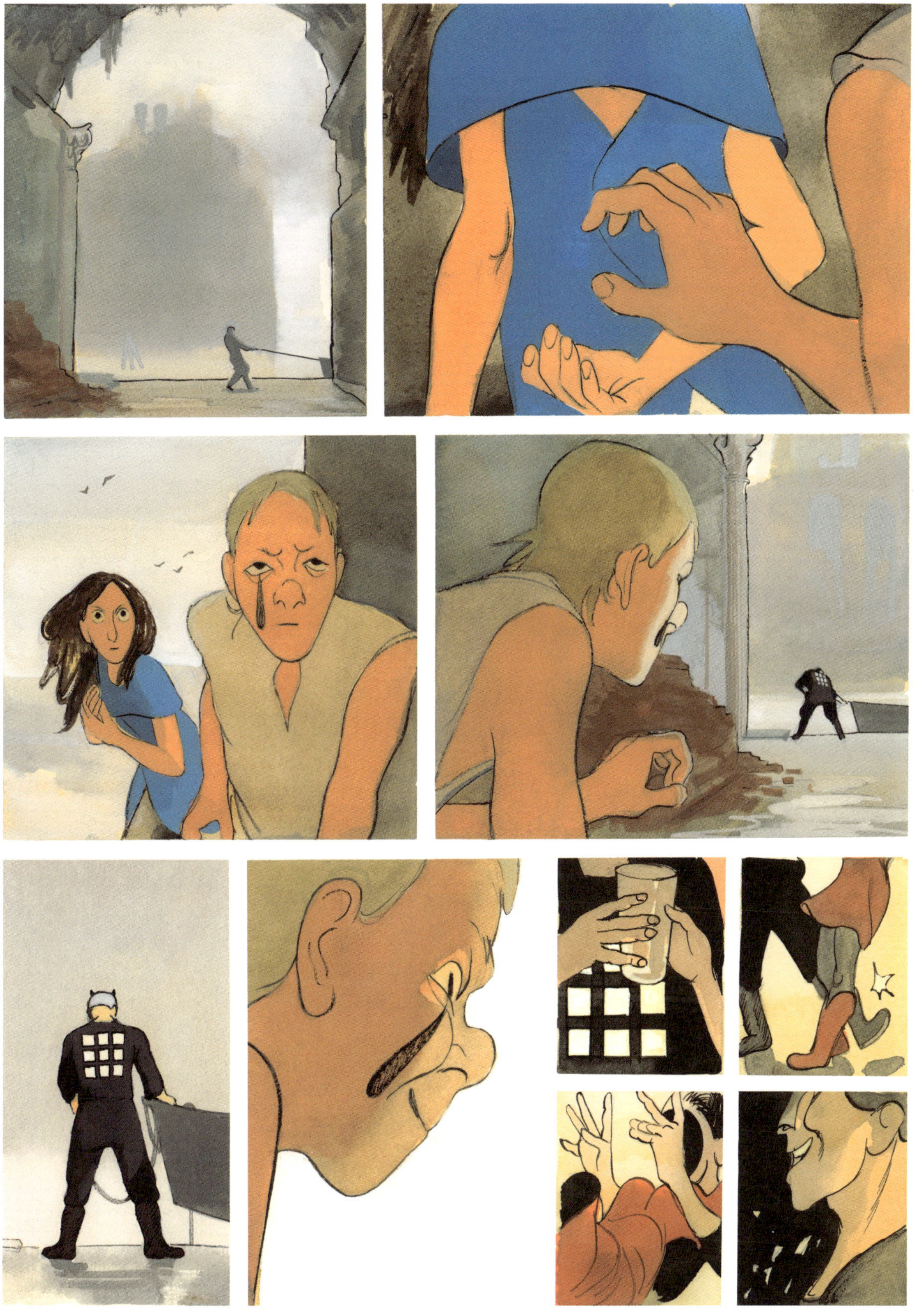

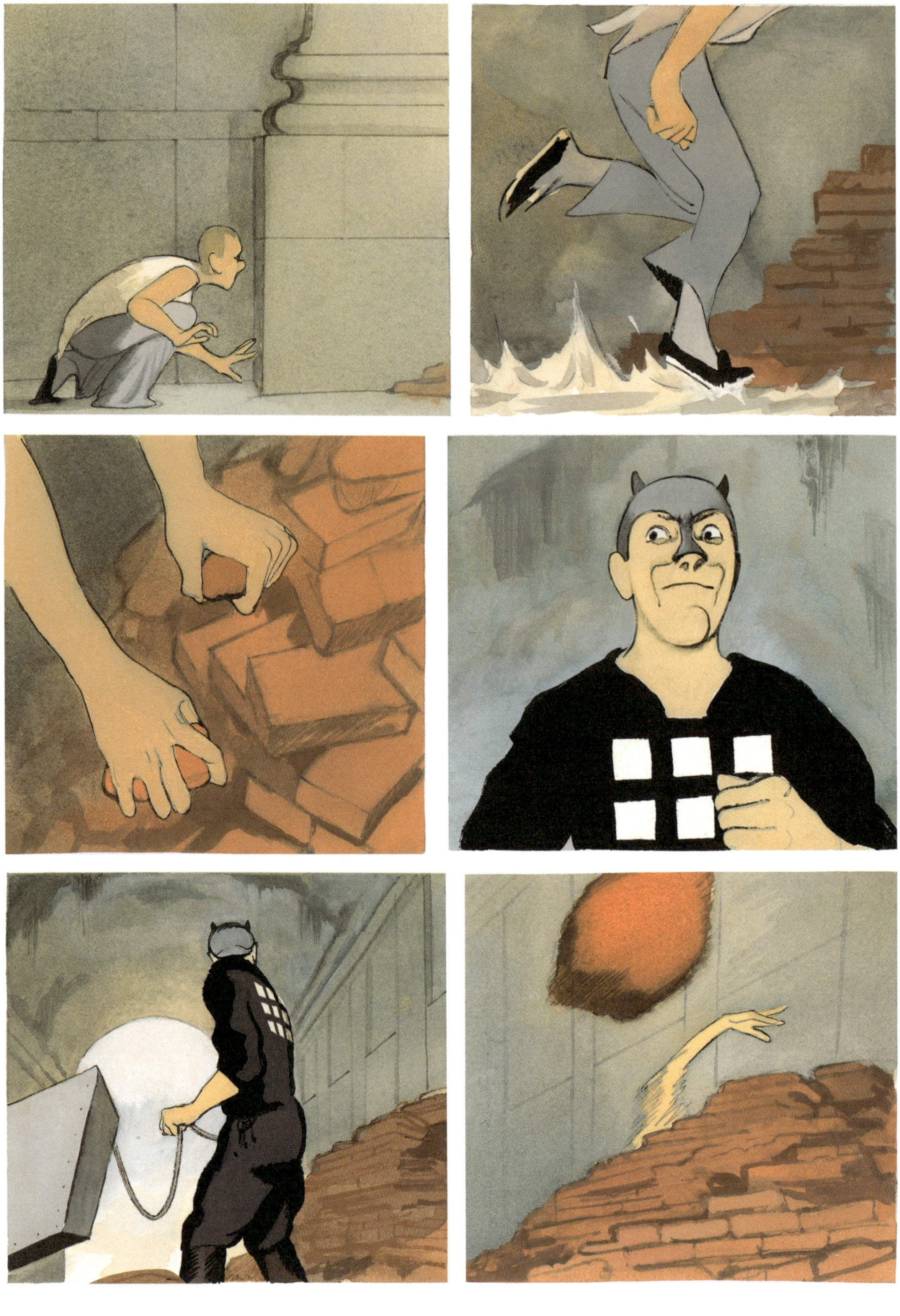

GAAAH!

PIERROT?!?

WHY YA DO THAT TO ME?

LET'S SEE IF YOU CAN FIGURE IT OUT.

BUT THAT WADDN'T ME...

THE BOSS TELL ME WHAT TO DO...

'CAUSE I TRIPPED THE GIRL...?

BRAVO, MONA.

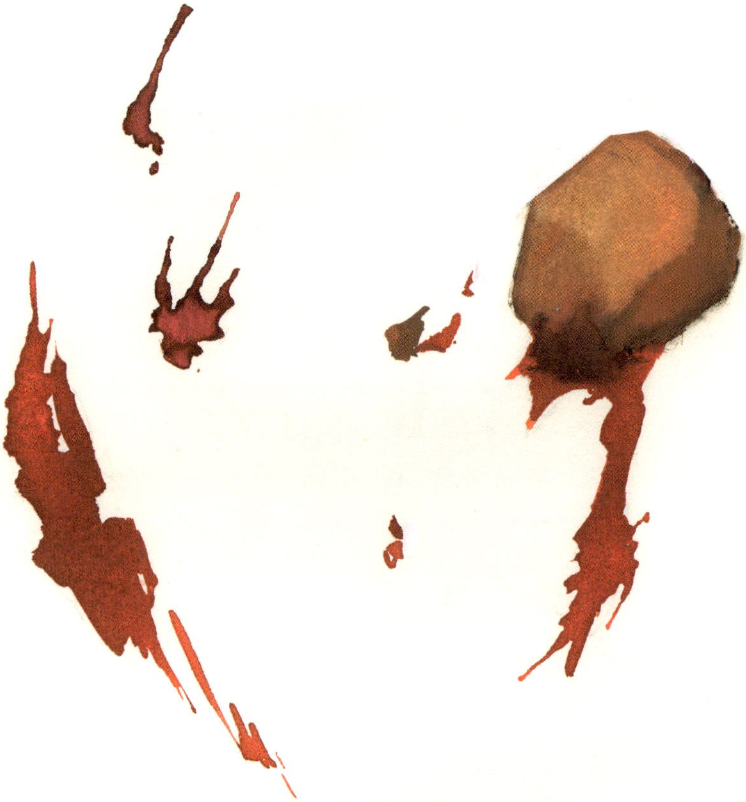

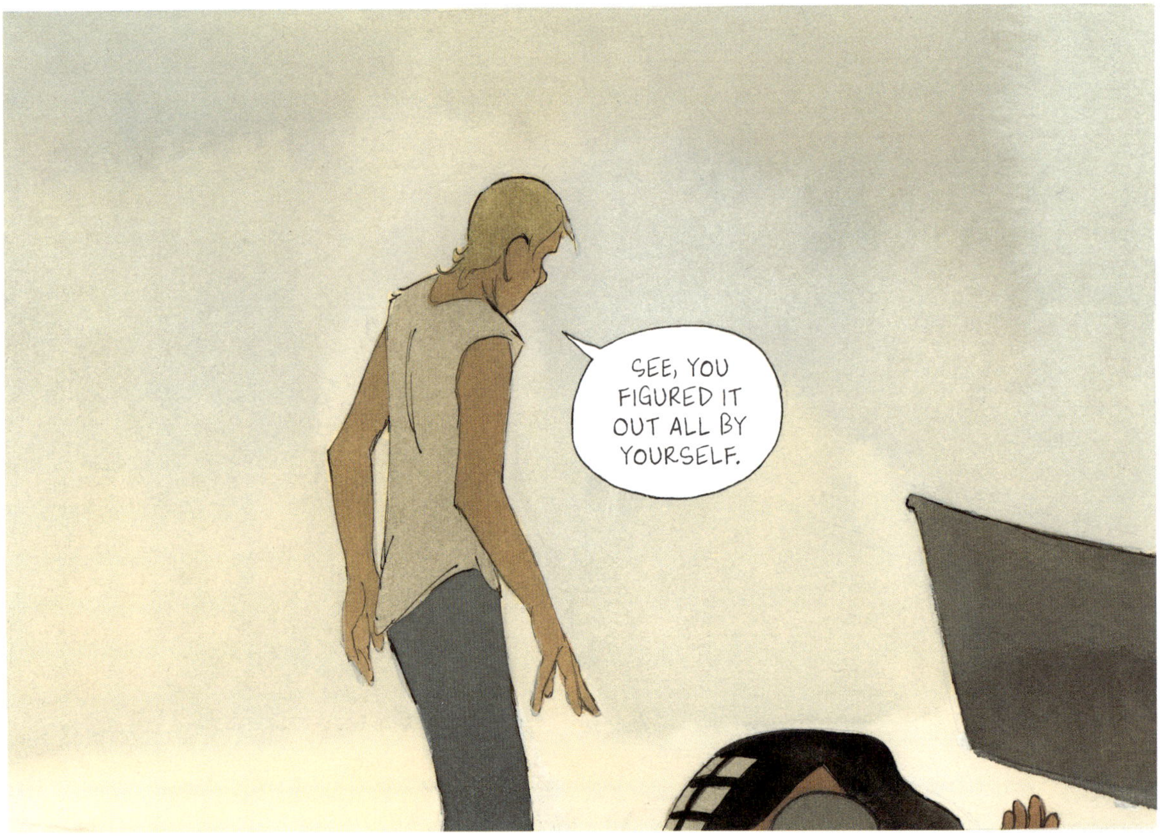
SEE, YOU FIGURED IT OUT ALL BY YOURSELF.

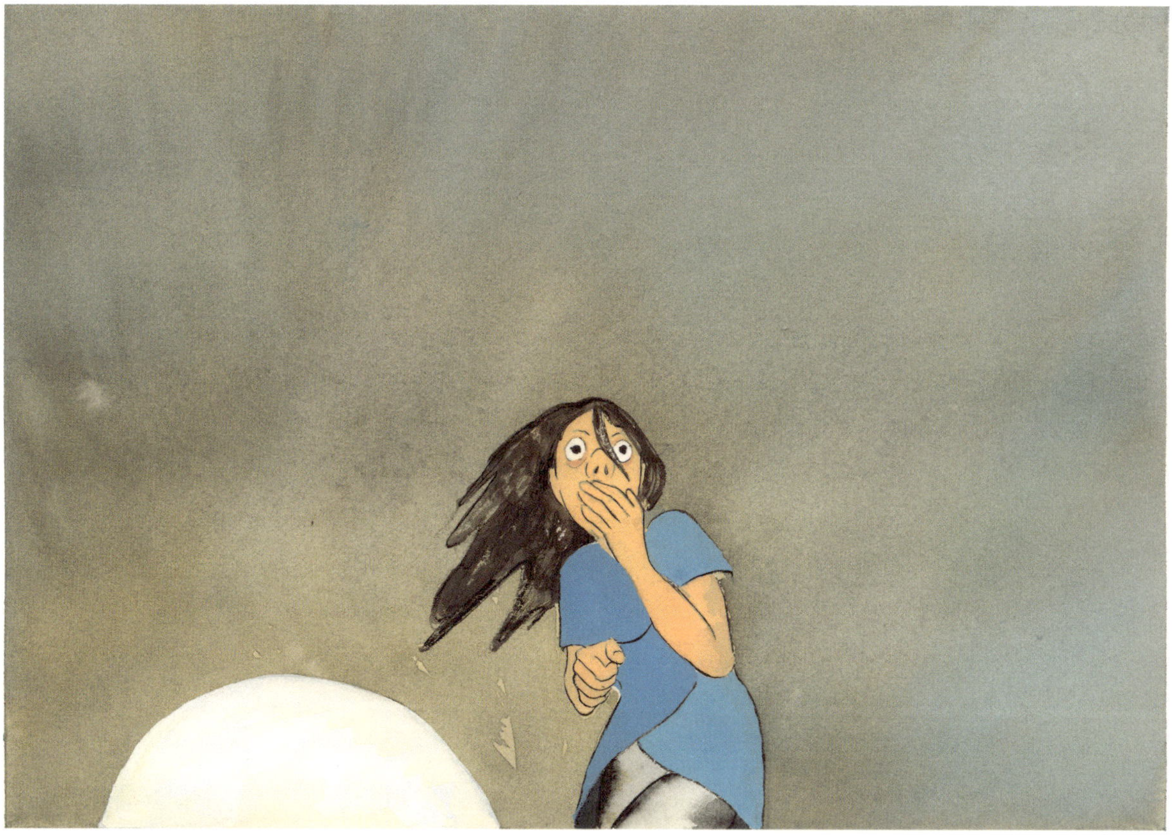

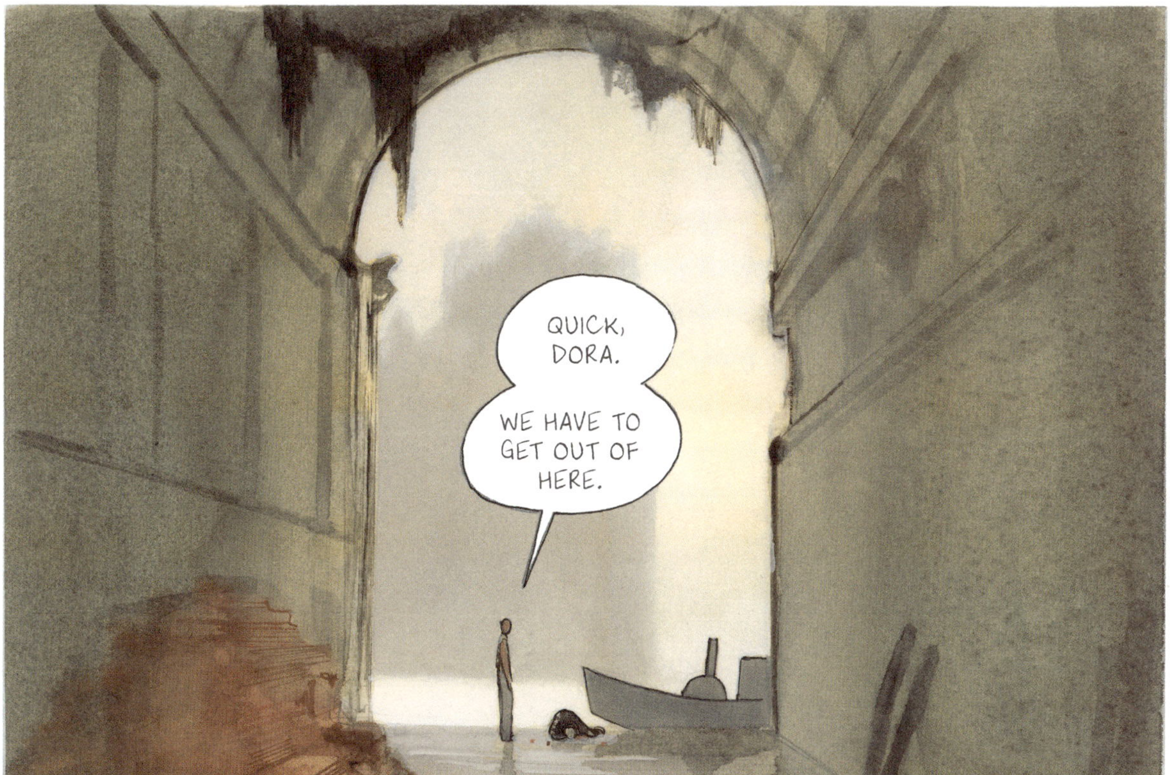
QUICK, DORA.
WE HAVE TO GET OUT OF HERE.

— I'M TELLIN' YA, MAN! HE PRACTICALLY STONED HIM!!!

— THAT DUDE'S MADDER 'N A HATTER!

— MONA LOST 'IM AN' EYE... POP! AN' ALL 'IS FRONT TEETH!

— HE GONE OVERBOARD THIS TIME. WE GOTTA DO SOMETHIN', MISTER.

— PASTA, ROUND UP THE BOYS. ASK AROUND THE GHETTO, TOO.

— SANDRO, YOU GO PICK UP THE STUFF. WE'RE GOING TO HANDLE THIS ONCE AND FOR ALL.

— CAN'T WAIT, MISTER.

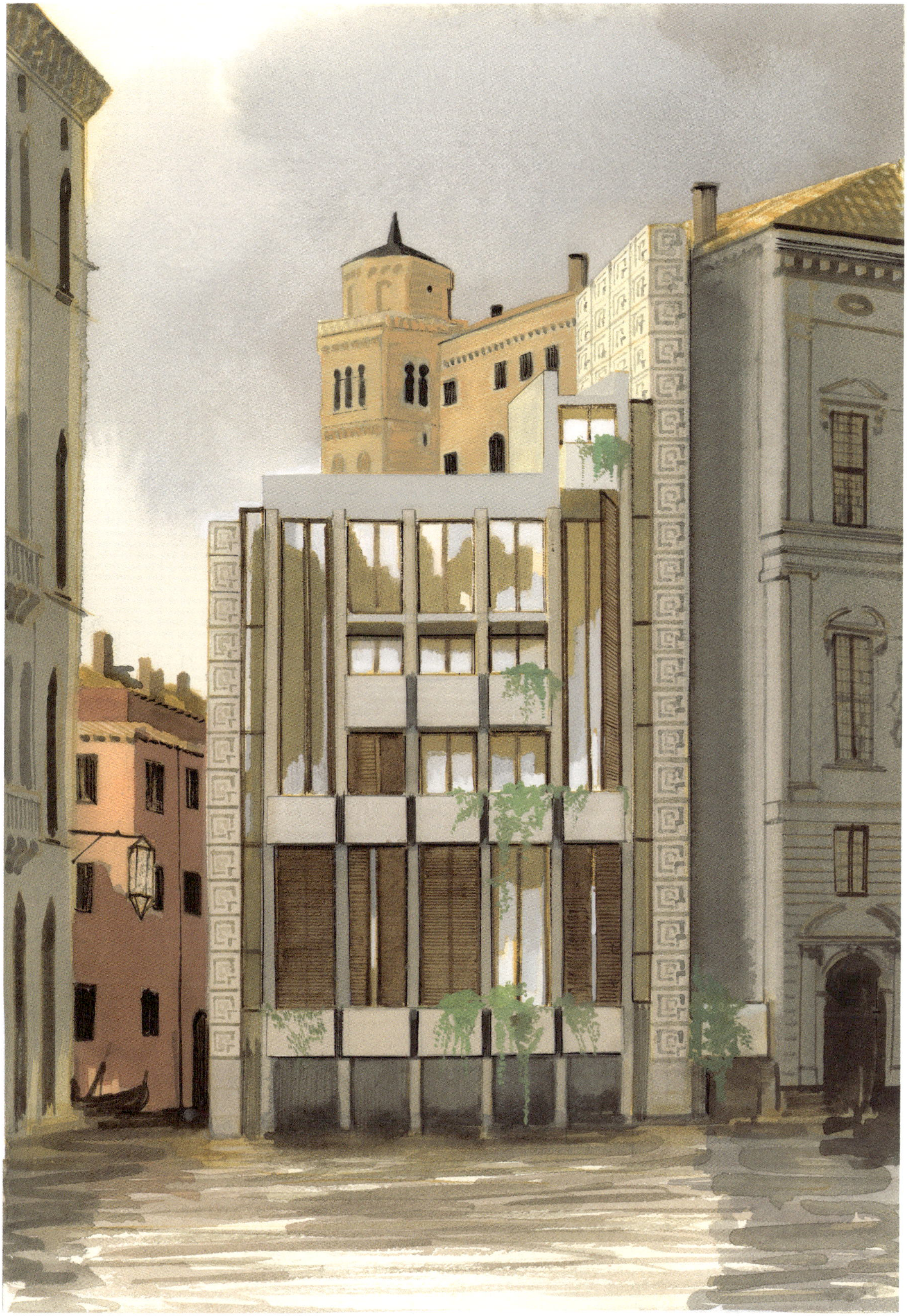

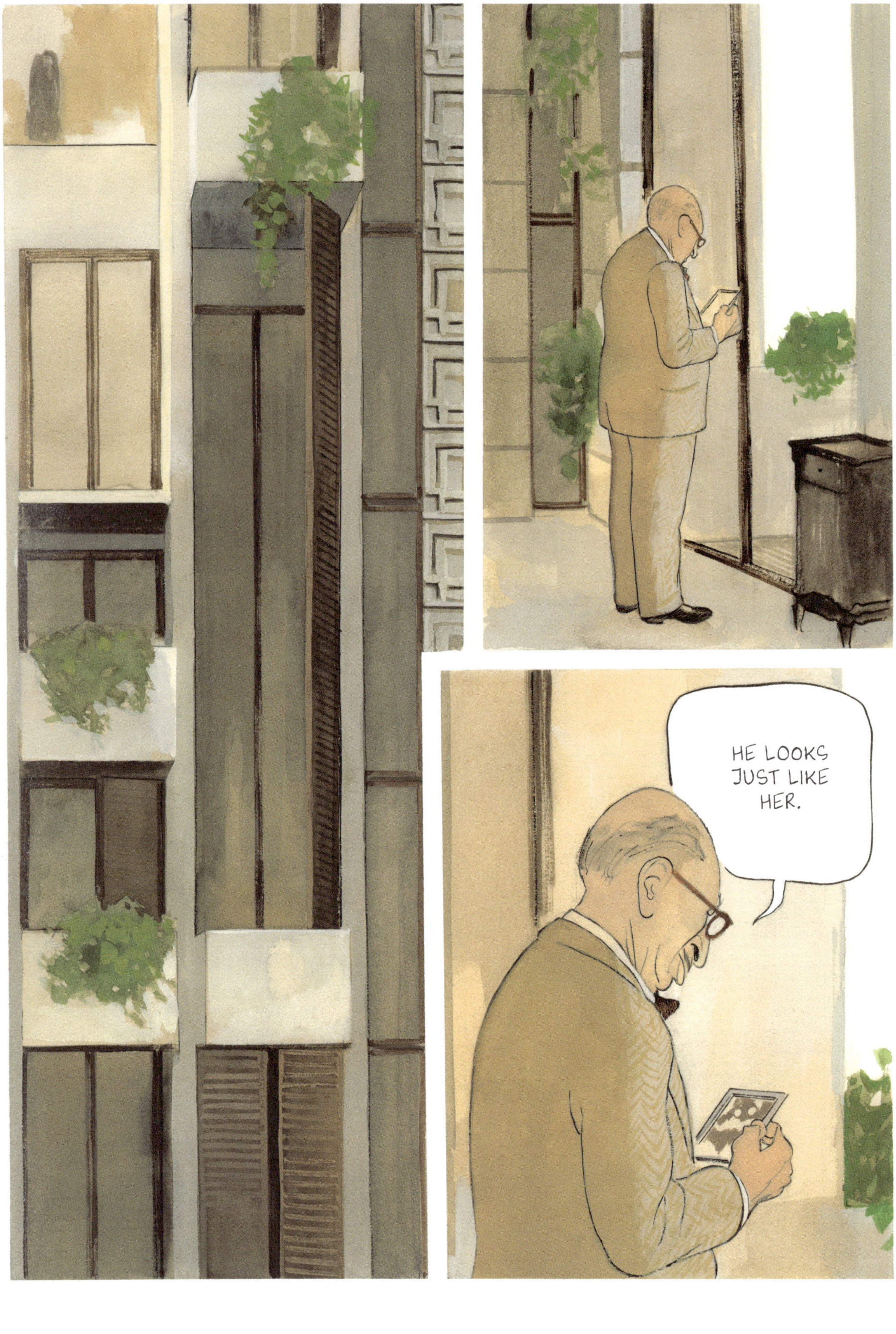
HE LOOKS JUST LIKE HER.

WHAT'S THAT?
NOTHING, I WAS JUST LOOKING AT SOME OLD PICTURES.
VERA, THE LOVE OF MY LIFE.
MY WIFE WAS A VERY INTELLIGENT, DETERMINED WOMAN.
WE WERE AMONG THE LAST TO BE BORN ON THE ISLAND.
DID YOU KNOW THAT?
IT WAS OUR IDEA TO BLOW UP THE BRIDGE.

WE WANTED TO CUT OURSELVES OFF FROM THE MAINLAND, PROTECT THE ISLAND FROM THE INVASION.
THE GREAT INVASION.
OUR TEAM WAS PLANTING THE LAST EXPLOSIVES, WHEN...
YOU WERE BOTH THERE...
A TRAGIC ACCIDENT.
BUT I SURVIVED IT.

"I'VE NEVER BEEN ABLE TO FORGIVE MYSELF."

"I LOST THE LOVE OF MY LIFE, AND PIERROT HIS MOTHER."

"HE WAS JUST A BOY."

"ALL TO SAVE THIS ISLAND."

"BUT SOME WERE ABLE TO CROSS THE MAINLAND..."

"AND TAKE REFUGE HERE..."

"US, FOR EXAMPLE."

"WE WERE LUCKY TO HAVE FOUND YOU."

"TO BE WELCOMED IN CELESTIA."

IT'S NORMAL, DON'T YOU THINK?
KINDRED SPIRITS ARE DESTINED TO MEET.
IN YOUR EYES, I SEE THE SAME DETERMINATION WE HAD THEN.
THE ILLUSION THAT EVERYTHING COULD START OVER FROM HERE...
ON THIS ISLAND OF STONE...
BUILT FROM NOTHING ON THE WATER, LIKE A VISION...
DESTINED TO CONQUER SEA AND EARTH...
SO LONG AGO,
BUT NOW...
NOW YOU ALL ARE THE VISIONARIES, OF A BOUNDLESS REALM:
THE MIND.

BUT THERE ARE SO FEW OF US AND WE DON'T...
GIVE ME YOUR HAND, ROSSELLA ...
YOU KNOW, FROM ABOVE, THIS ISLAND IS IN THE SHAPE OF TWO HANDS INTERTWINED.
NOW SQUEEZE MY HAND. HARD!
GOOD!
DON'T BE SCARED!
HARDER!
I DON'T UNDERSTAND WHAT...
TAKE COMMAND OF CELESTIA.
ALL TOGETHER.

PLEASE.

DOCTOR? HERE WE ARE.

PERFECT, LET'S GET STARTED.

SUCH A LOVELY TEAM.

VERY WELL.

READY FOR ACTION?

JUST A FEW POINTS BEFORE WE GO SEARCHING FOR DORA.

IT'S STILL LOW TIDE.

WITHIN TWENTY-FOUR HOURS IT'LL GO UP ABOUT SIX FEET.

THE WHOLE ISLAND WILL BE FLOODED.

FAMILIAR PATHS WILL BECOME BOTTOMLESS WELLS.

I DON'T WANT TO FISH OUT YOUR BODIES COME LOW TIDE.

BE VERY CAREFUL.

KEEP AWAY FROM PEOPLE IN MASKS, THEY'RE VERY DANGEROUS.

BUT DON'T LOSE CONTACT WITH PIERROT.

MY SON WAS NEVER EASY TO GET ALONG WITH.

I KNOW HE ISN'T EVERYONE'S FAVORITE.

BUT WE NEED HIM.

NO ONE KNOWS THIS ISLAND'S SECRETS BETTER.

...AND MOST IMPORTANTLY, HE HAS A STRONG BOND WITH DORA.

SHE'S THE ONLY PERSON HE'S EVER LET GET CLOSE TO HIM.
IN HIS OWN WAY, I THINK HE LOVES HER.
BUT WHAT IF SHE LEFT THE ISLAND?
SHE COULDN'T HAVE DONE IT ALONE.
AND IF SO, SHE WOULDN'T LAST LONG...
OUT OF CELESTIA, THERE'S HARDLY ANYONE LEFT.

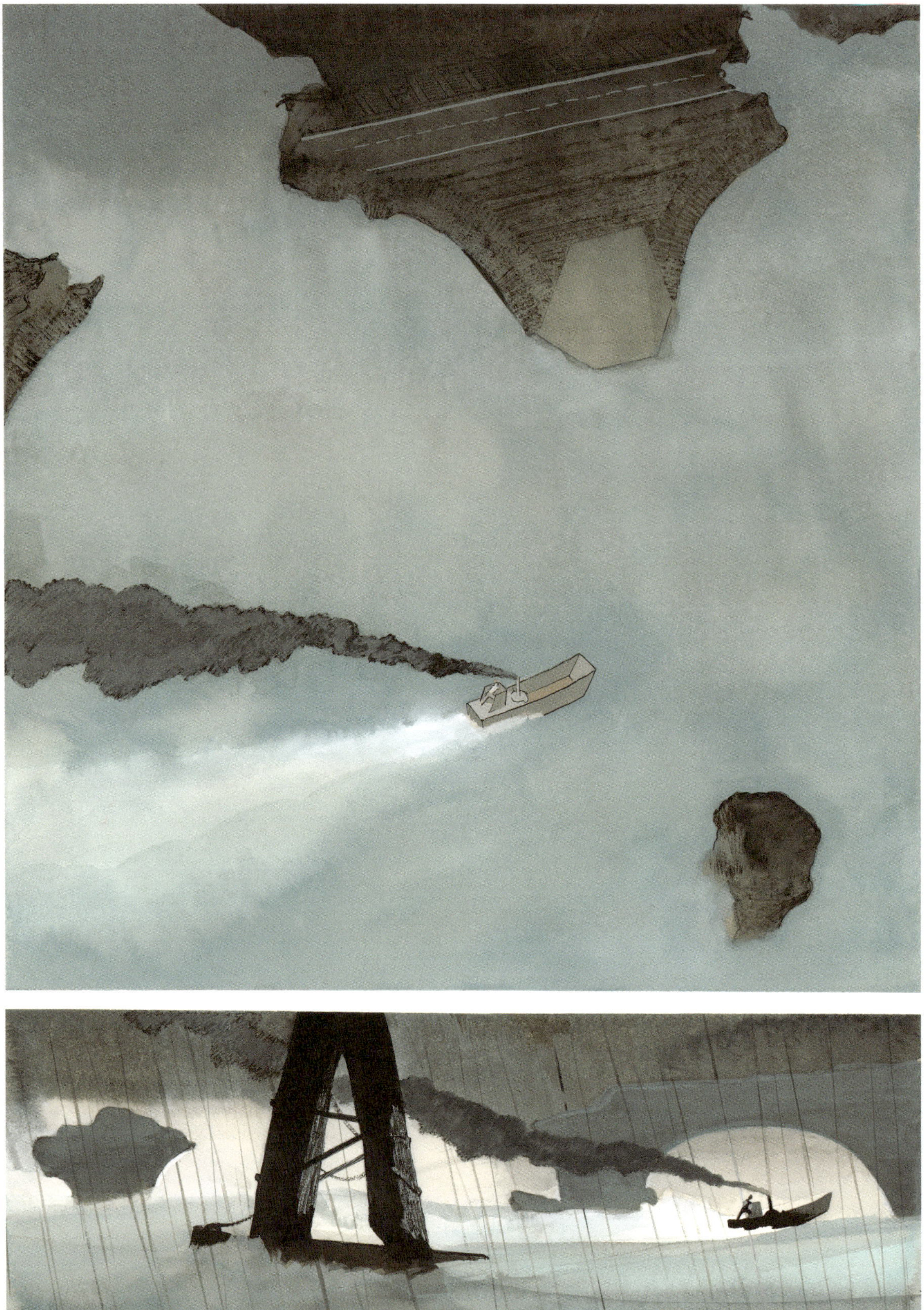

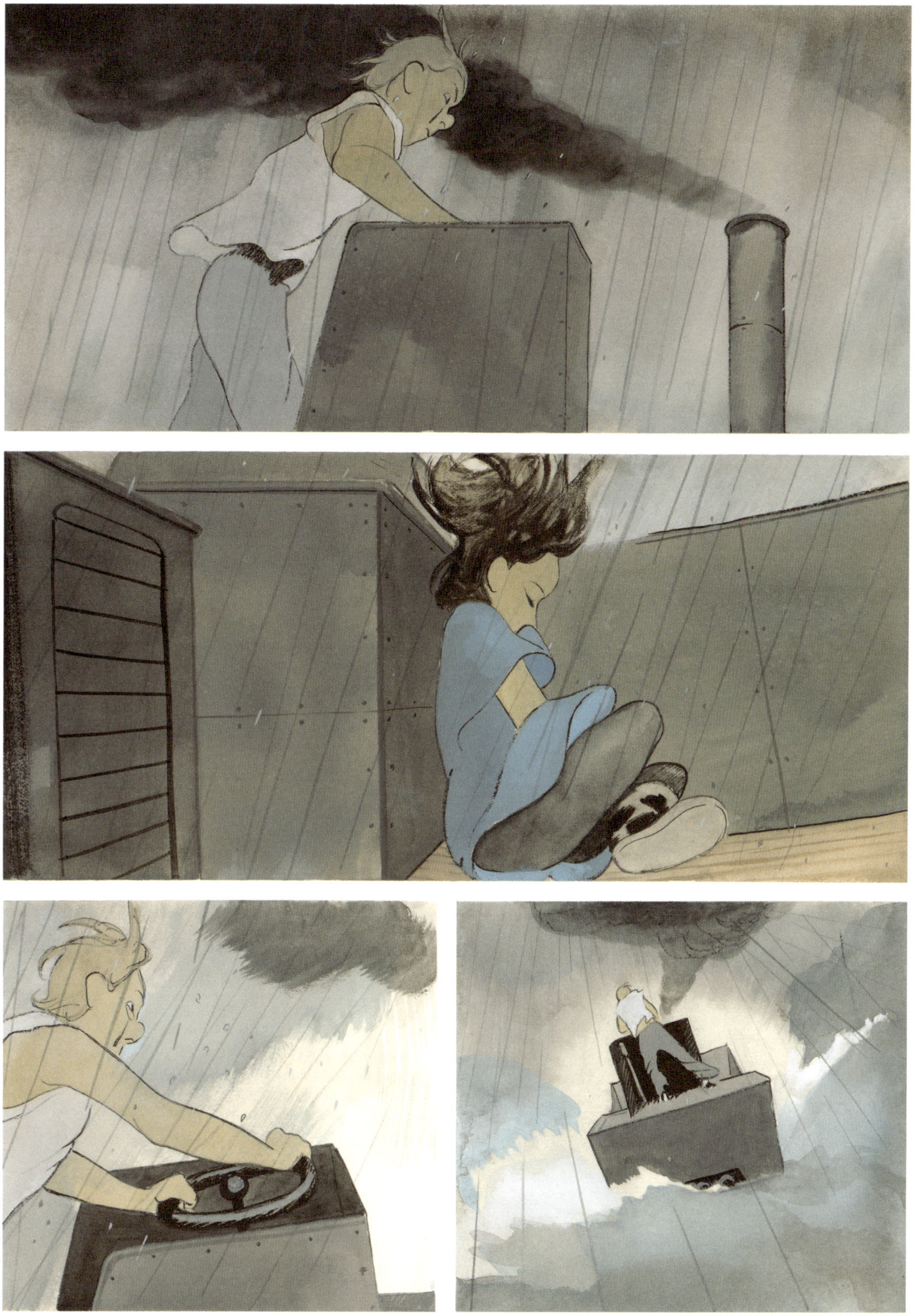

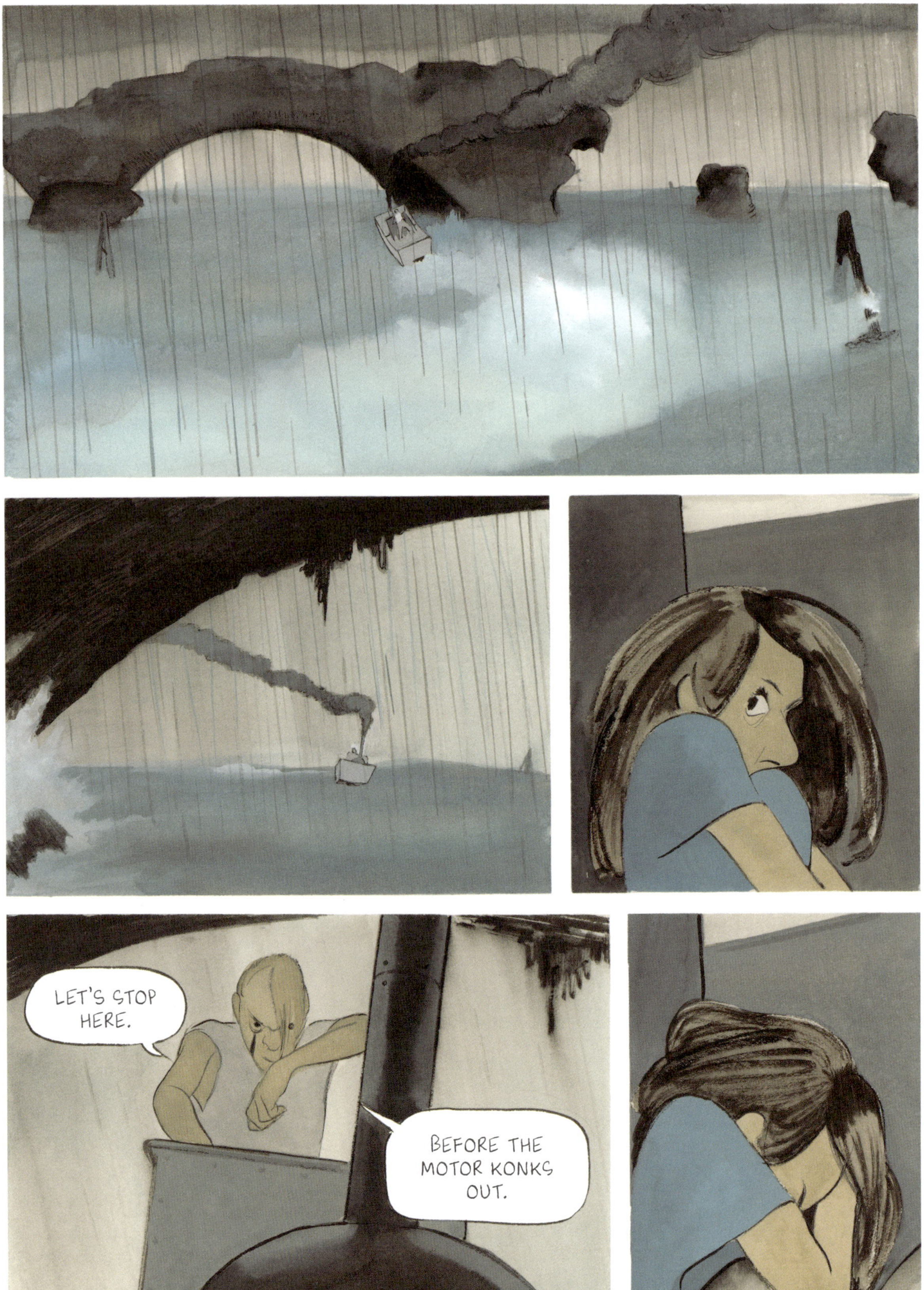
LET'S STOP HERE.
BEFORE THE MOTOR KONKS OUT.

I'M HUNGRY.
LET'S SEE WHAT'S IN THE LARDER.
FUCK ALL!
AND WHAT'S WITH ALL YOUR SNIVELING?!?
WELL? SPEAK UP!
WHY ARE YOU ALWAYS SULKING AT ME?!
YOU SCARE ME.

DO YOU NOT REALIZE WHO WE'VE JUST SICCED ON US?!?
DON'T THOSE PEOPLE SCARE YOU?
WHAT'S IT GOT TO DO WITH ME?!?
PIERROT, PLEASE... TWO WEEKS, I'VE BEEN WANDERING...
DID YOU REALLY HAVE TO TAKE ME WITH YOU???
WASN'T THAT YOU?!
WASN'T THAT YOU?!?
STOP!
JUST LEAVE ME ALONE!
OK?

OK?!

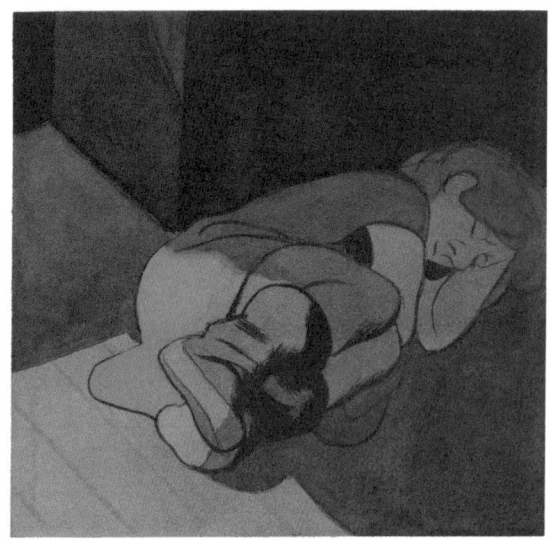

IT STOPPED RAINING.

LET'S GO.

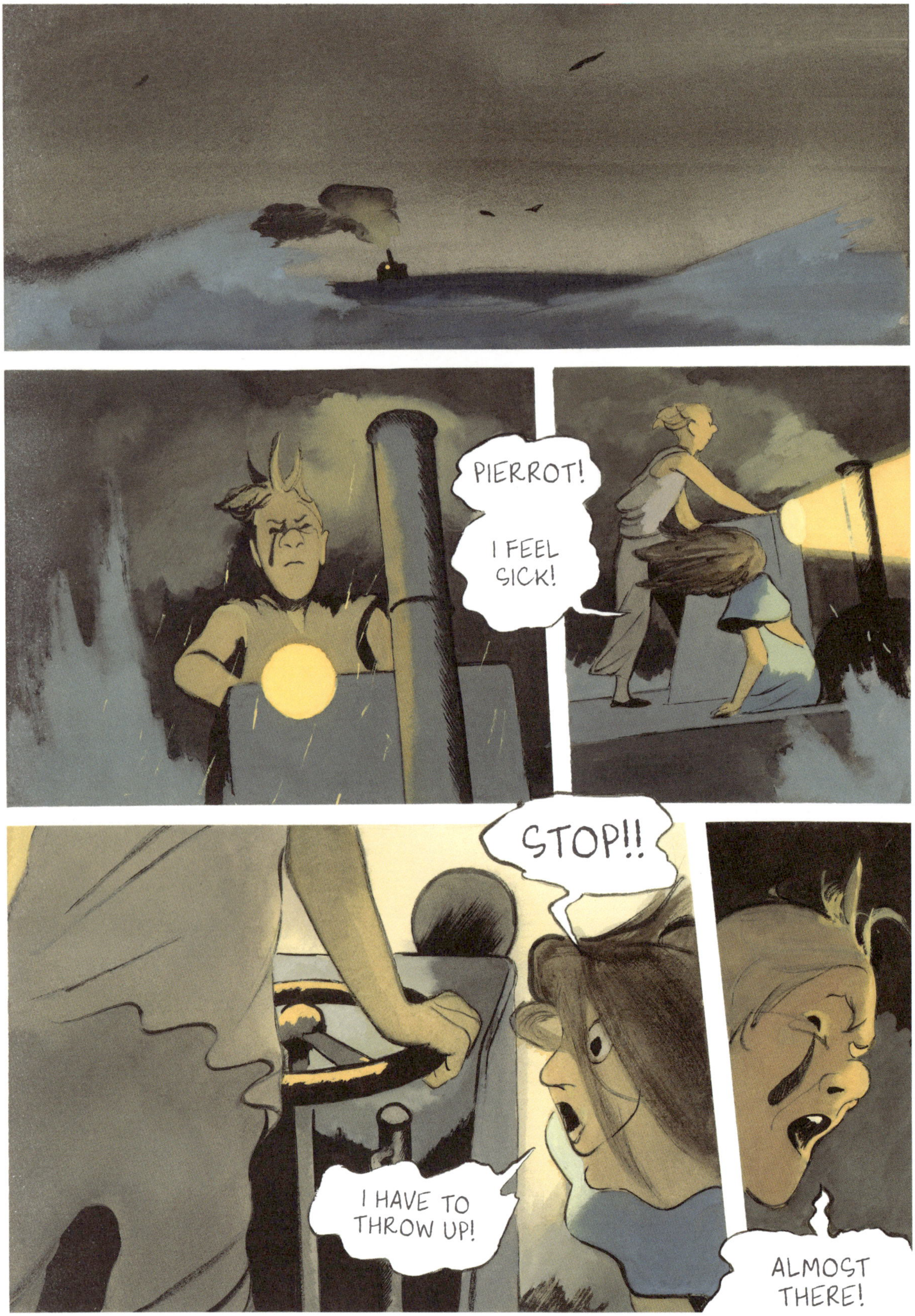
PIERROT!
I FEEL SICK!
STOP!!
I HAVE TO THROW UP!
ALMOST THERE!

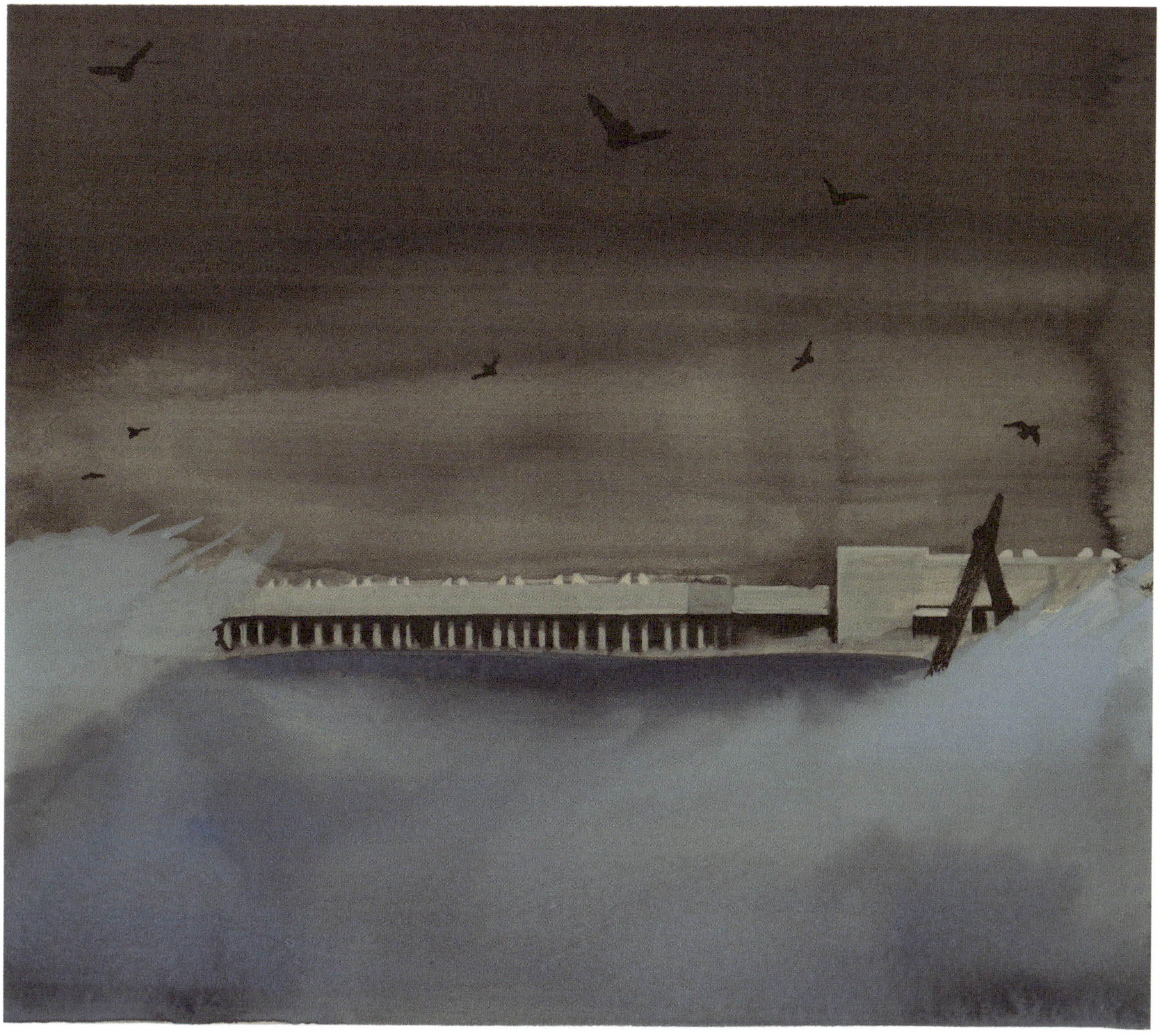

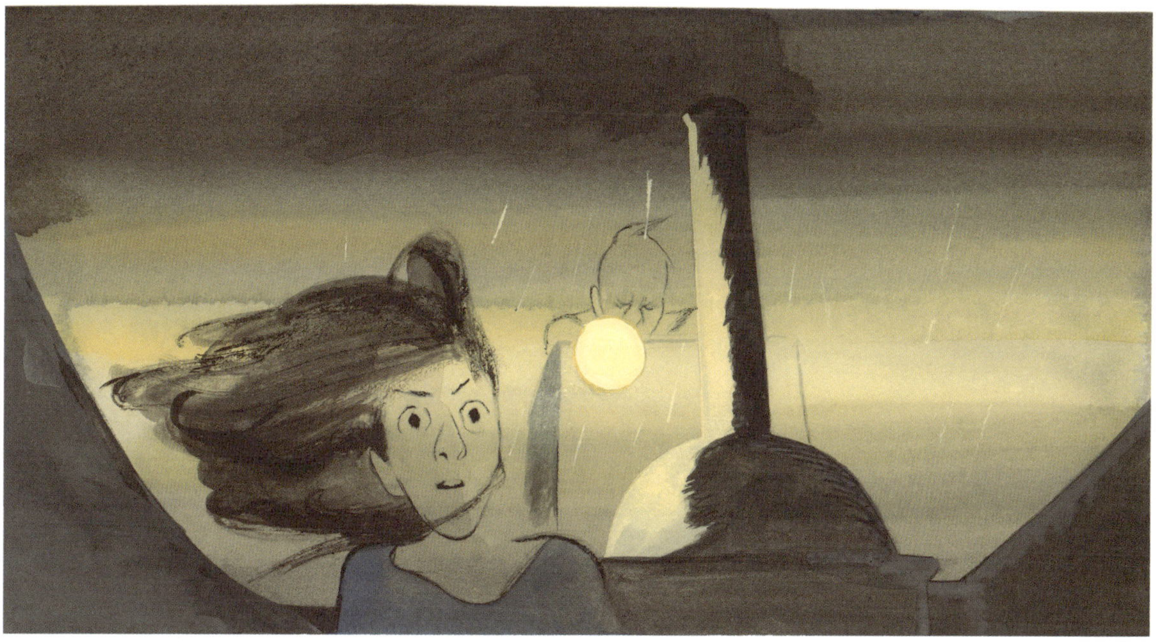

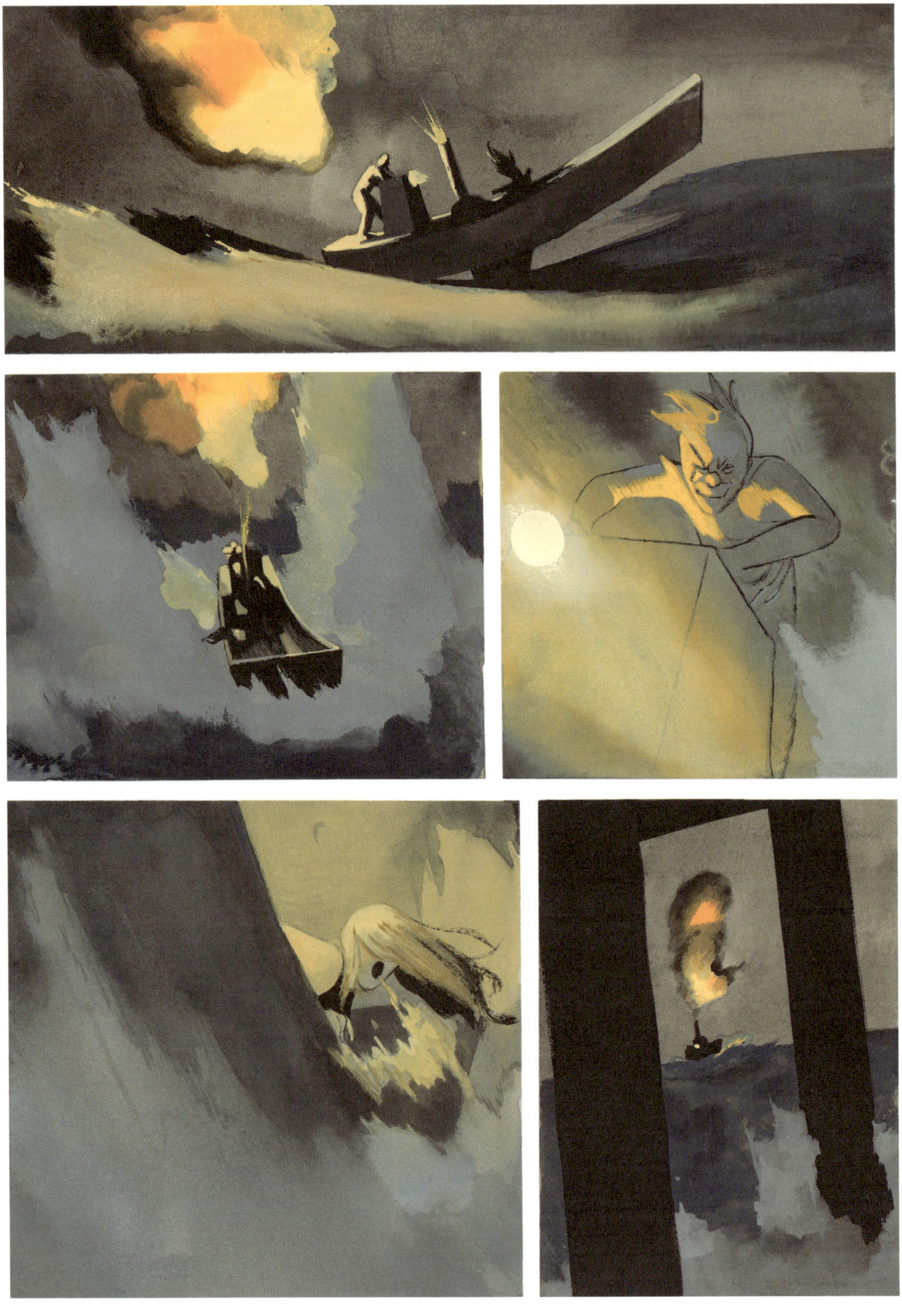

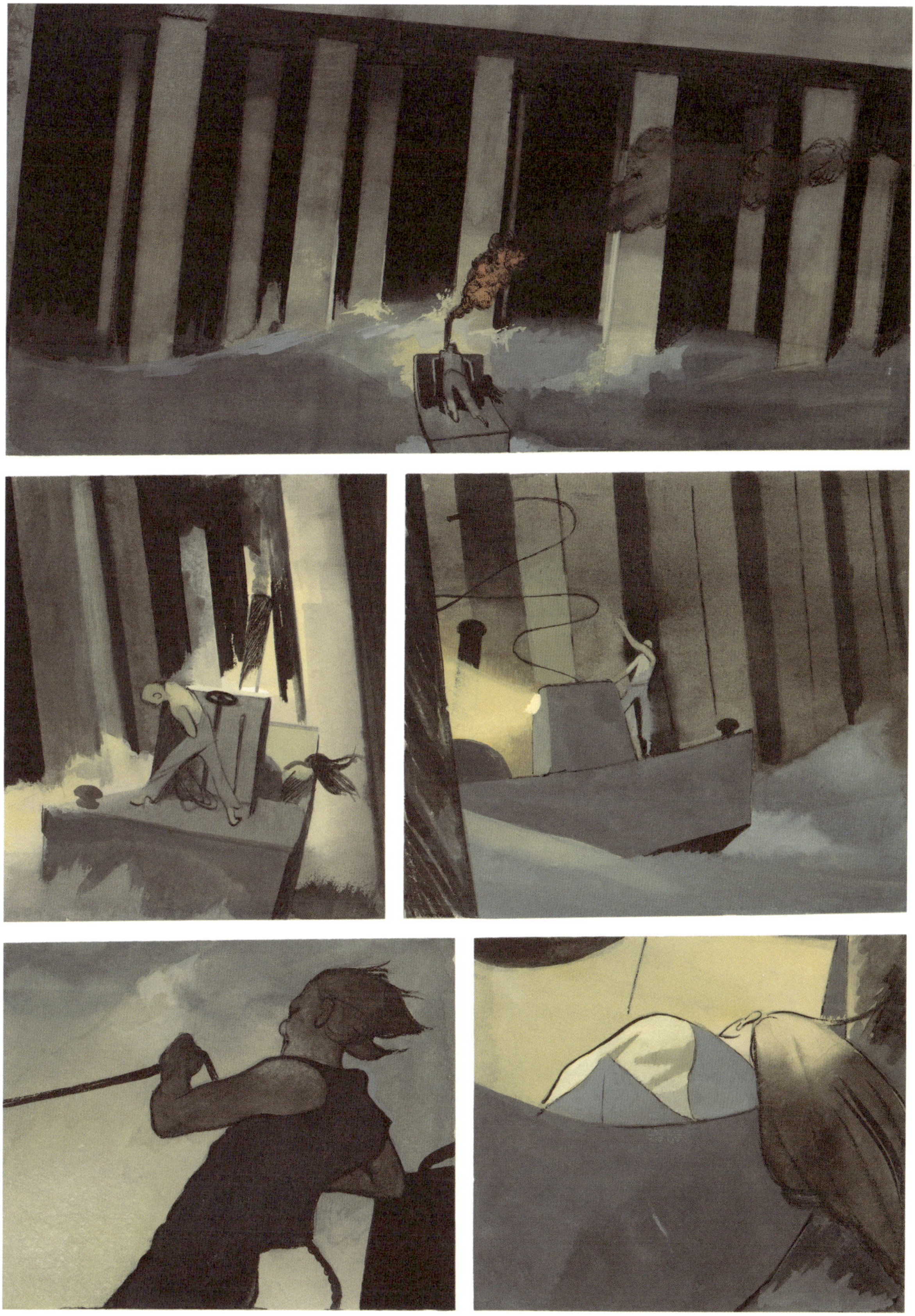

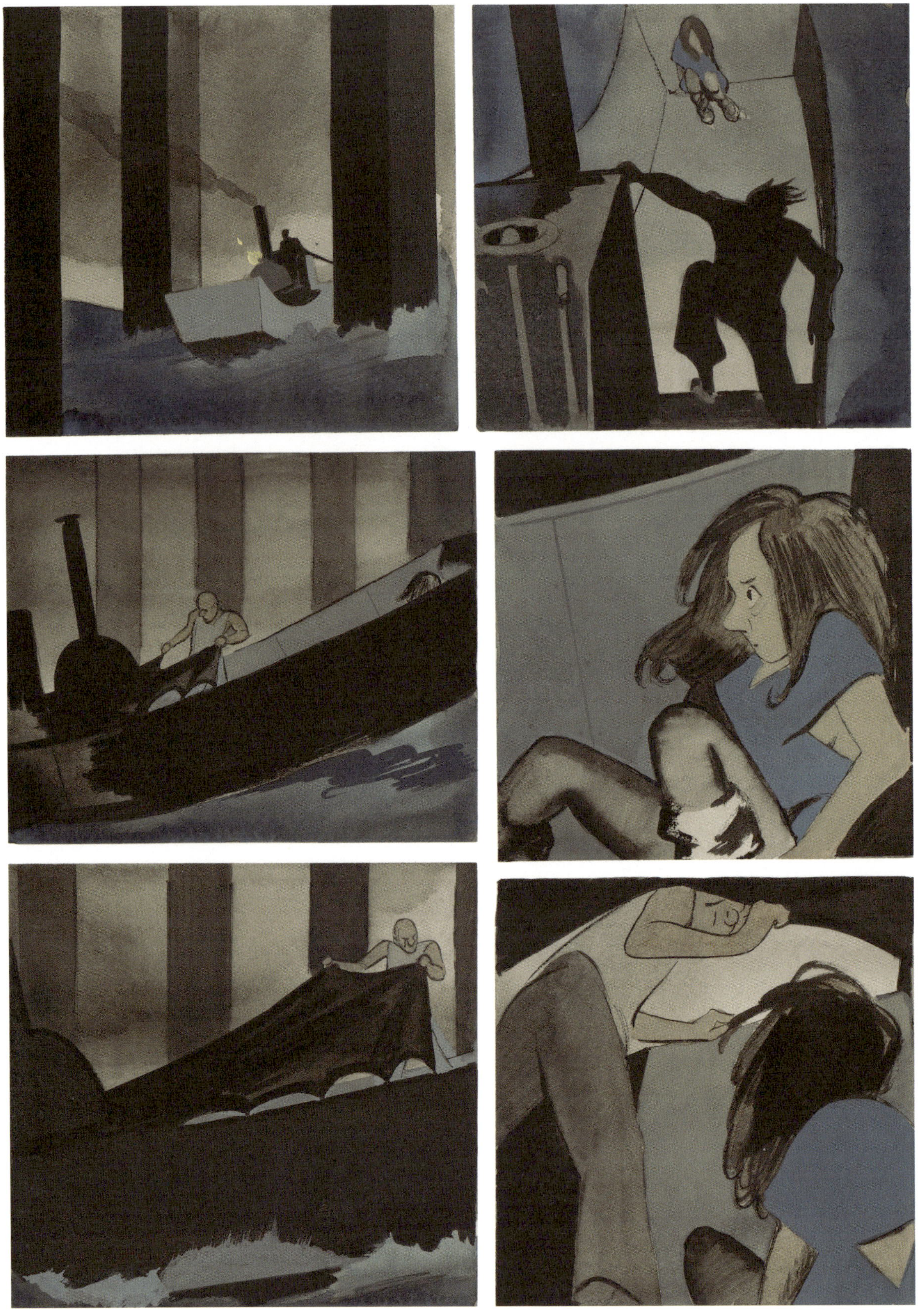

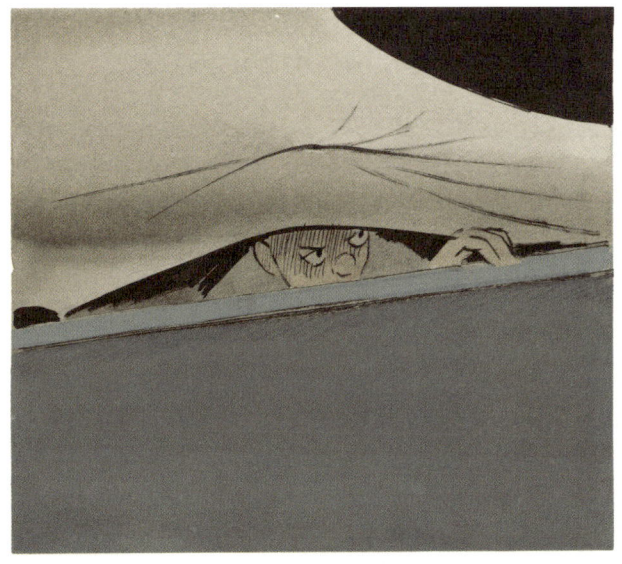

CLICK

WE CAN SLEEP HERE.

WE'LL EAT TOMORROW.

I FOUND A BLANKET IN CARGO.

WE'LL HAVE TO SHARE.

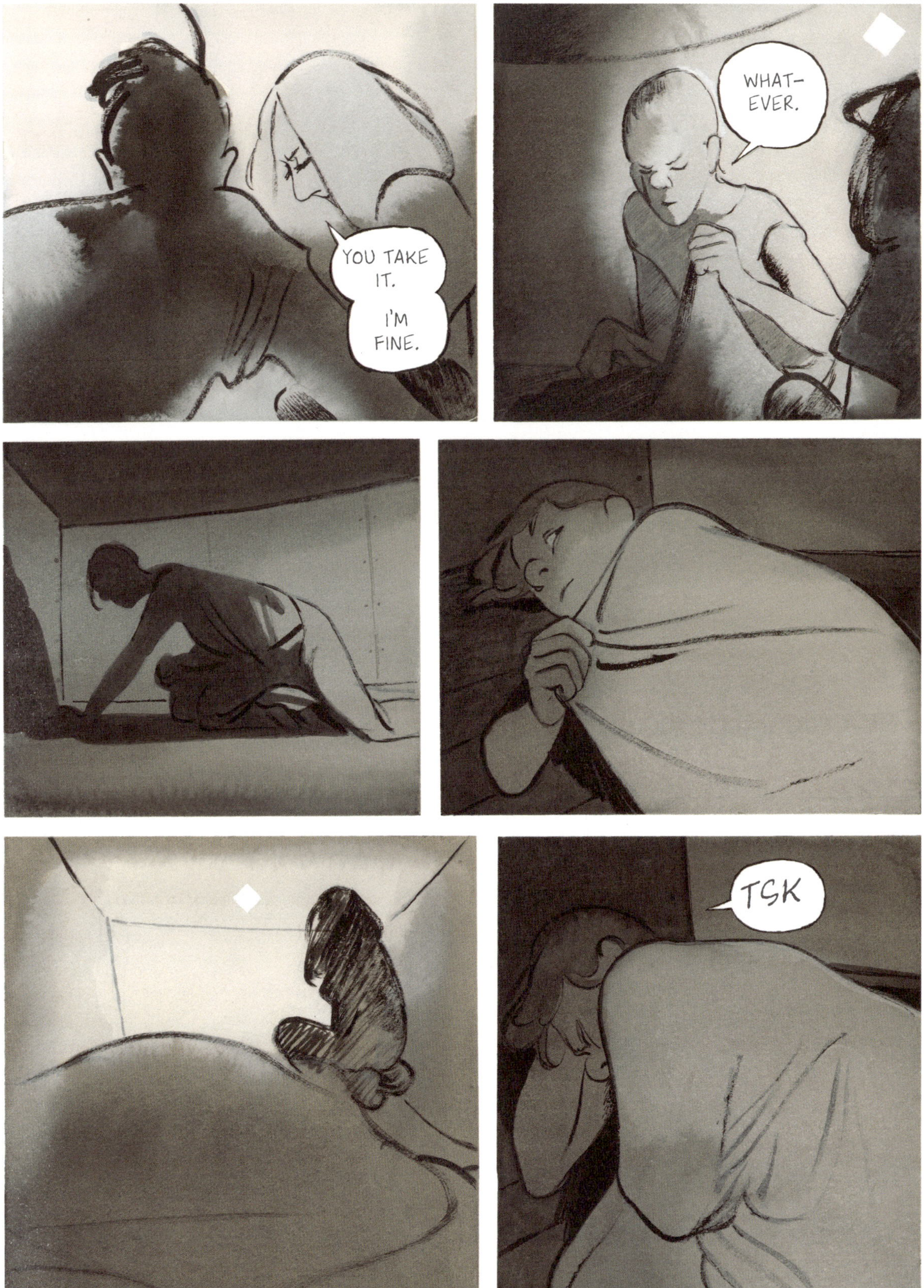
YOU TAKE IT.
I'M FINE.
WHAT-EVER.
TSK

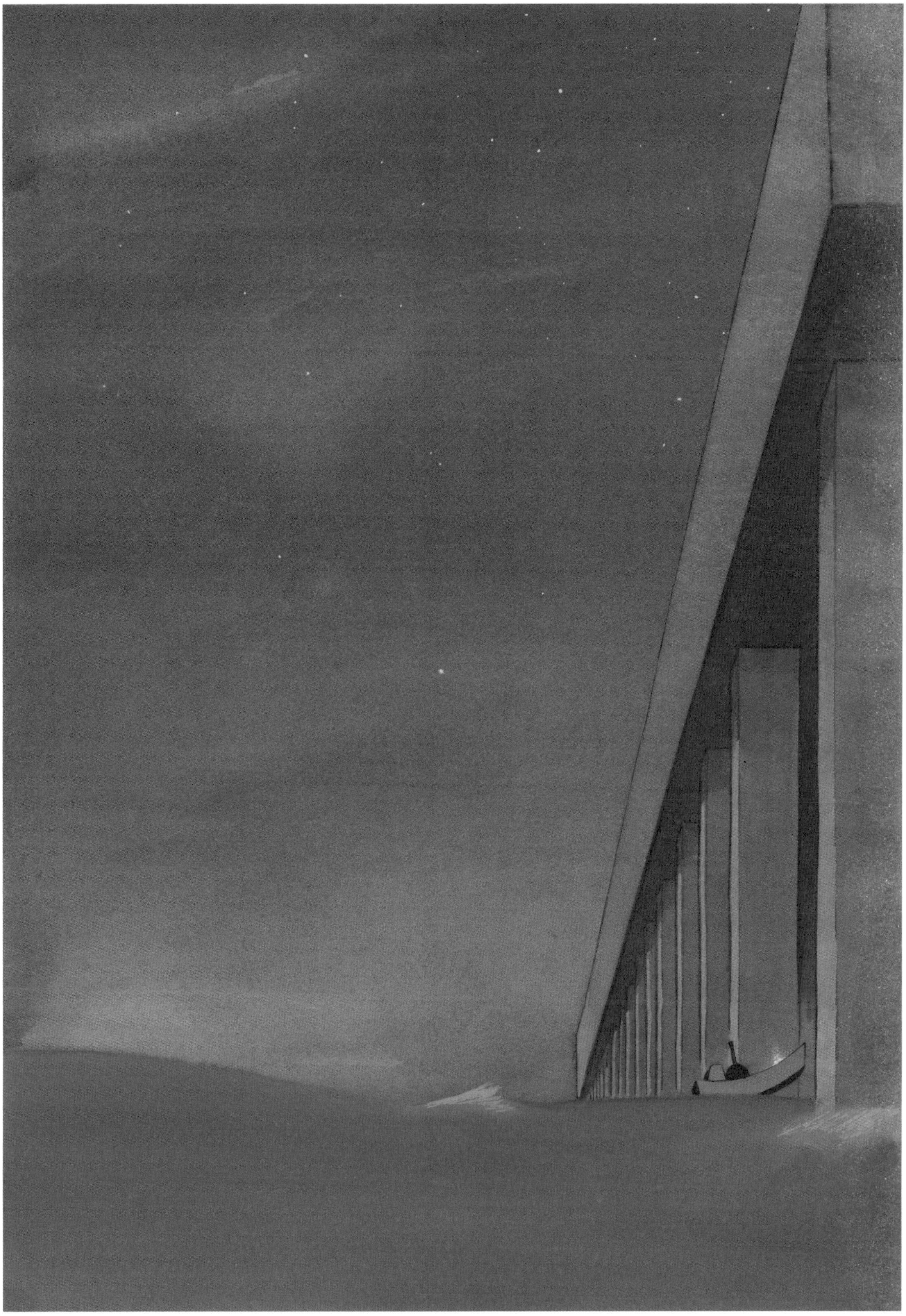

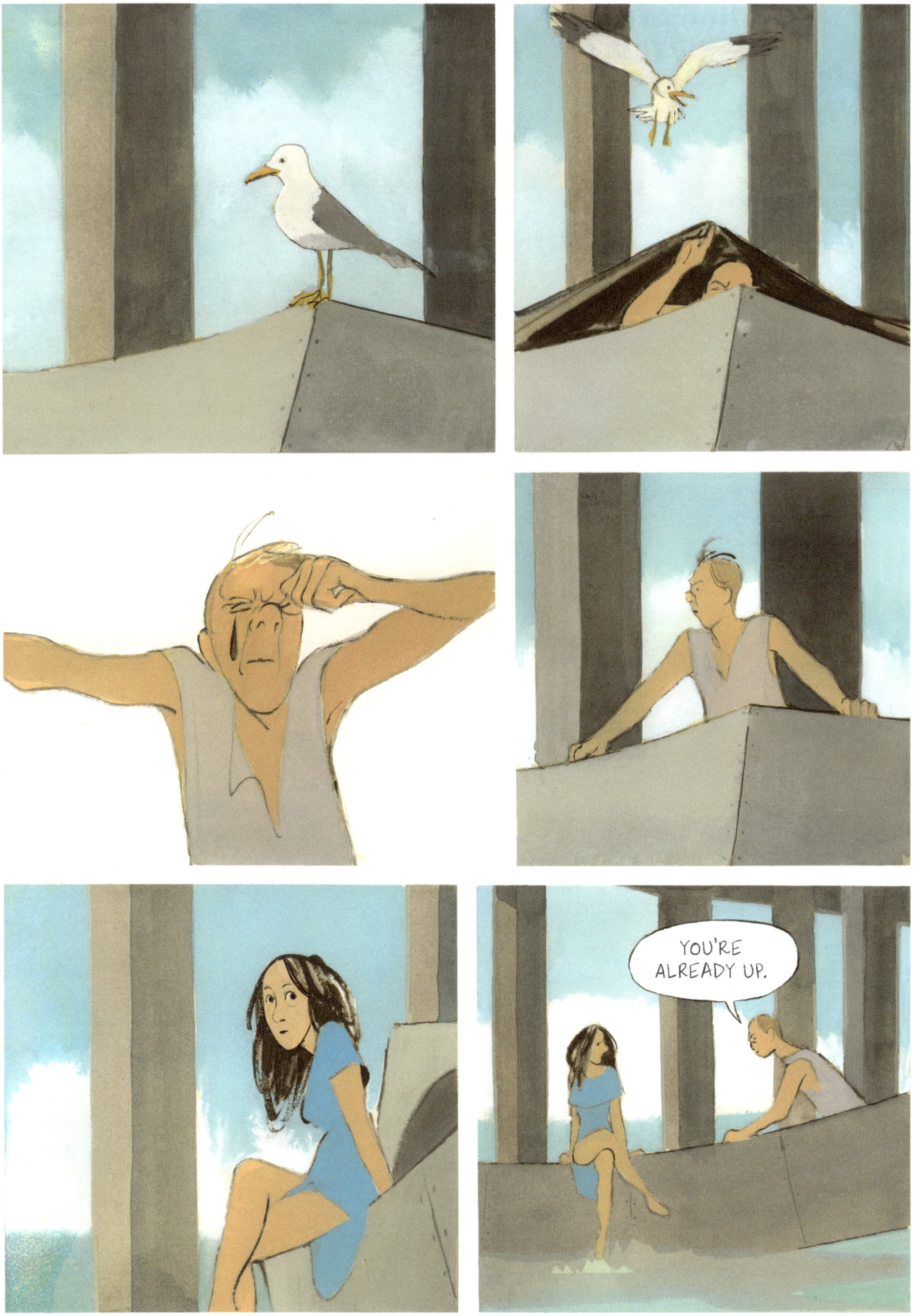
YOU'RE ALREADY UP.

WHAT IS THIS PLACE?
IT USED TO BE A HOSPITAL.
MY MOTHER WORKED THERE.

WAS YOUR MOTHER A DOCTOR?	KINDA.

LISTEN, PIERROT, I'M SORRY.

FOR ALL OF THIS...

I PROMISE I'LL BE MORE CAREFUL.

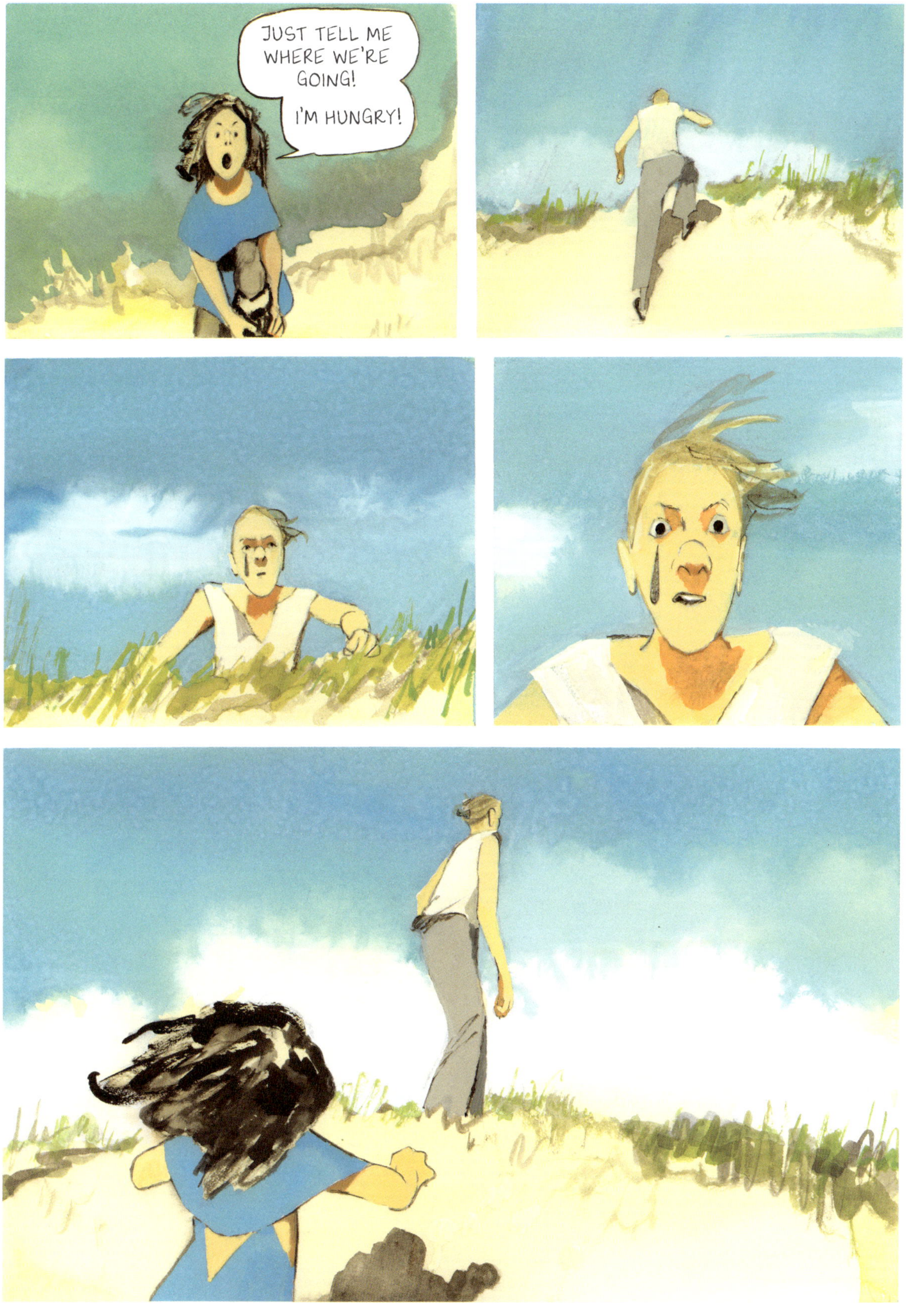
JUST TELL ME WHERE WE'RE GOING!
I'M HUNGRY!

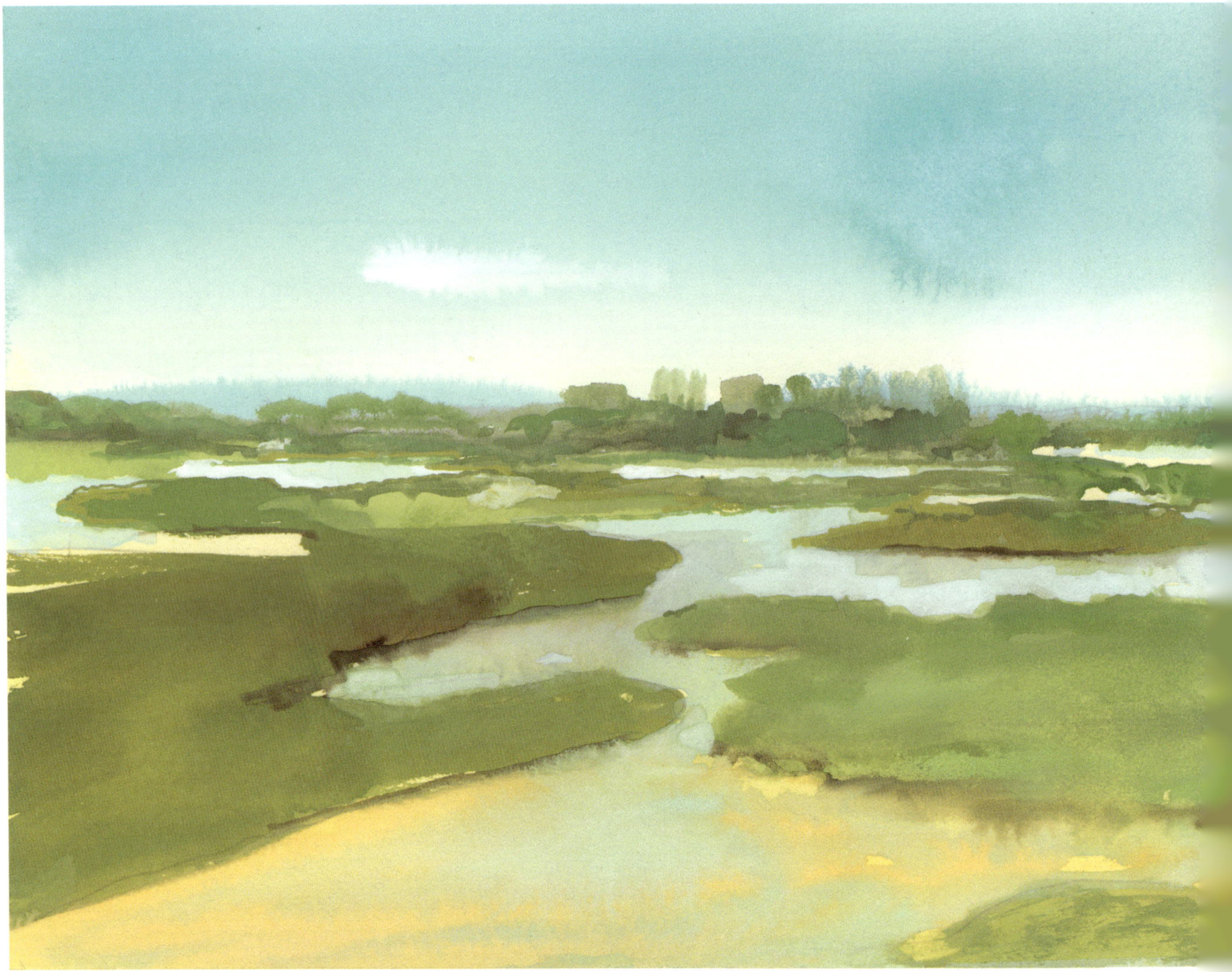

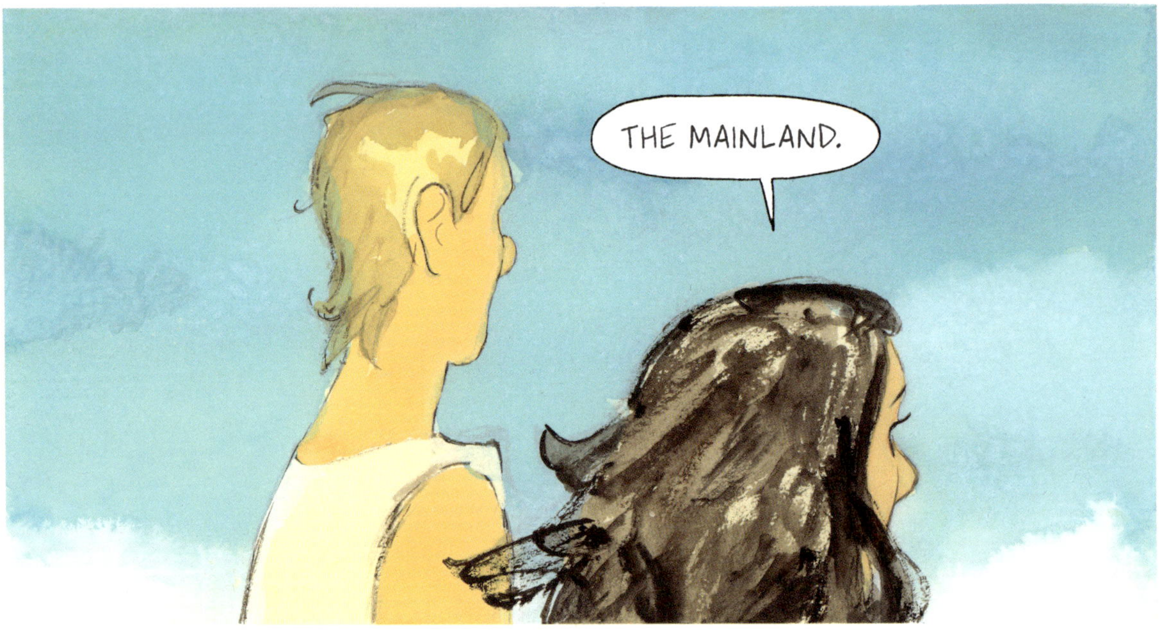
THE MAINLAND.

FROM ALL THE STORIES, I IMAGINED WORSE.
WAIT, PIERROT!
IF THE BOAT IS DEAD, HOW ARE WE GOING TO GET BACK?

YOU DON'T HAVE TO FOLLOW ME, YOU KNOW!
GO WHERE YOU LIKE, DO WHAT YOU PLEASE.
WE CAN DEAL WITH OUR PROBLEMS SEPARATELY!
EVEN TWO'S TOO MANY IN THIS MUCK.

AND BY NOW I'VE REALIZED THAT YOU'RE BAD LUCK!

BUT IF YOU TOO FEEL A GAPING HOLE
WHETHER IN YOUR BELLY OR IN YOUR SOUL

COME ALONG WITH ME ON A MISSION
TO SEE WHAT THIS CASTLE HOLDS WITHIN IT.

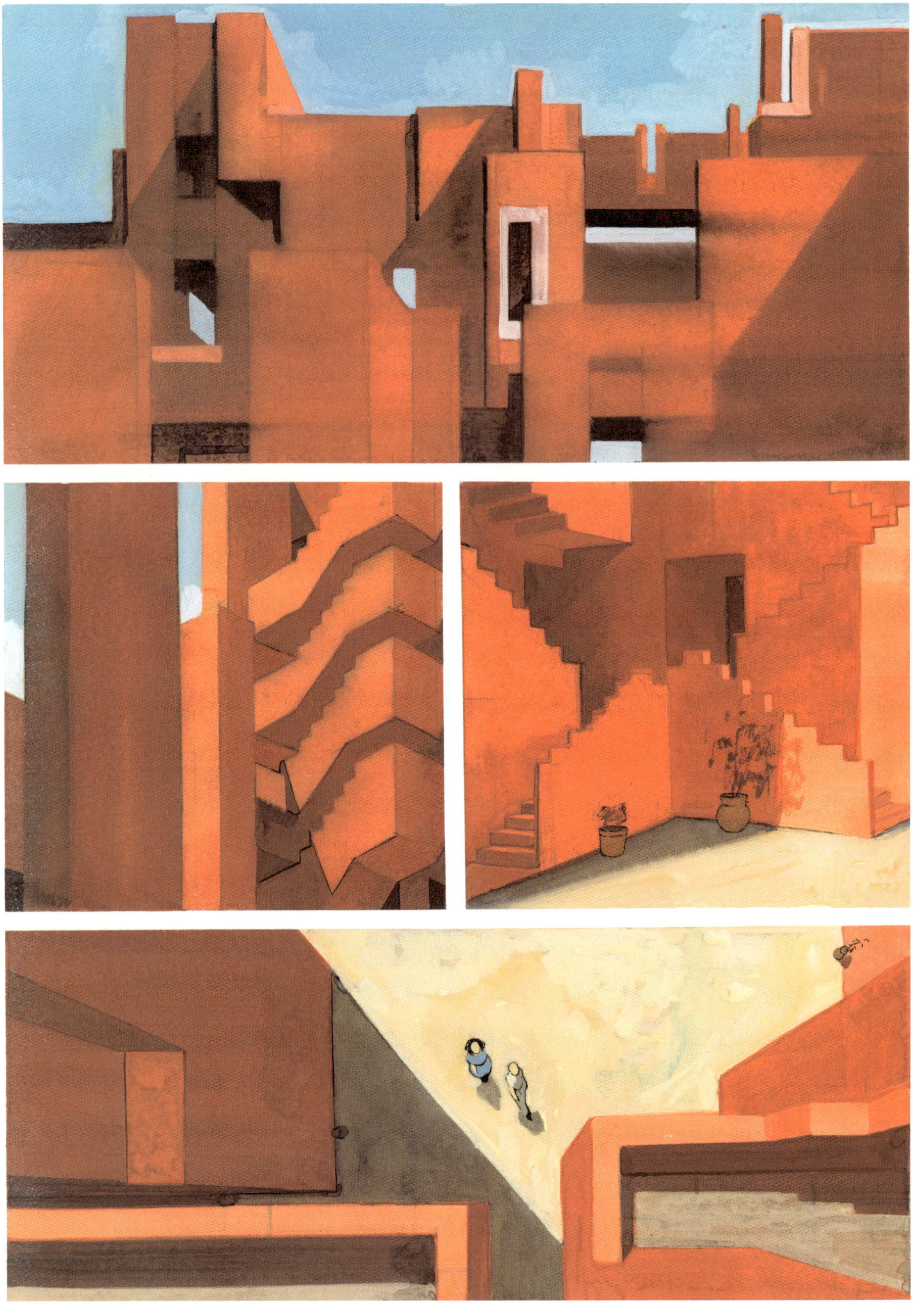

HELLO THERE!
YOU'RE A LITTLE EARLY.
WAS SOMEONE EXPECTING US?
NO, NO ONE.

BUT SINCE YOU ARRIVED LAST NIGHT, THERE AREN'T MANY OTHER PLACES YOU COULD HAVE GONE.

YOU KNEW WE ARRIVED?

ME? OF COURSE NOT! HOW COULD I HAVE?

I DON'T EVEN KNOW WHO YOU ARE.

CARE FOR A COFFEE?

THERE'S NO SUGAR.

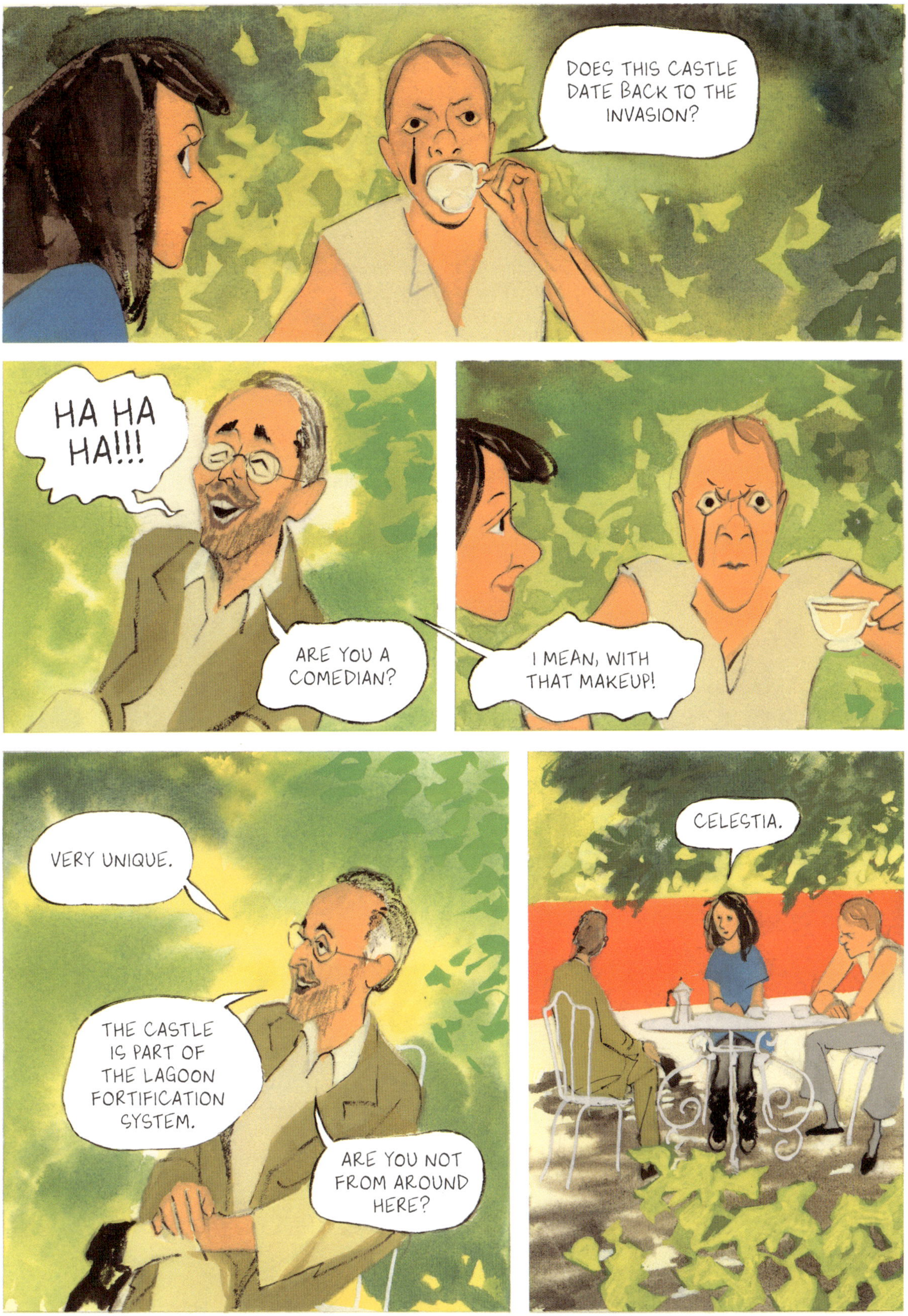
DOES THIS CASTLE DATE BACK TO THE INVASION?
HA HA HA!!!
ARE YOU A COMEDIAN?
I MEAN, WITH THAT MAKEUP!
VERY UNIQUE.
THE CASTLE IS PART OF THE LAGOON FORTIFICATION SYSTEM.
ARE YOU NOT FROM AROUND HERE?
CELESTIA.

NICE. VERY HUMID, THOUGH.

I DON'T THINK I COULD STAND IT.

MORE COFFEE?

THEN IF YOU DON'T MIND, WE CAN GET GOING.

WHERE?

WHAT DO YOU MEAN, WHERE? WHY ELSE ARE YOU HERE?

WE DIDN'T COME FOR ANY REASON, WE JUST

ESCAPED.

FROM CELESTIA.

TOO HUMID FOR YOU TOO, I SEE.

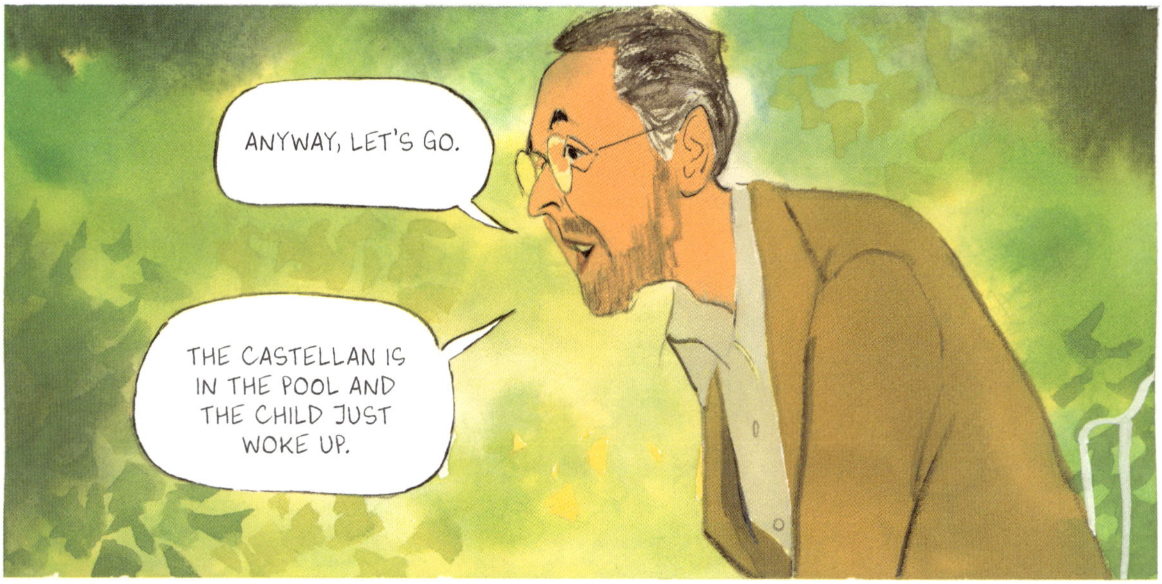
ANYWAY, LET'S GO.
THE CASTELLAN IS IN THE POOL AND THE CHILD JUST WOKE UP.

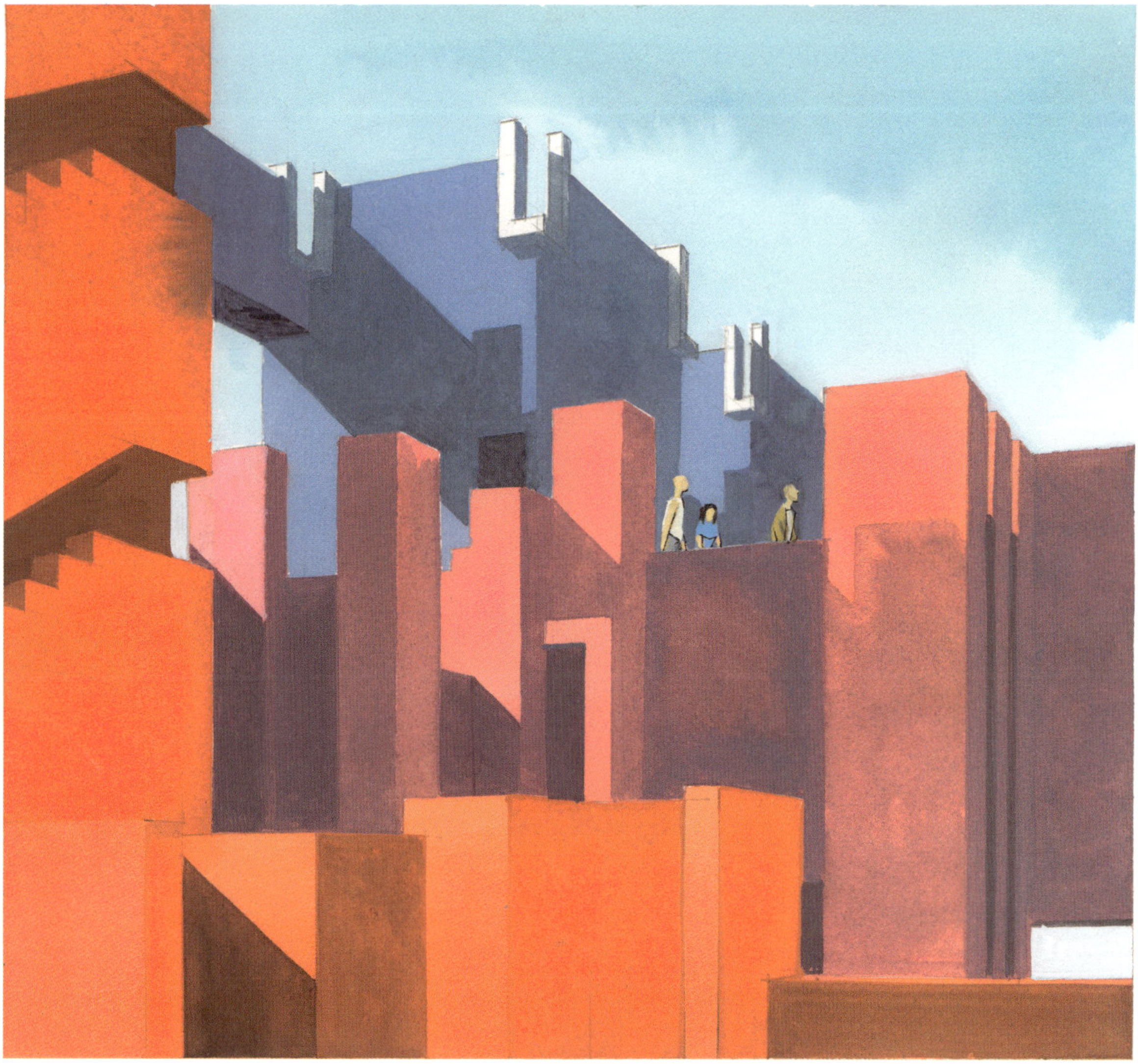

WHERE ARE ALL THE INHABITANTS OF THIS PLACE?

THERE ARE NONE.

"ESCAPED."

HEHE.

THERE WERE LOTS OF PEOPLE, TONS OF WORK, I ASSURE YOU.

THEN ALMOST EVERYONE PREFERRED TO LEAVE.

HOW COME?

IT'S NOT EASY TO LIVE LOCKED UP IN A CASTLE.

NO MATTER HOW COLORFUL, IT'S STILL THE SAME FOUR WALLS...

EVEN THOUGH...

HERE WE'RE SAFE, ABSOLUTELY NOTHING COULD HAPPEN TO US...

NO REASON TO BE SCARED.

SCARED OF WHAT?

"TO TELL YOU THE TRUTH, I DON'T REMEMBER ANYMORE. IT'S BEEN SO LONG..."

"BUT YOU STAYED!"

"WHAT ELSE WAS I TO DO?"

"YOU COULD HAVE LEFT!"

"LEFT THE CASTLE?"

"I CAN'T DO THAT."

"I'M THE GUARDIAN, HADN'T YOU FIGURED?"

"OF COURSE I STAYED.

IT'S NICE HERE. IT'S A PEACEFUL PLACE.

BESIDES, LET'S JUST SAY IT, WHERE WOULD I GO?"

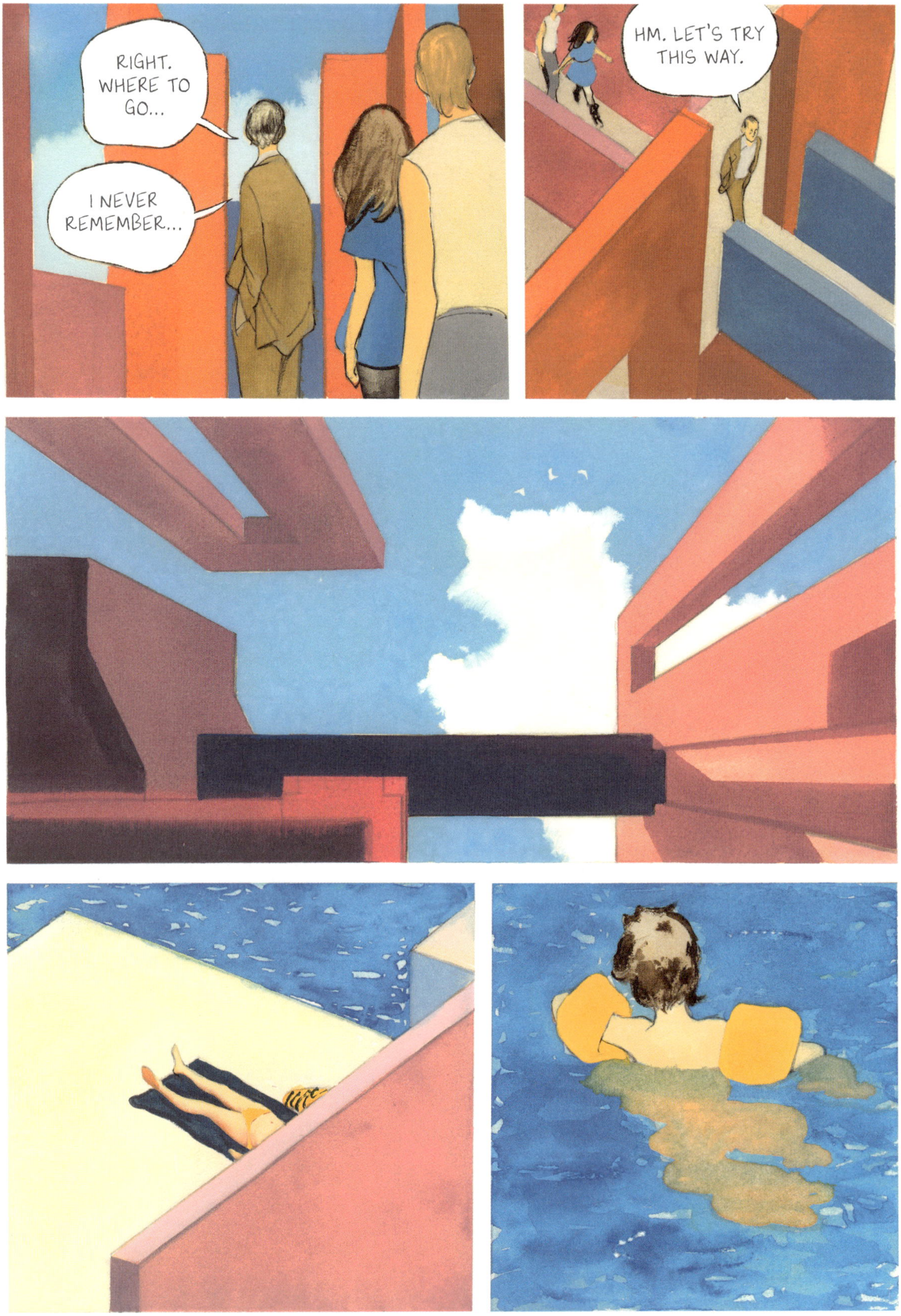
RIGHT. WHERE TO GO...
I NEVER REMEMBER...
HM. LET'S TRY THIS WAY.

MISS CASTELLAN.

WE HAVE VISITORS.

HOW DELIGHTFUL. WHO ARE THEY?

I HAVE NO IDEA.

THEY'RE DORA AND PIERROT.

FANCY THAT... I JUST SAW THEM IN A DREAM...

I DOZED OFF AFTER MY SWIM, IT WAS SO NICE...

WHY DON'T YOU TAKE A DIP?

THEY ESCAPED CELESTIA BECAUSE OF THE HUMIDITY.
WE'D BETTER GET OUT OF HERE!
YOU'D NEVER BE ABLE TO FIND YOUR WAY OUT OF THE CASTLE.
YOU WOULD GET LOST.
MY SON. HE ALWAYS SAYS STRANGE THINGS.
MUST BE BORED.
HE NEVER SEES ANYONE. EXCEPT ME AND THE GUARDIAN.

— DOES EITHER OF YOU KNOW HOW TO DRIVE A CAR?

— SEE WHAT I MEAN?

— I... I THINK I REMEMBER!

— GOOD.

— MAMMA, I HAVE TO GO. I'LL BE AWAY FOR A WHILE, I DON'T KNOW WHEN I'LL SEE YOU AGAIN.

— THAT'S TOO BAD, HONEY.

COME, LET ME DRY YOU OFF FIRST.
SCAMP.
HOW MUCH DO YOU LOVE YOUR MAMMA?
TONS.
GOOD BOY.
AND NOW FOR A SWIM.
IT'S SO HOT OUT.

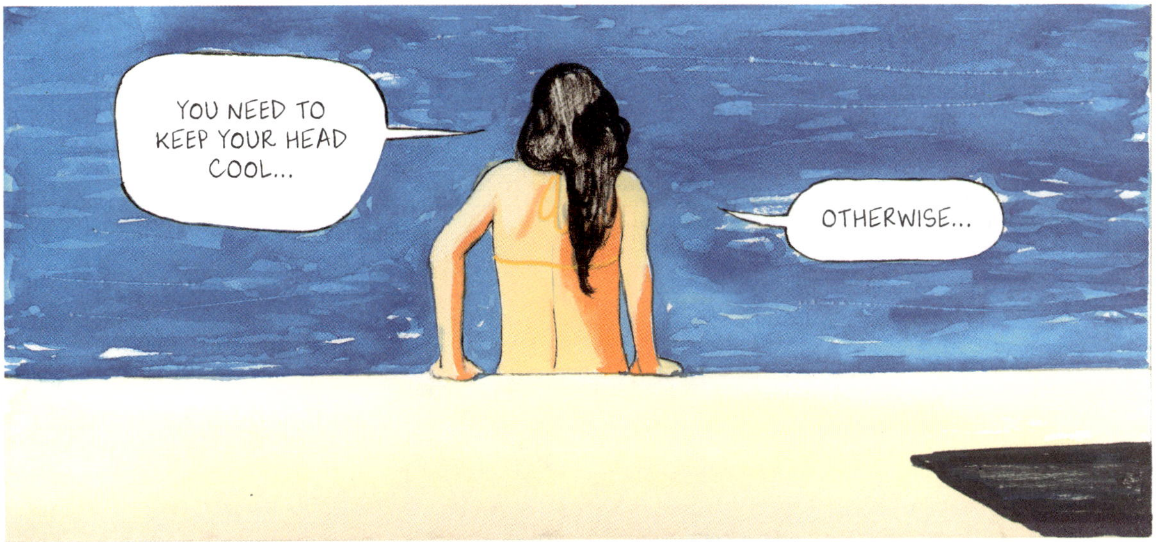
YOU NEED TO KEEP YOUR HEAD COOL...
OTHERWISE...

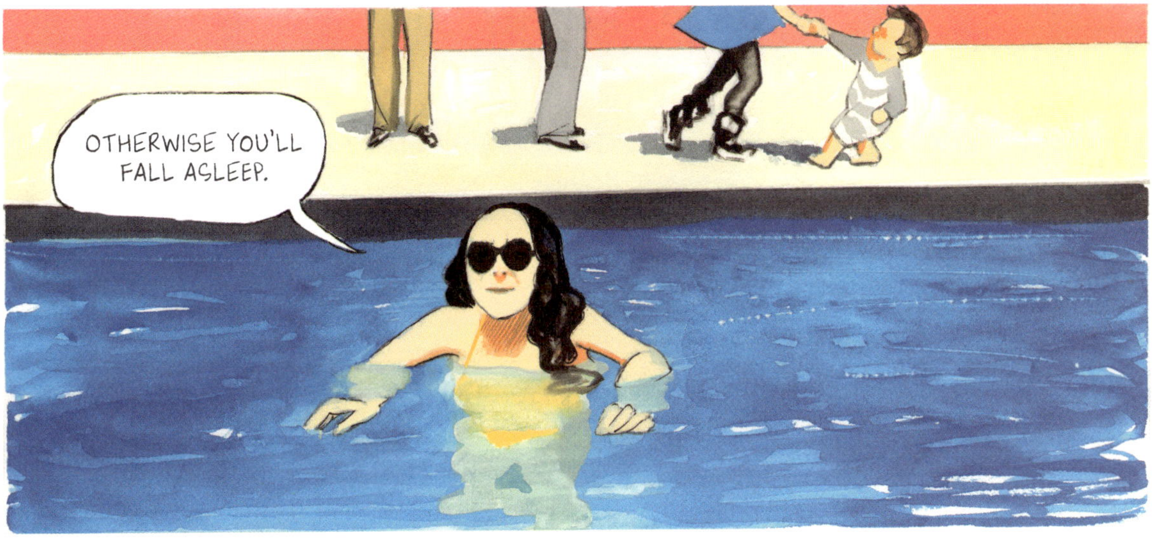
OTHERWISE YOU'LL FALL ASLEEP.

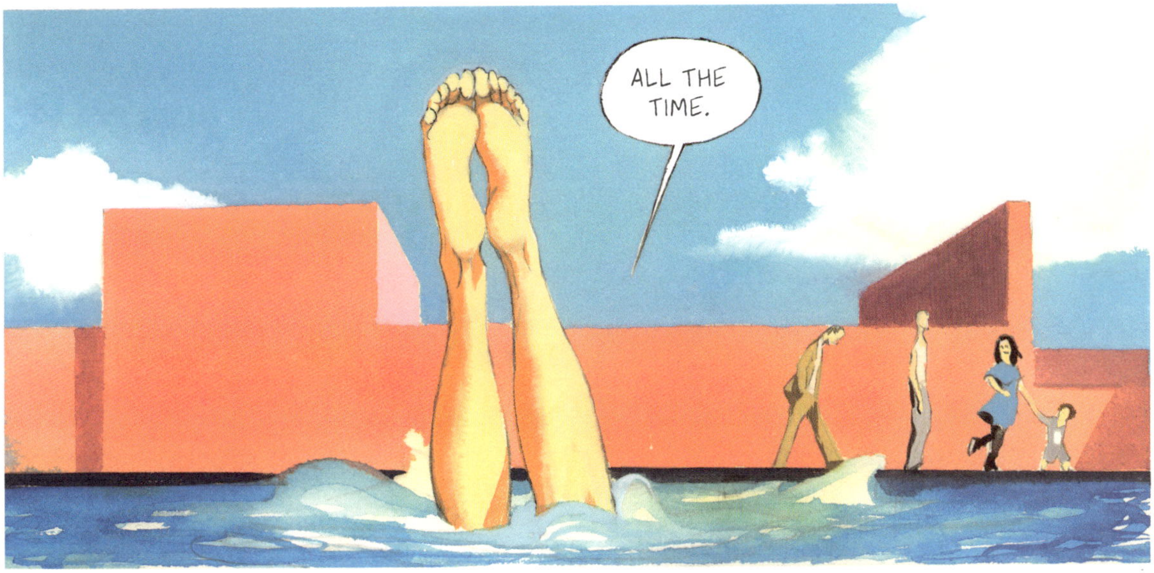
ALL THE TIME.

IT'S AN OLD SOLAR-POWERED MODEL, REGISTERED ON THE MAINLAND.

BEEN PARKED FOR ALMOST THIRTY YEARS.

THE BATTERY COULD'VE GONE DEAD. BUT WE SHOULD HAVE A SPARE IN STORAGE.

TRUST ME, I'D HAVE NO PROBLEM DRIVING IT MYSELF...

BUT MY FEET CAN'T REACH THE PEDALS.

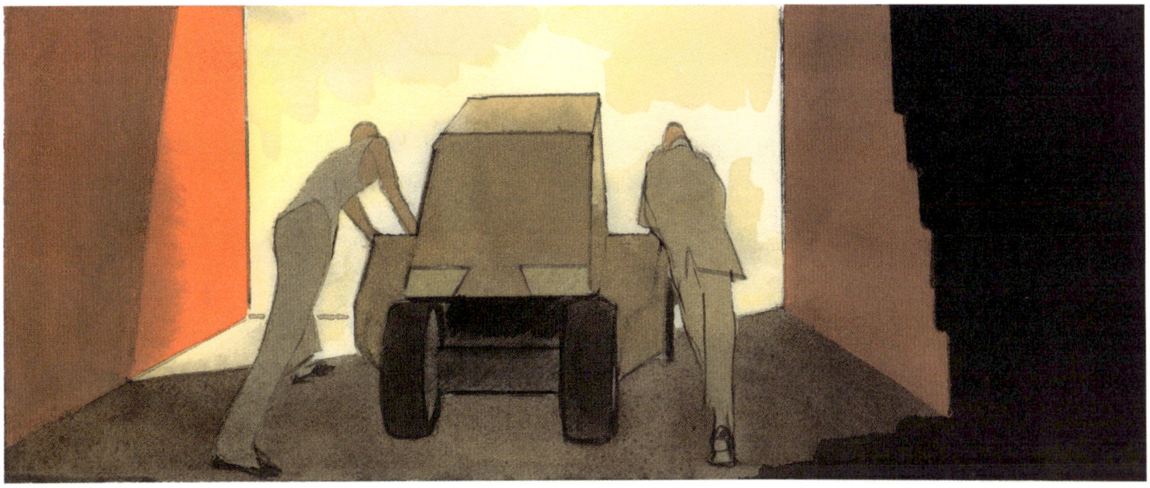

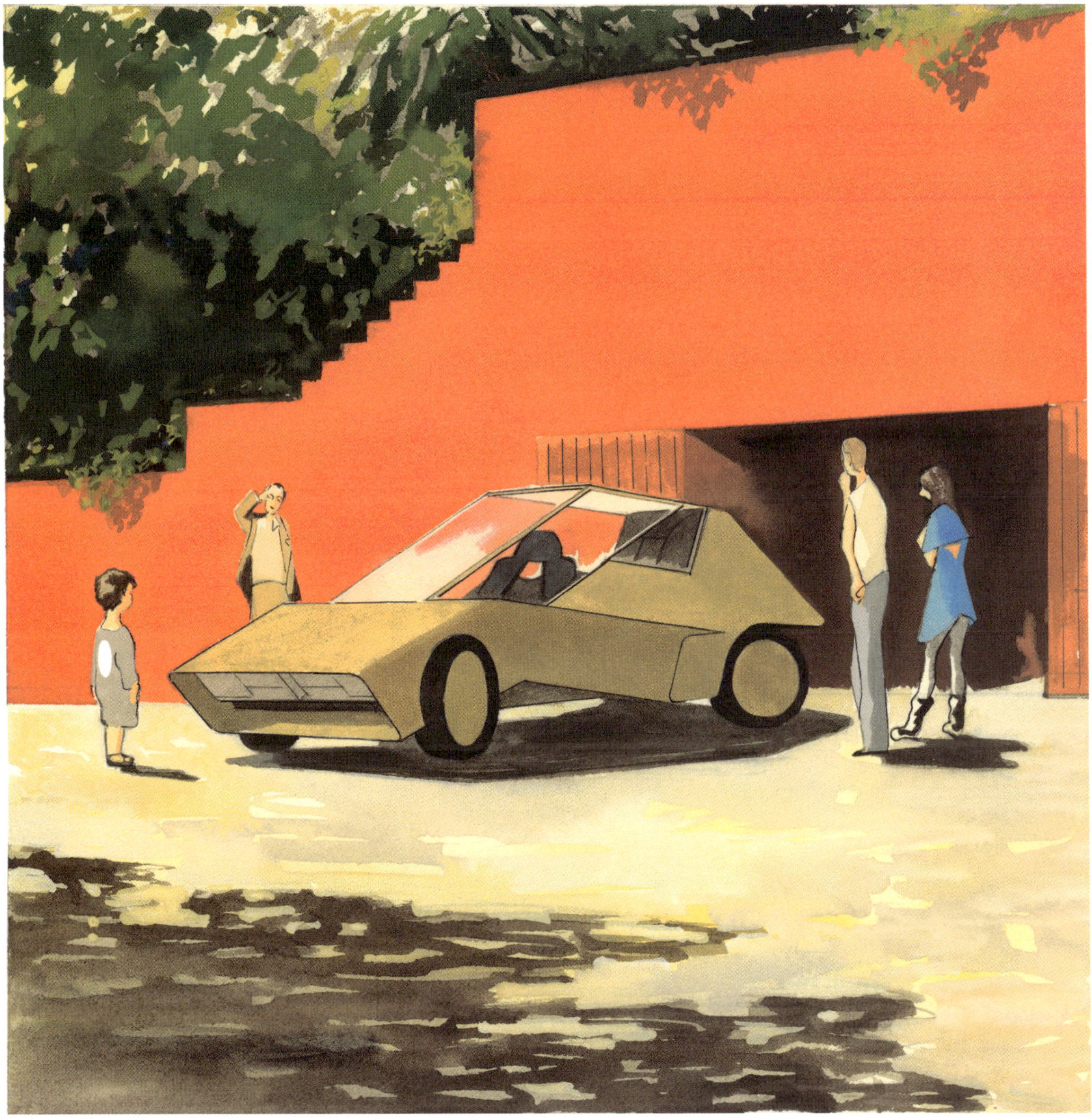

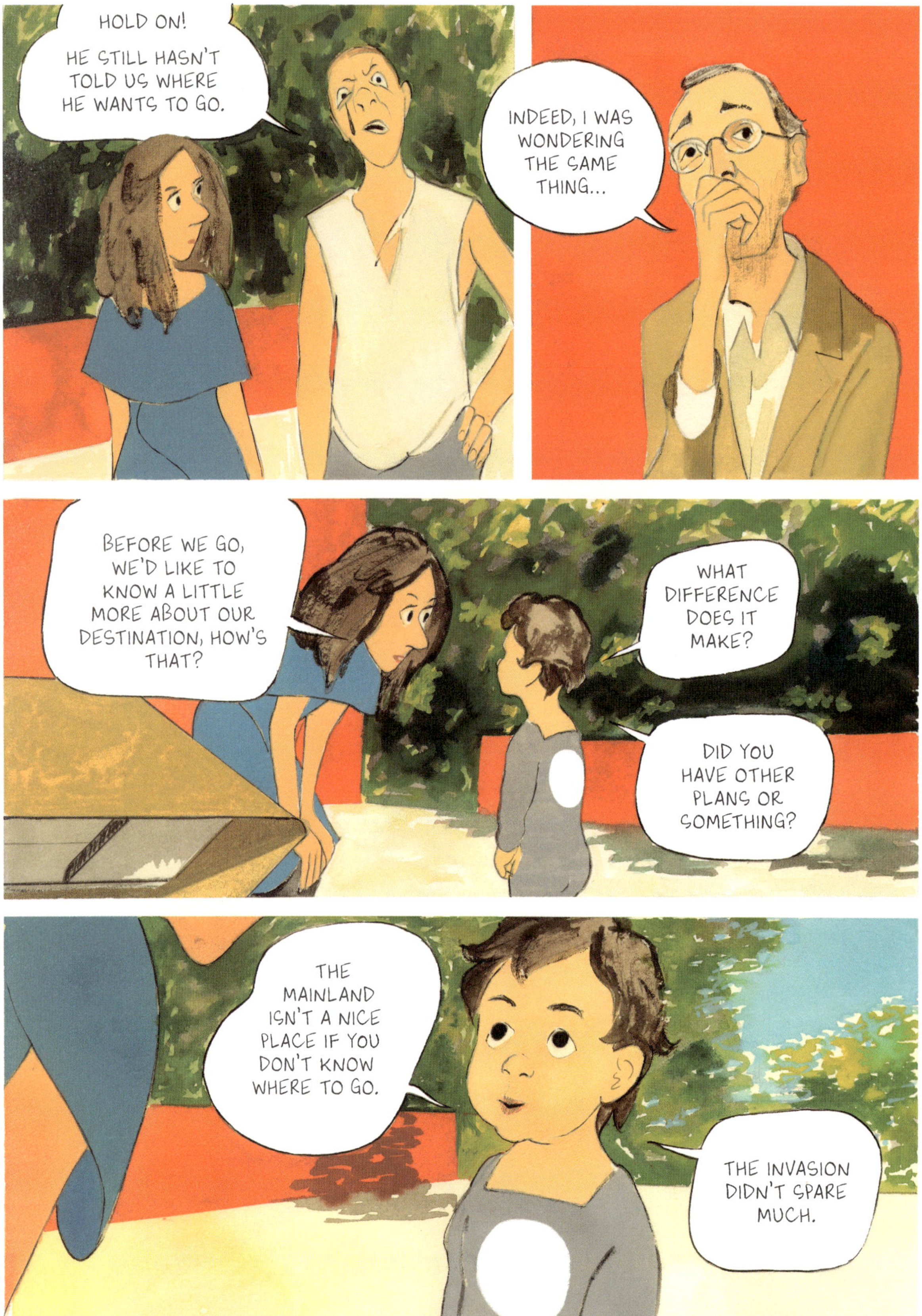
HOLD ON!
HE STILL HASN'T TOLD US WHERE HE WANTS TO GO.
INDEED, I WAS WONDERING THE SAME THING...
BEFORE WE GO, WE'D LIKE TO KNOW A LITTLE MORE ABOUT OUR DESTINATION, HOW'S THAT?
WHAT DIFFERENCE DOES IT MAKE?
DID YOU HAVE OTHER PLANS OR SOMETHING?
THE MAINLAND ISN'T A NICE PLACE IF YOU DON'T KNOW WHERE TO GO.
THE INVASION DIDN'T SPARE MUCH.

I WASN'T BORN YET, OF COURSE, BUT THE PEOPLE WHO LIVED HERE...
THEY'VE BEEN THROUGH ALL KINDS OF STUFF.
THEY NEED HELP, I TRY TO DO WHAT I CAN.
THESE TWO ARE VIRTUALLY IRRECUPERABLE.
IF THEY REMEMBER THEIR NAMES, IT'S A LOT.
HEY, DON'T DISRESPECT YOUR MOTHER, LITTLE ONE.

THAT WOMAN IS NOT MY MOTHER, MR. PIERROT.	
I JUST LET HER THINK SHE IS.	
	YOU LITTLE MONSTER!
IF I HADN'T TAKEN HER UNDER MY WING, SHE'D STILL BE WANDERING IN SEARCH OF HER SON.	GET IN THE BACK, I'LL SIT ON YOUR LAP.
I TOOK IT UPON MYSELF TO FIX YOU SOME SANDWICHES FOR THE TRIP...	SINCE YOU DIDN'T HAVE ANYTHING TO EAT.
	HOW KIND OF YOU.

OK THEN.
LET'S SEE IF I REMEMBER.
PINK BUTTON.
IT WORKS!
HAVE A NICE TRIP!
I...
I'LL STAY HERE.
ANYWAY... WHERE ELSE WOULD I GO?
WHERE? MAYBE...
NO, NO.
TOO HUMID.

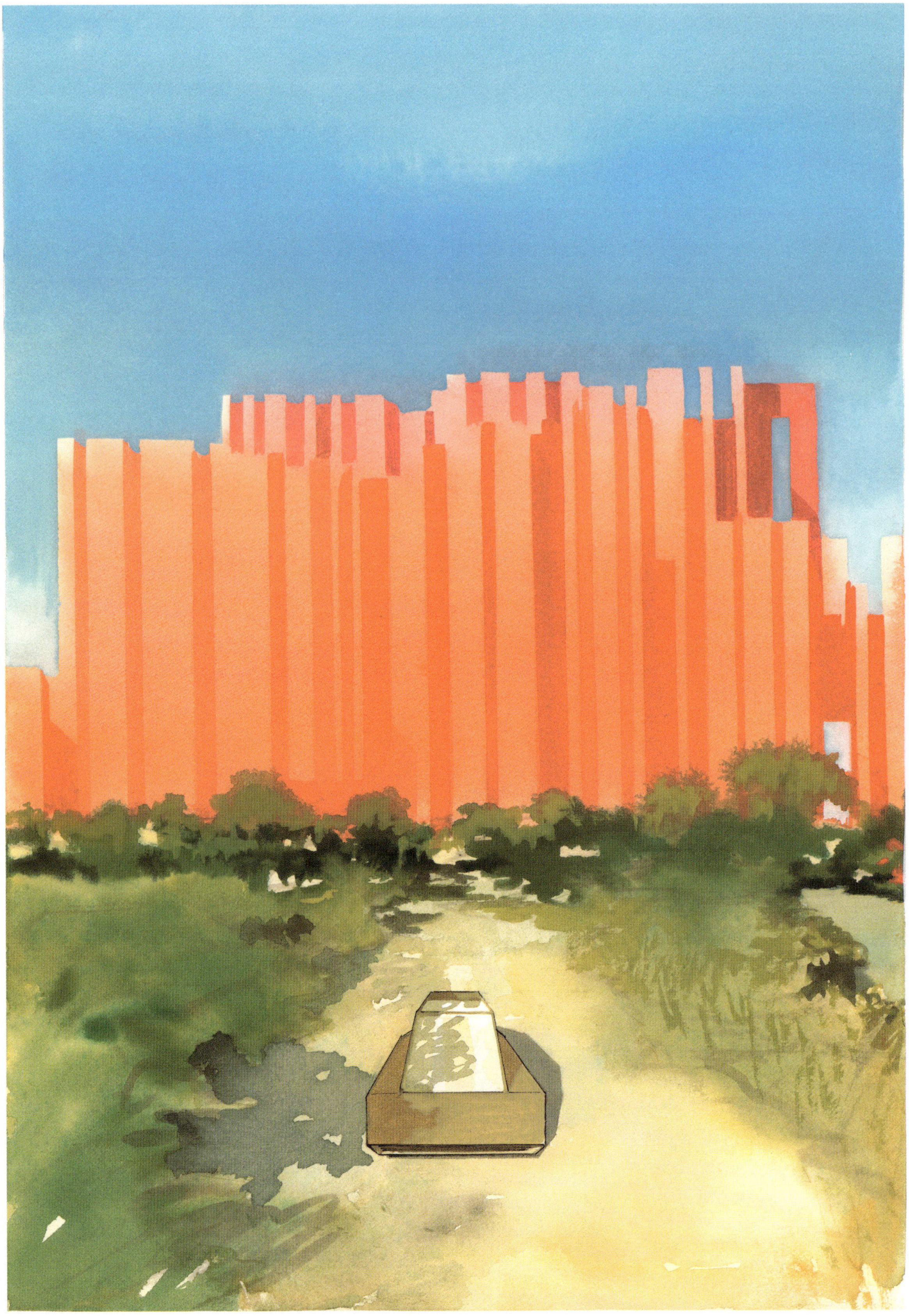

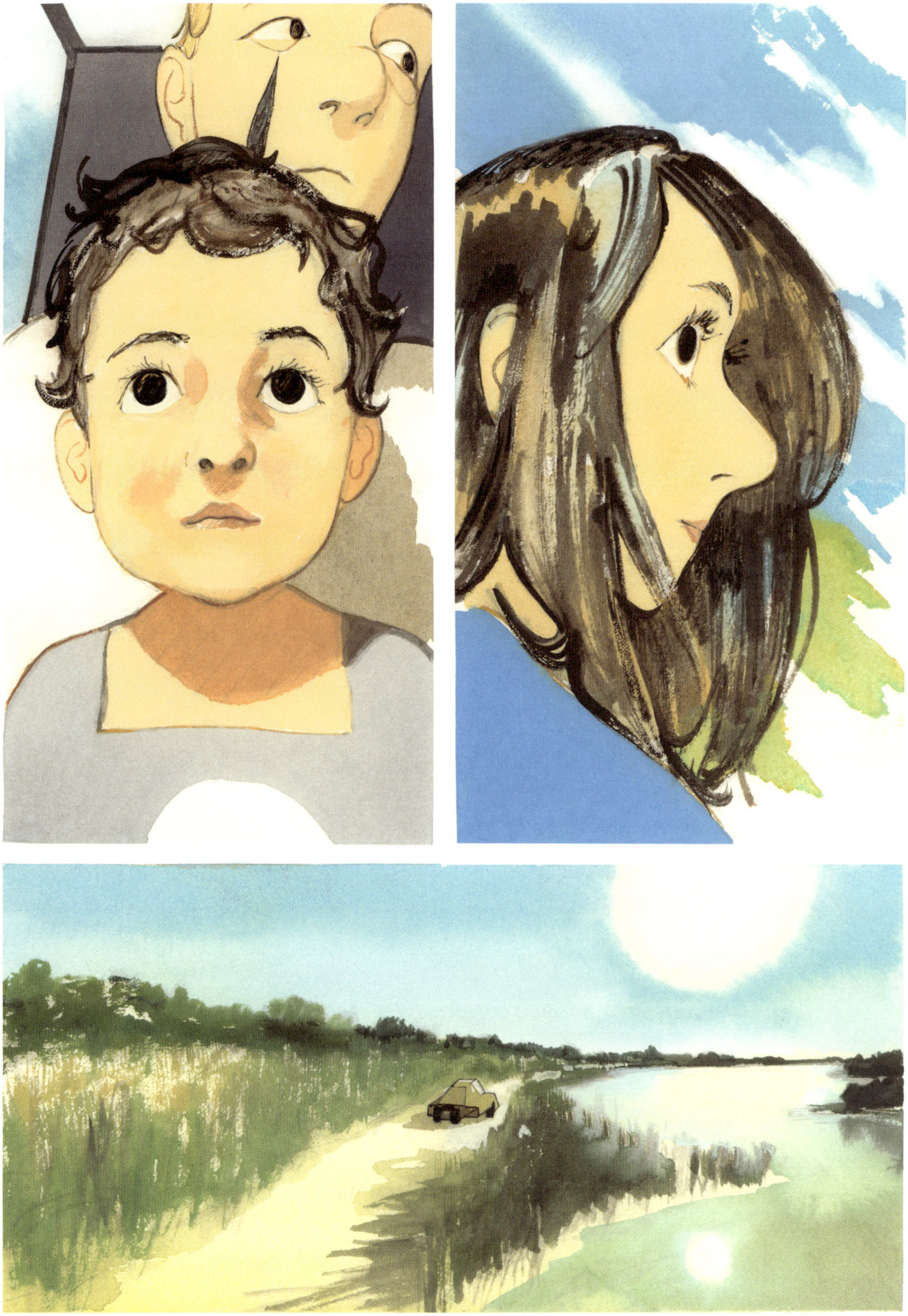

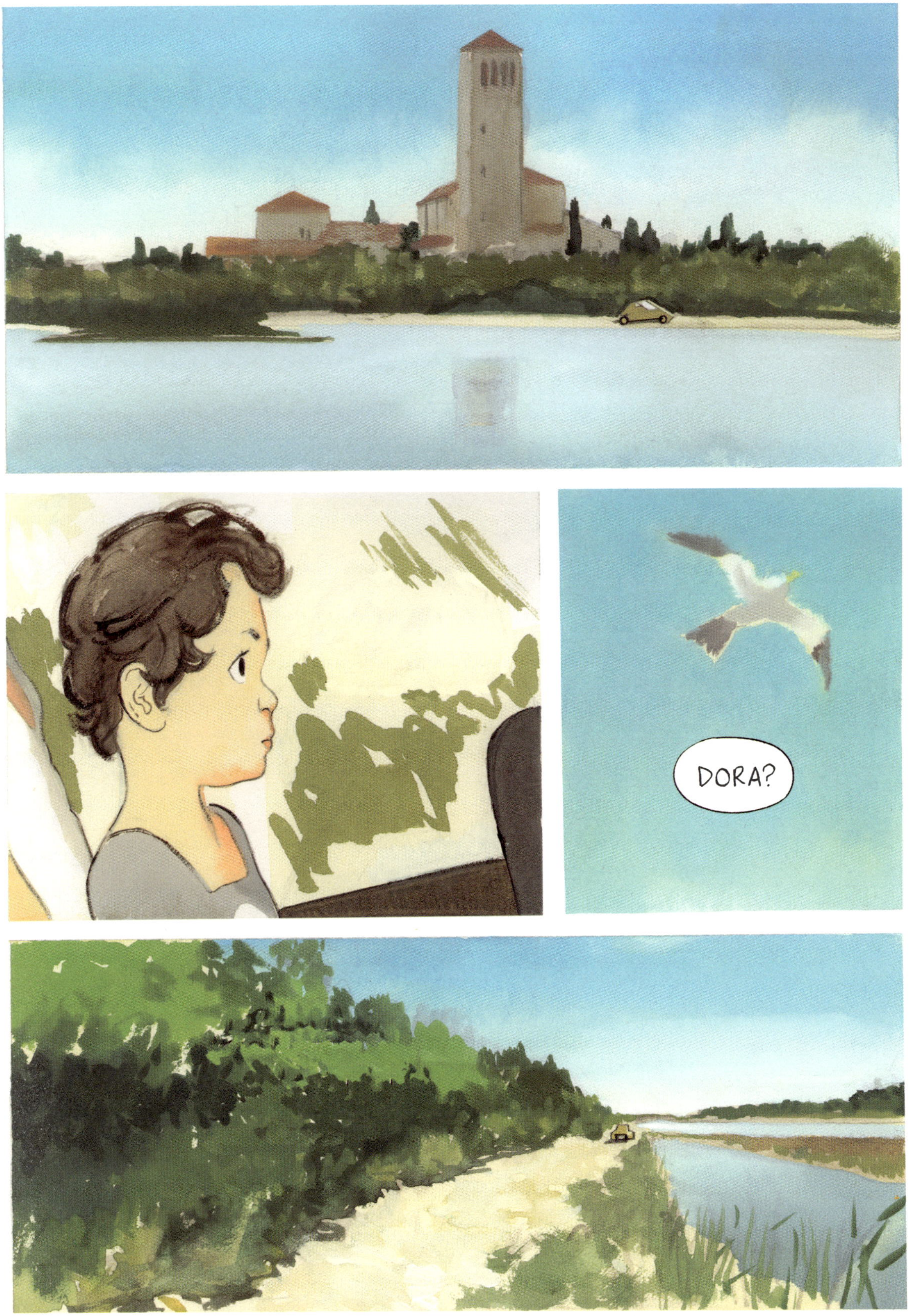
DORA?

DORA, DO YOU HEAR ME?
CAN ONE OF YOU TELL ME WHERE WE'RE GOING?
SHHT.
THE CHILD IS GUIDING ME.

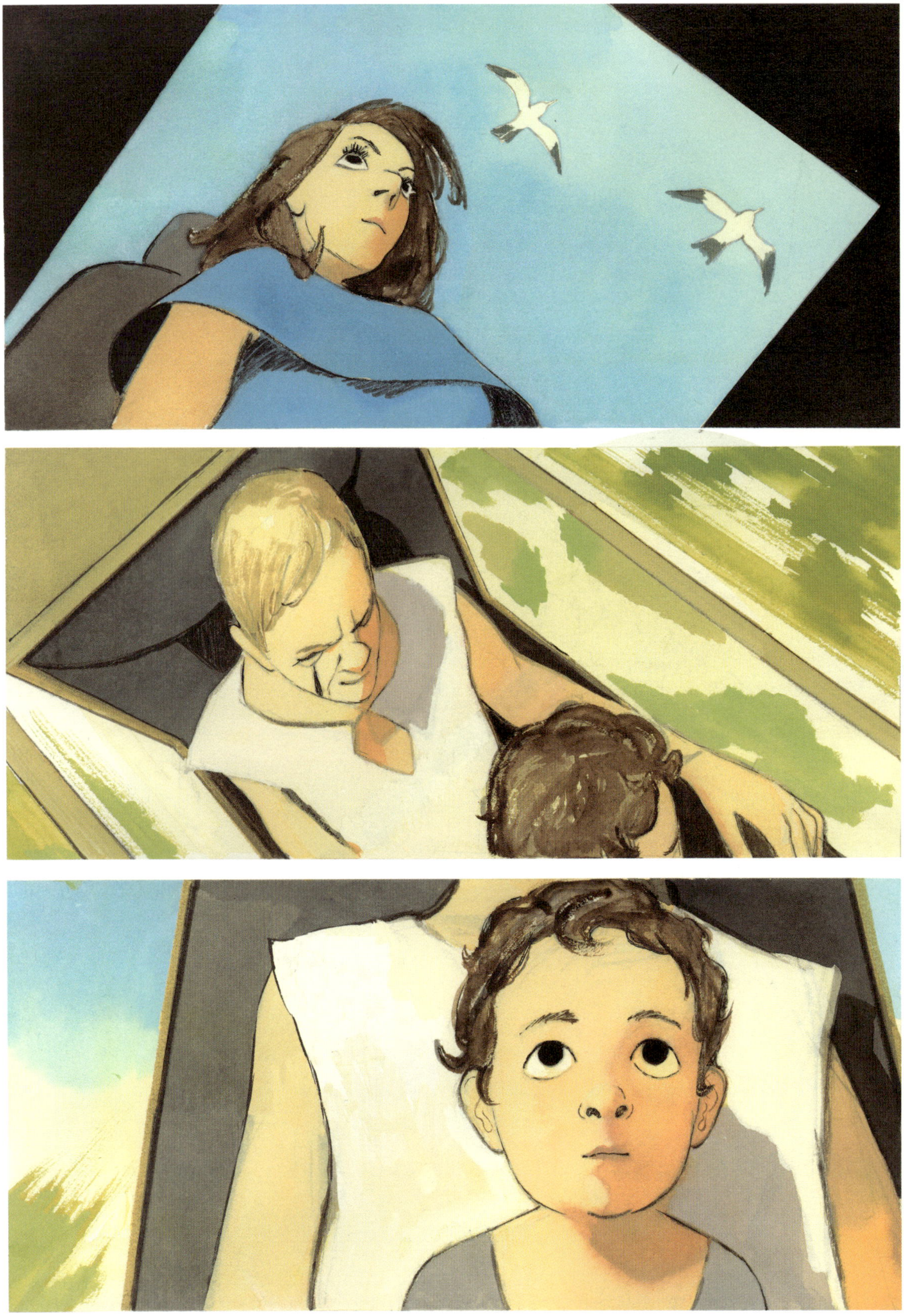

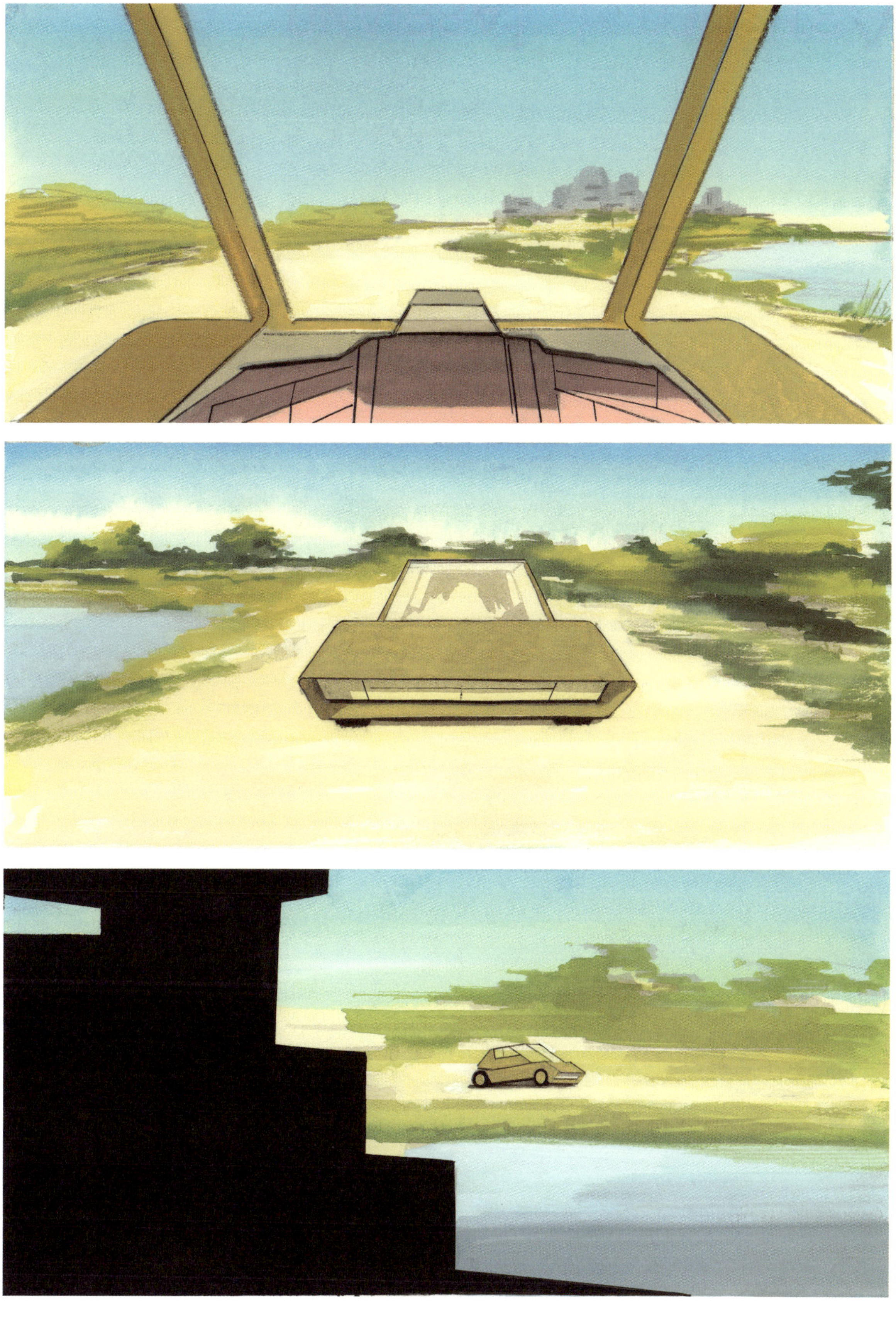

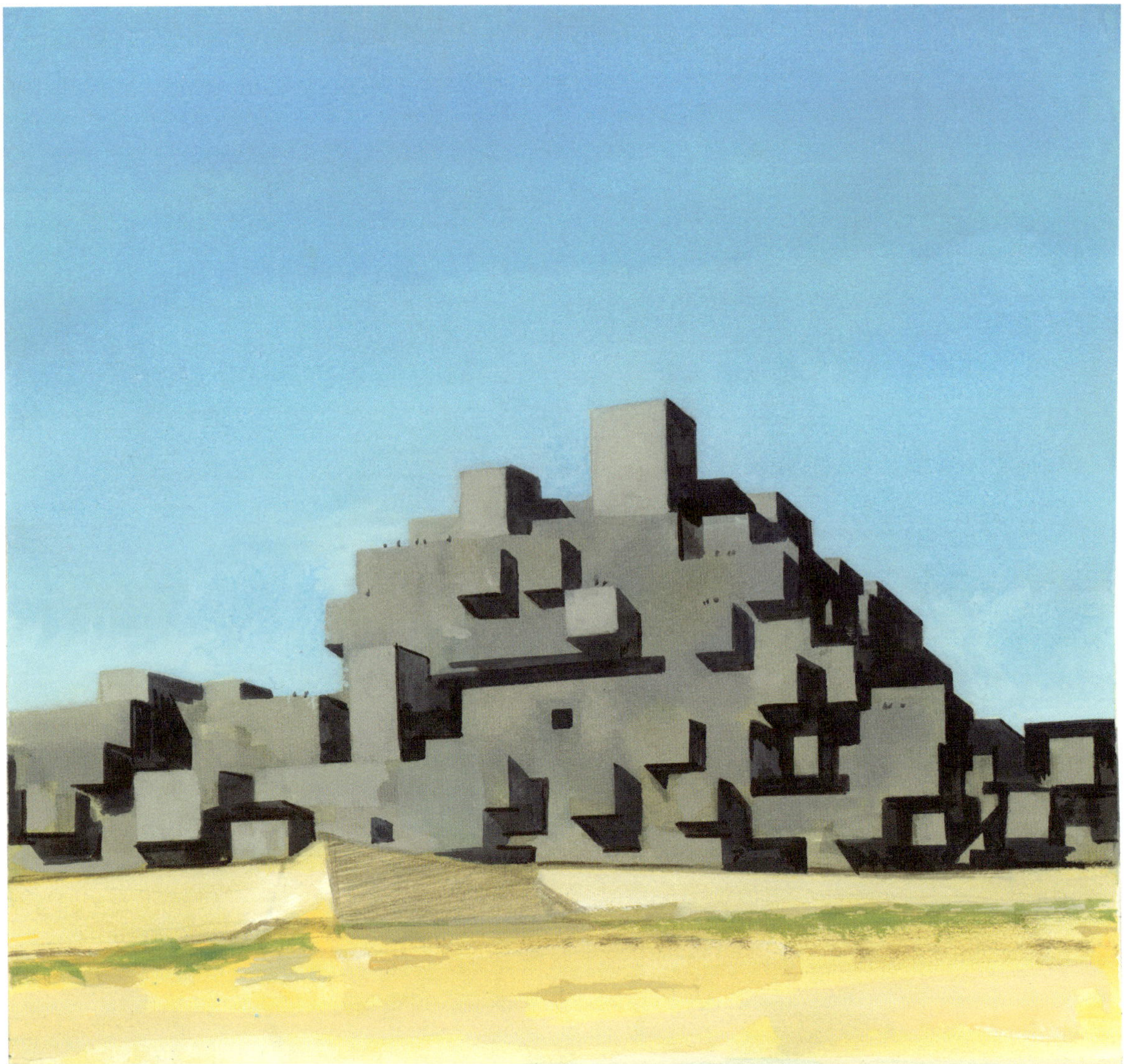

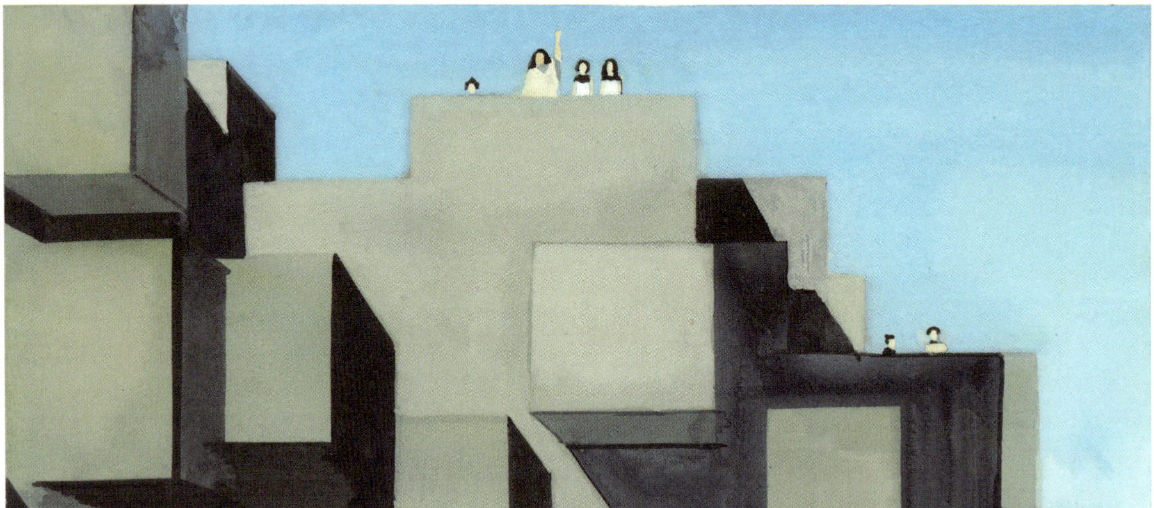

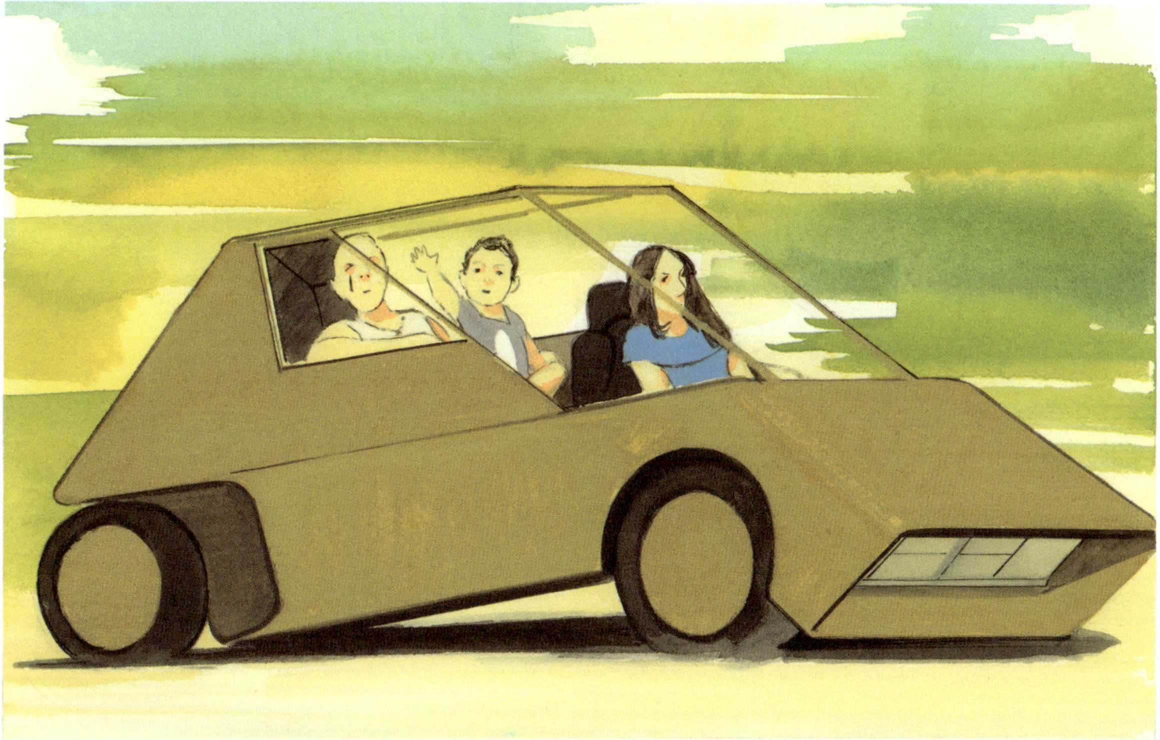

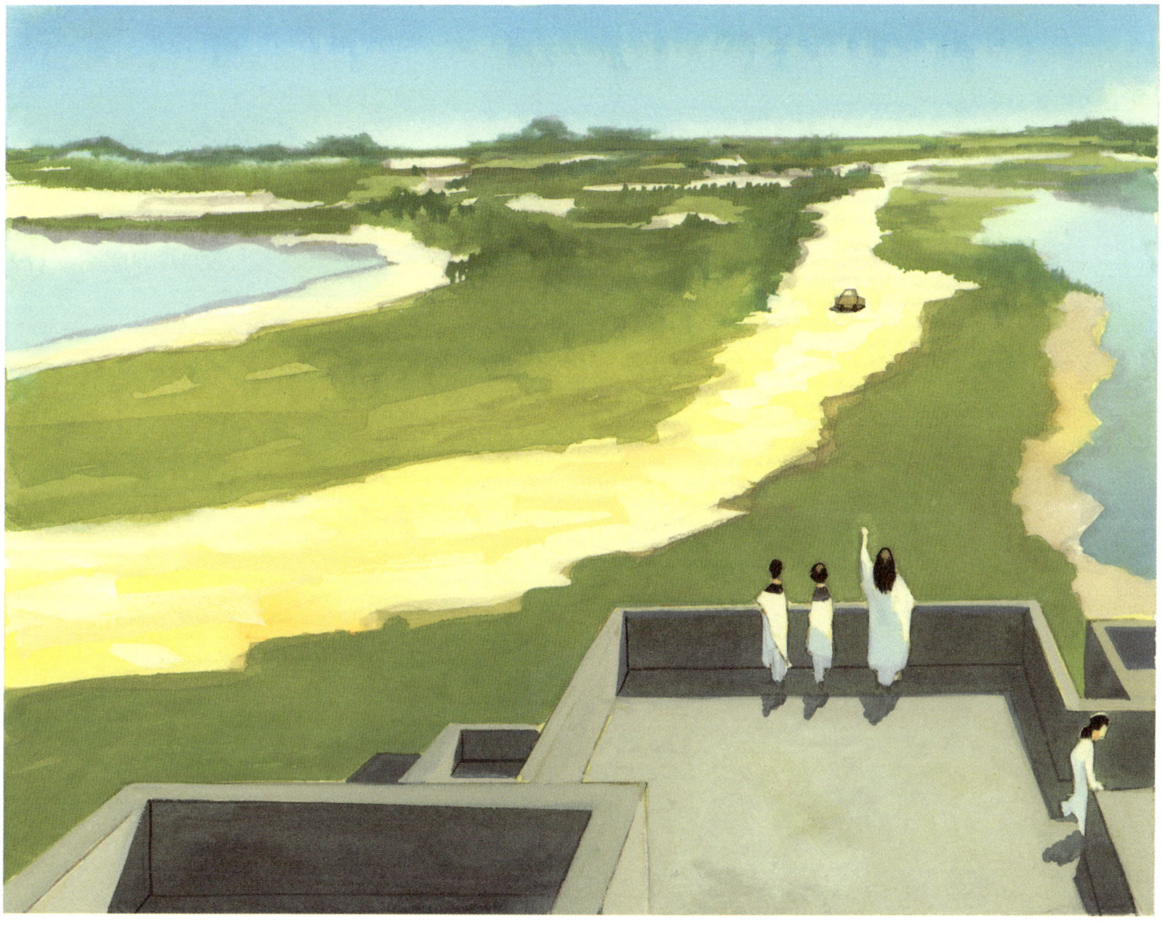

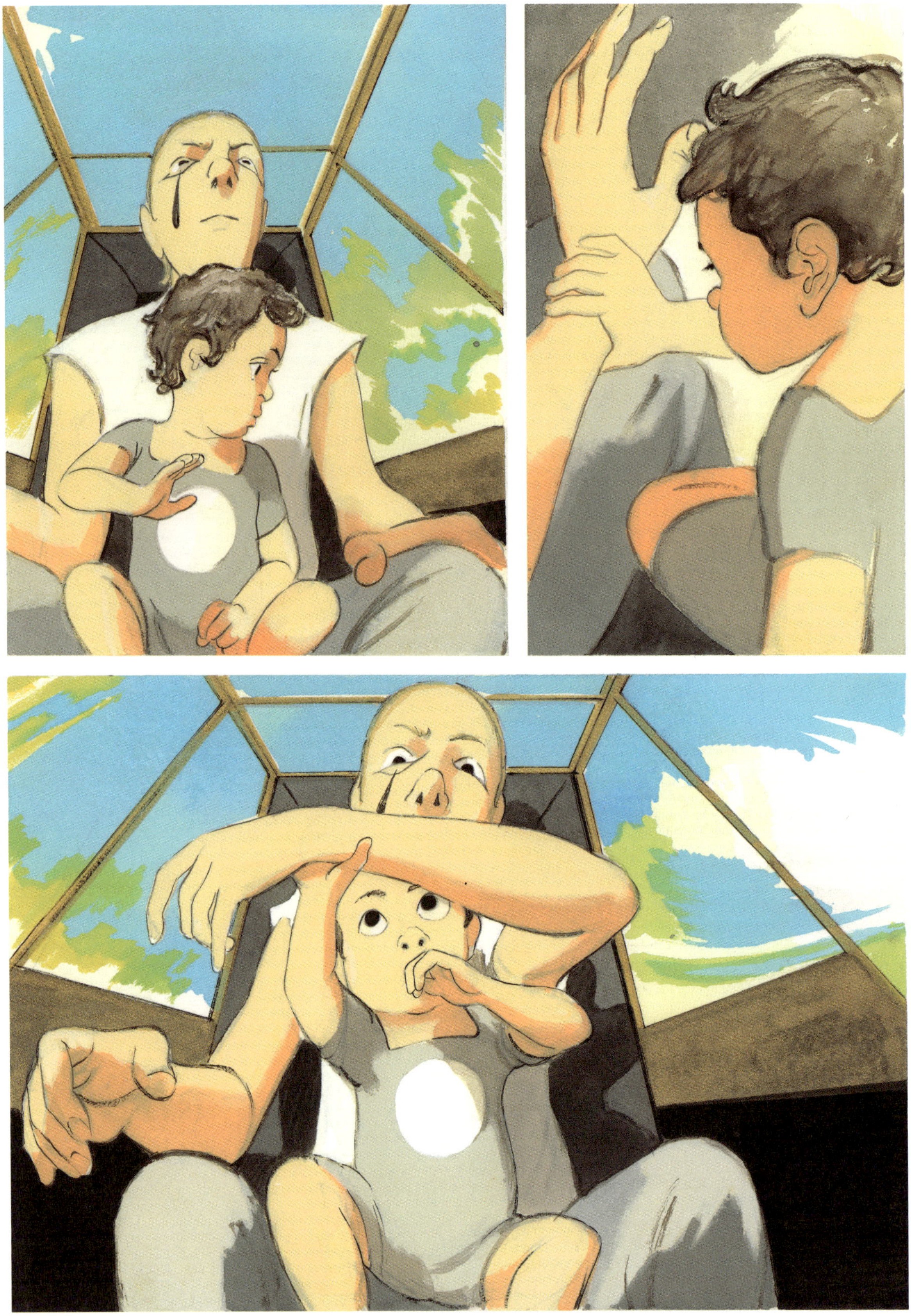

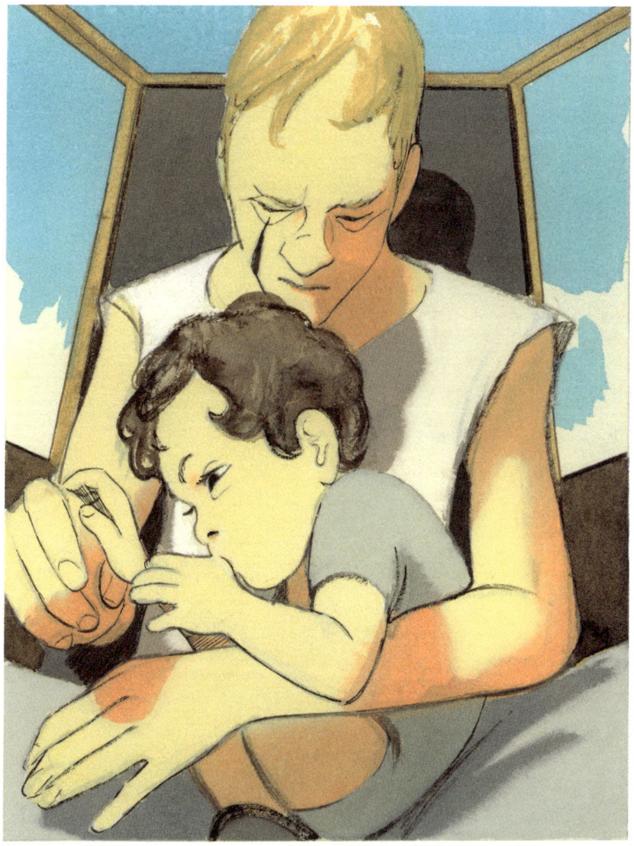

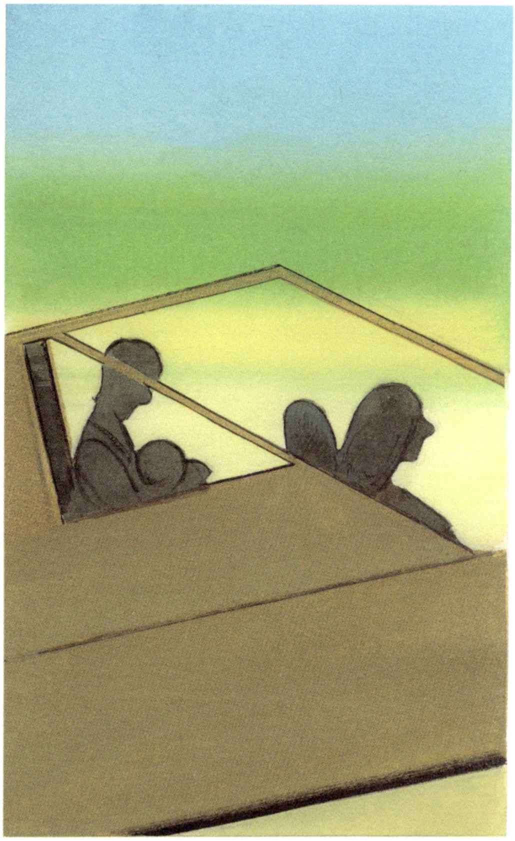

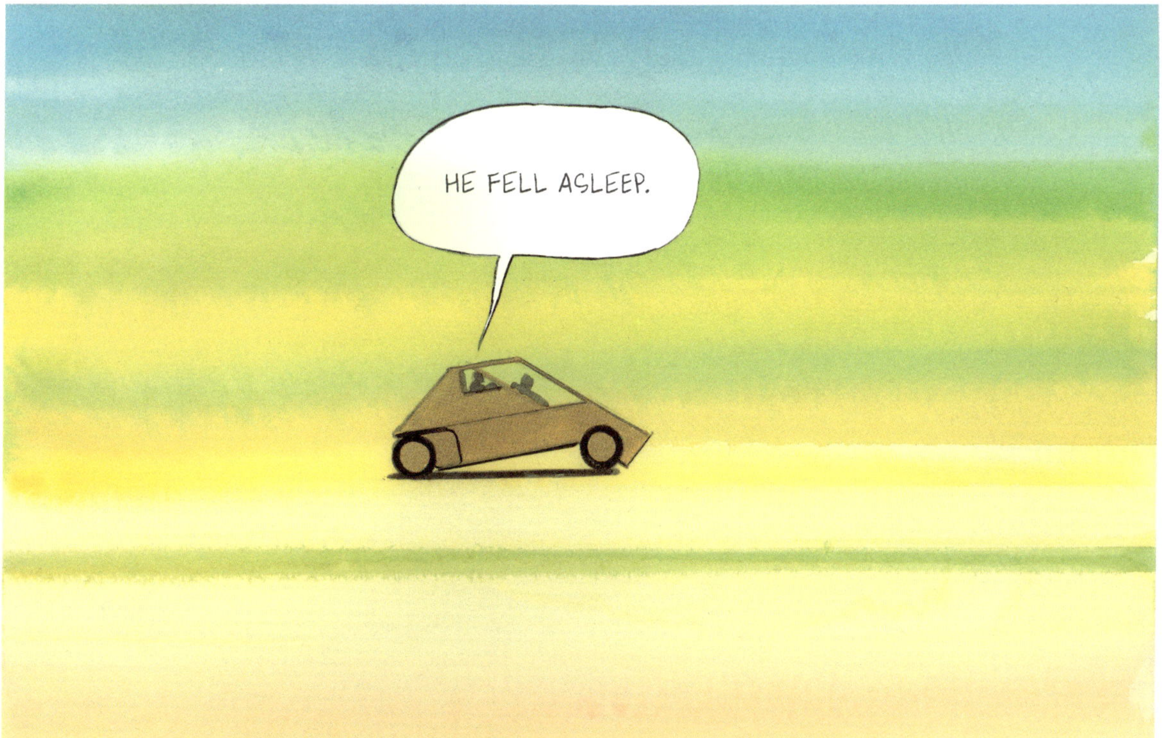
HE FELL ASLEEP.

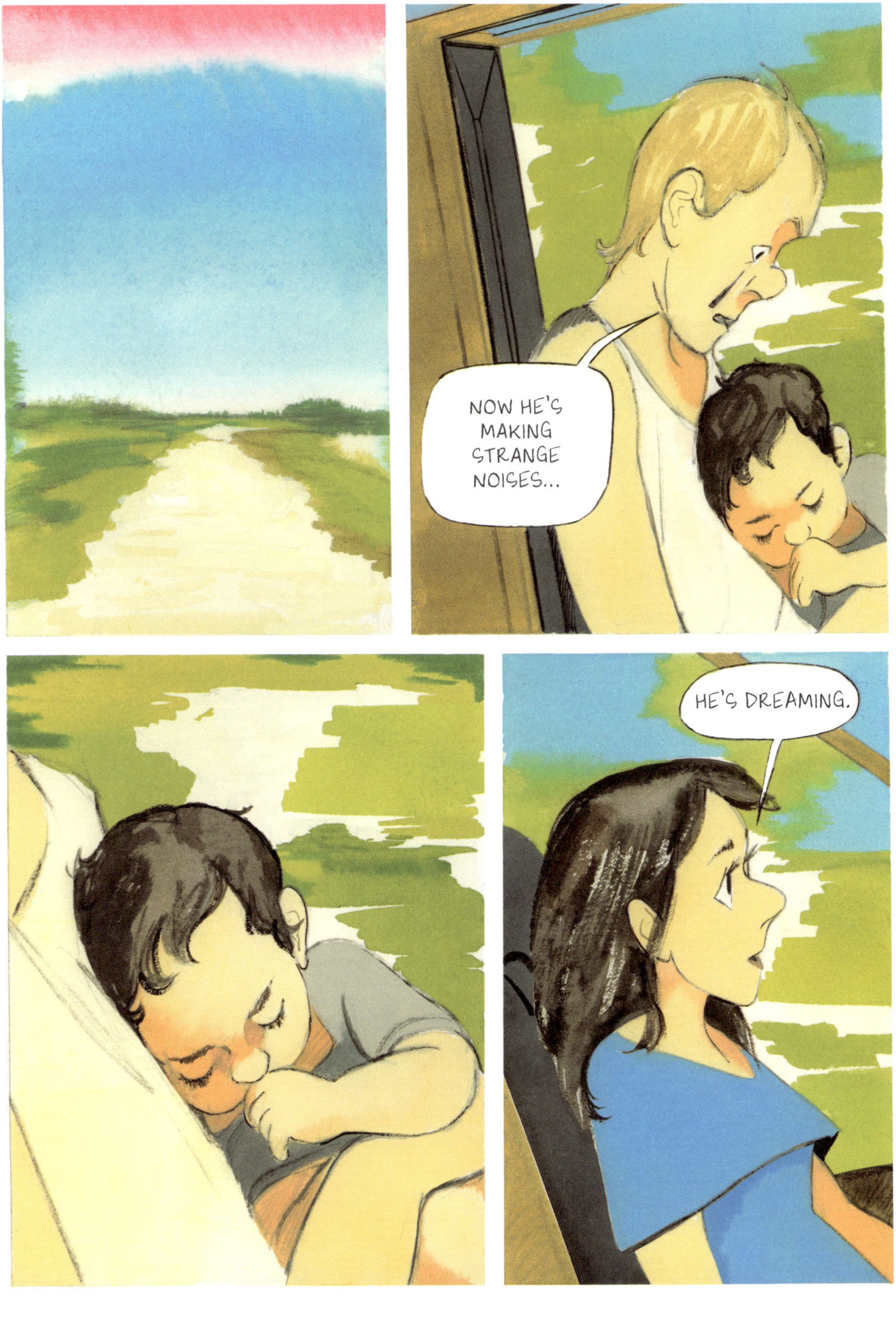
NOW HE'S MAKING STRANGE NOISES...
HE'S DREAMING.

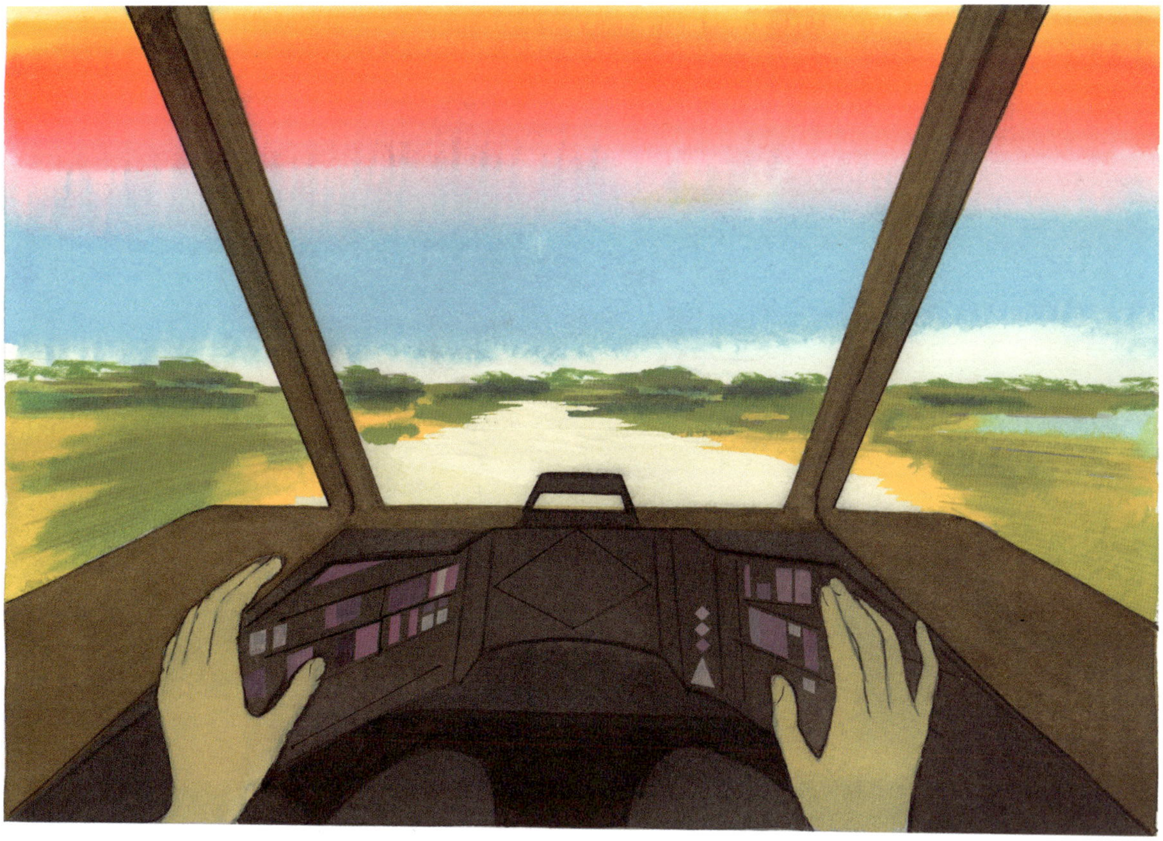

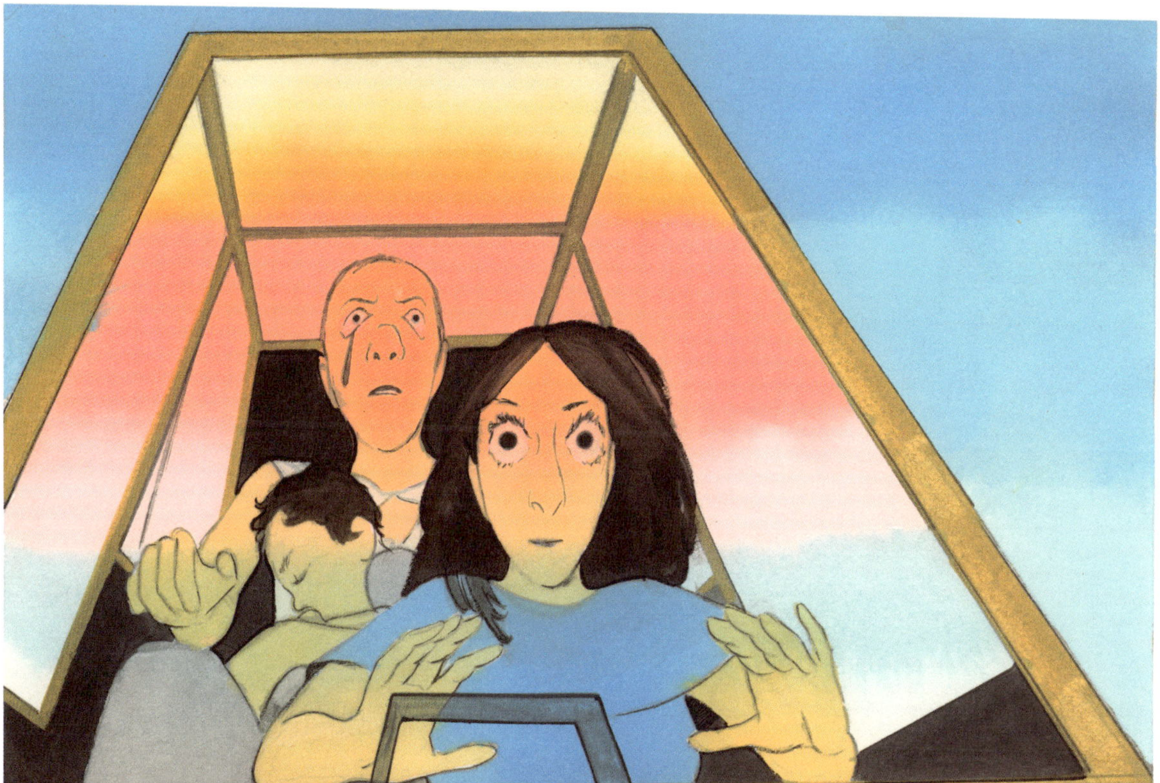

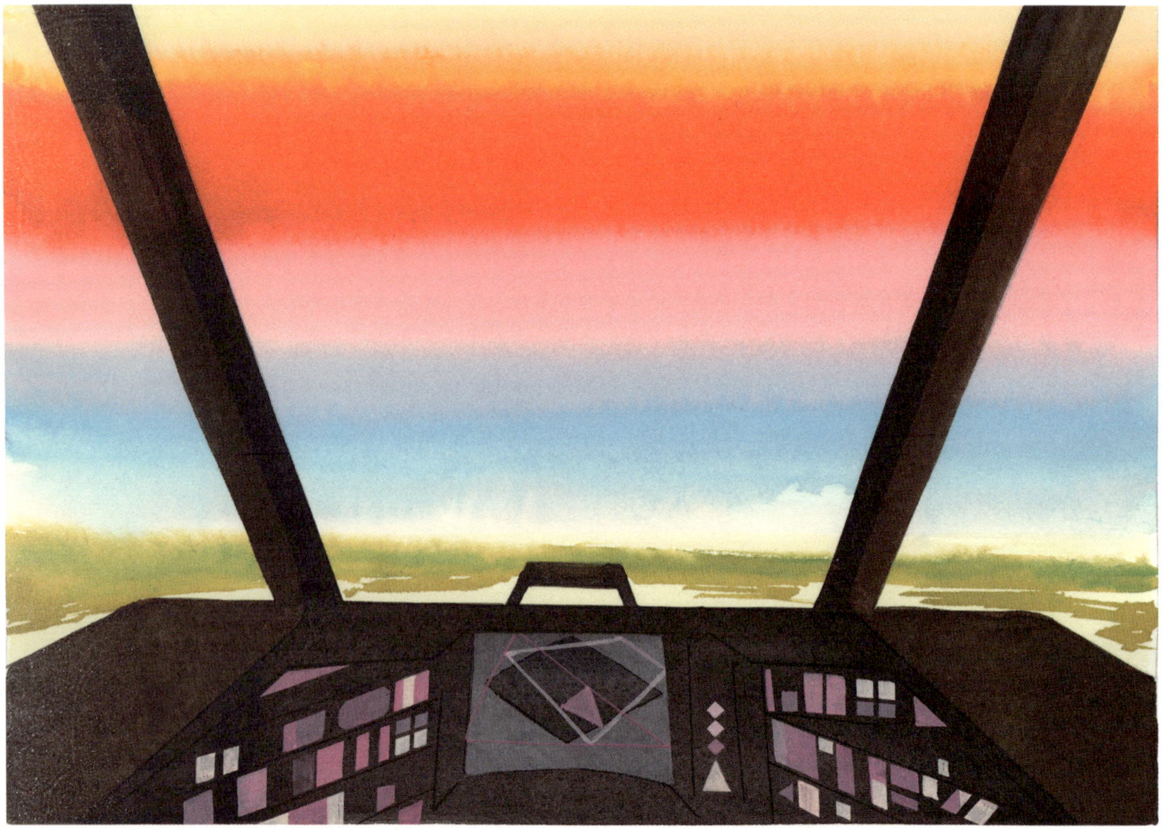

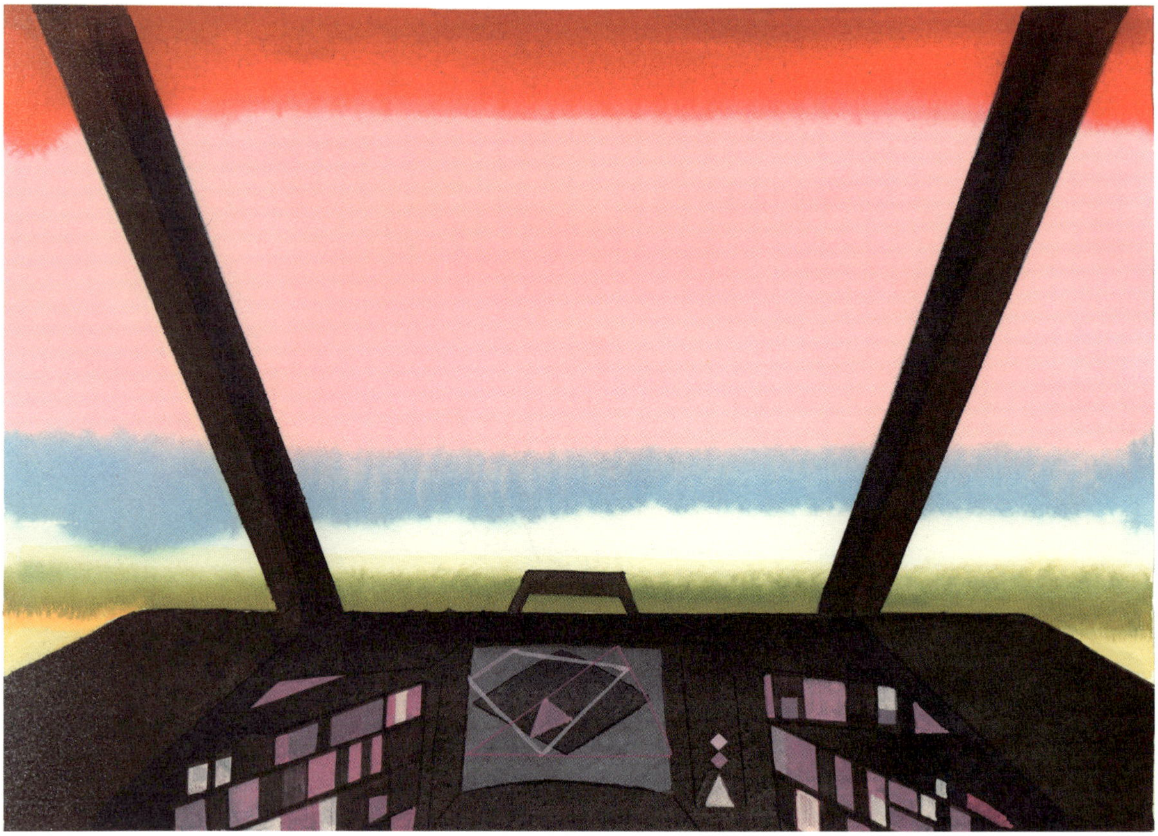

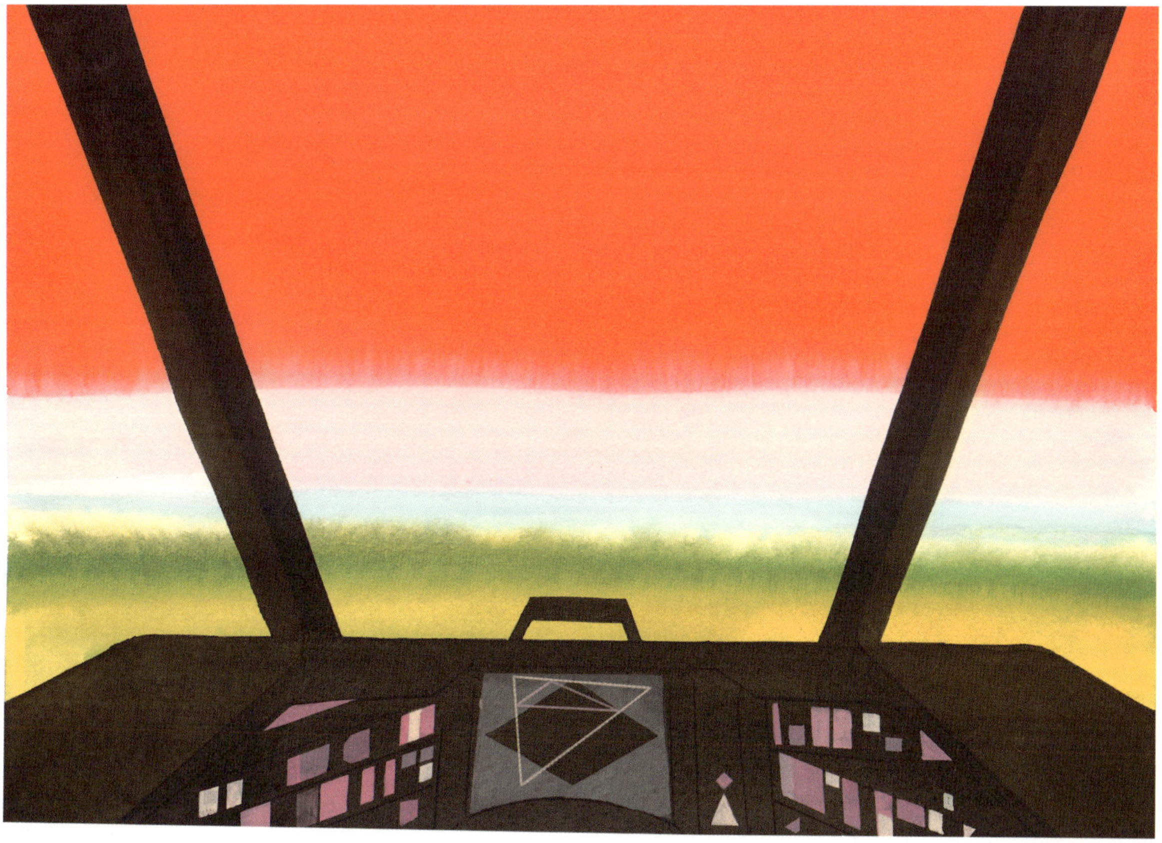

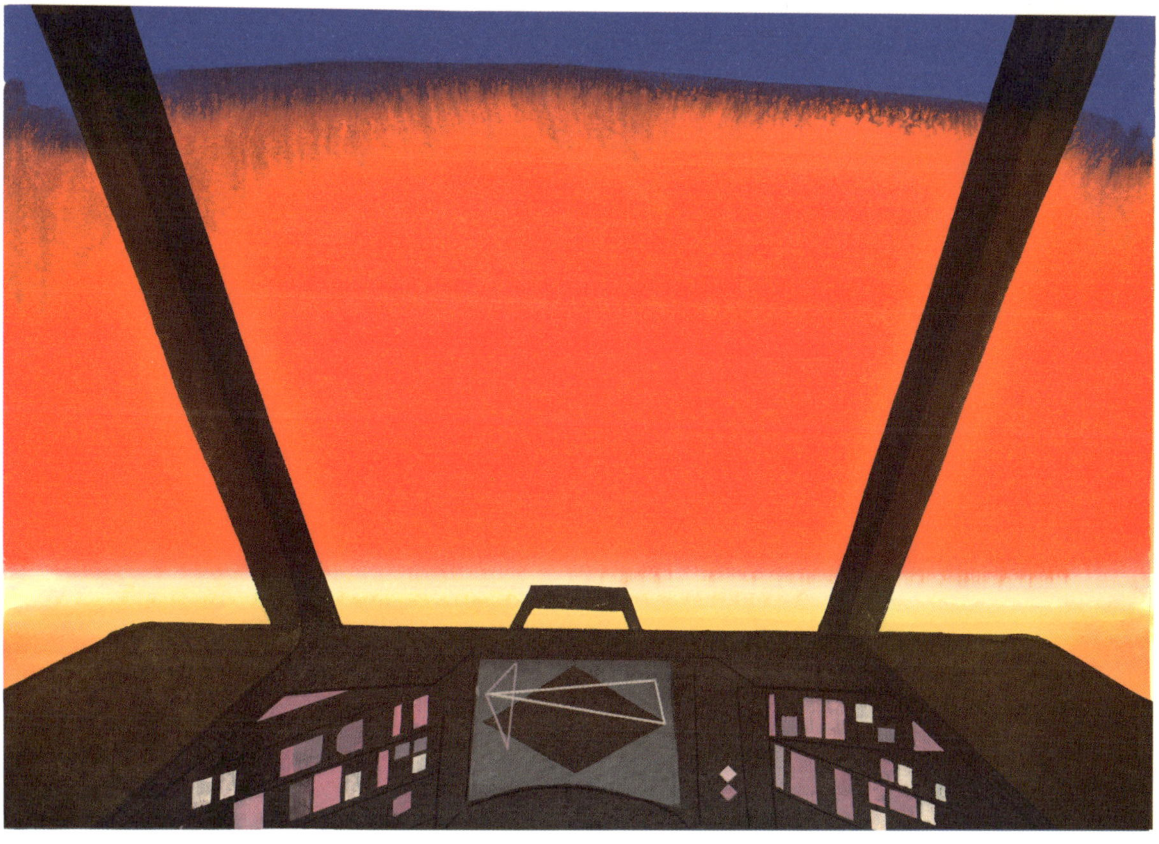

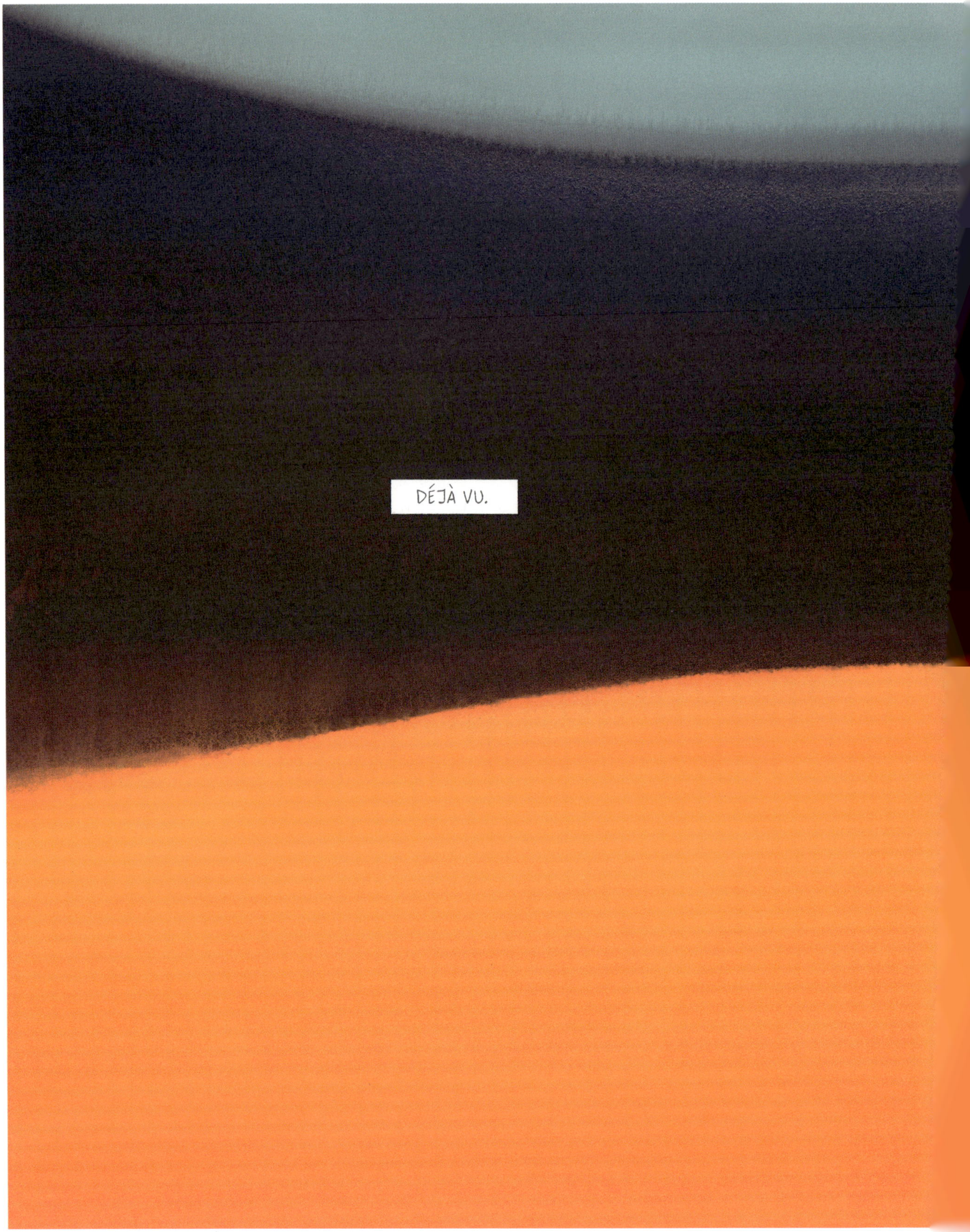
DÉJÀ VU.

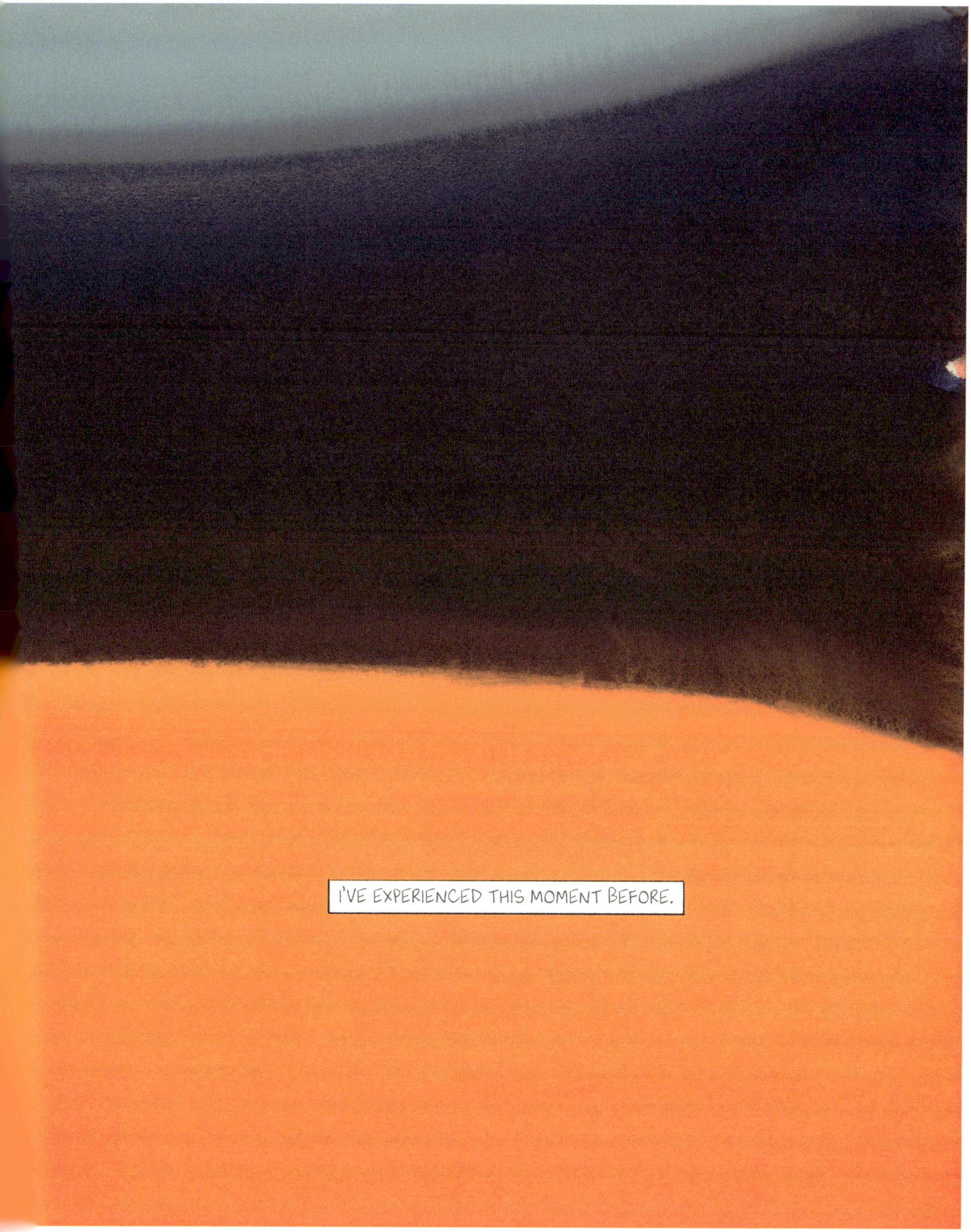
I'VE EXPERIENCED THIS MOMENT BEFORE.

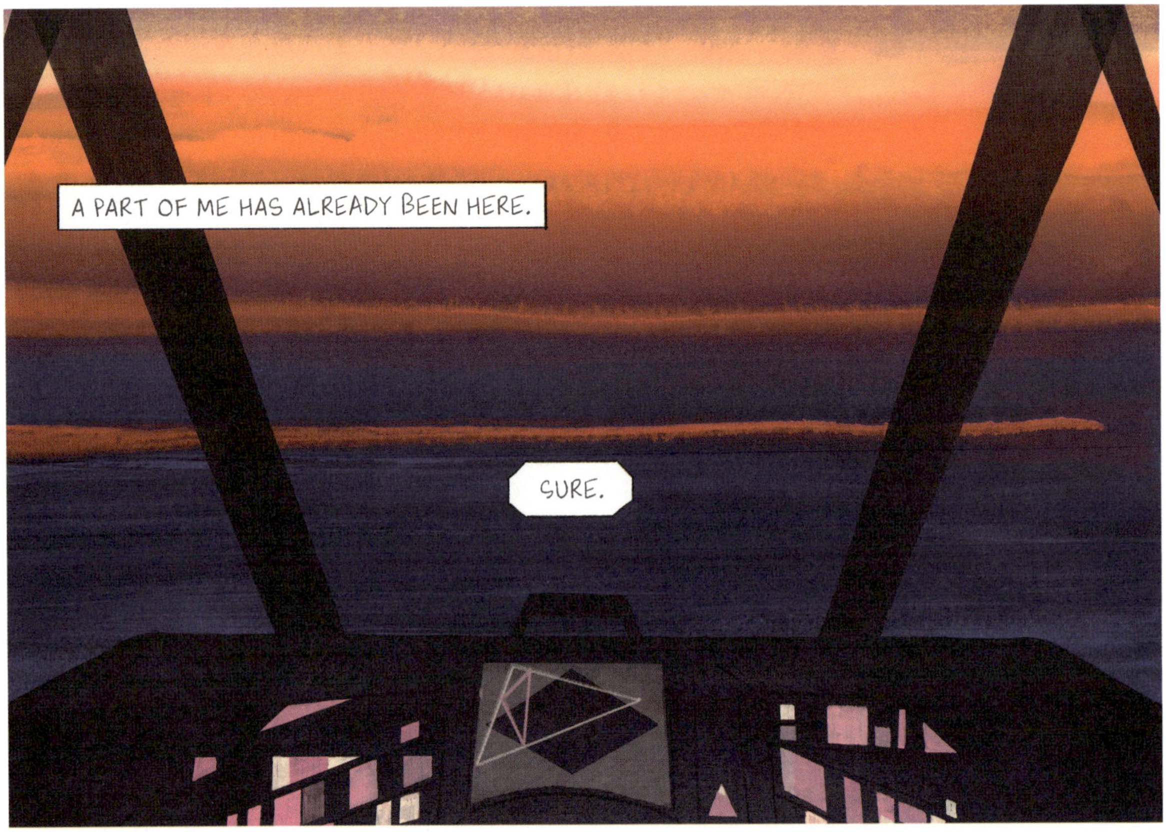
A PART OF ME HAS ALREADY BEEN HERE.
SURE.

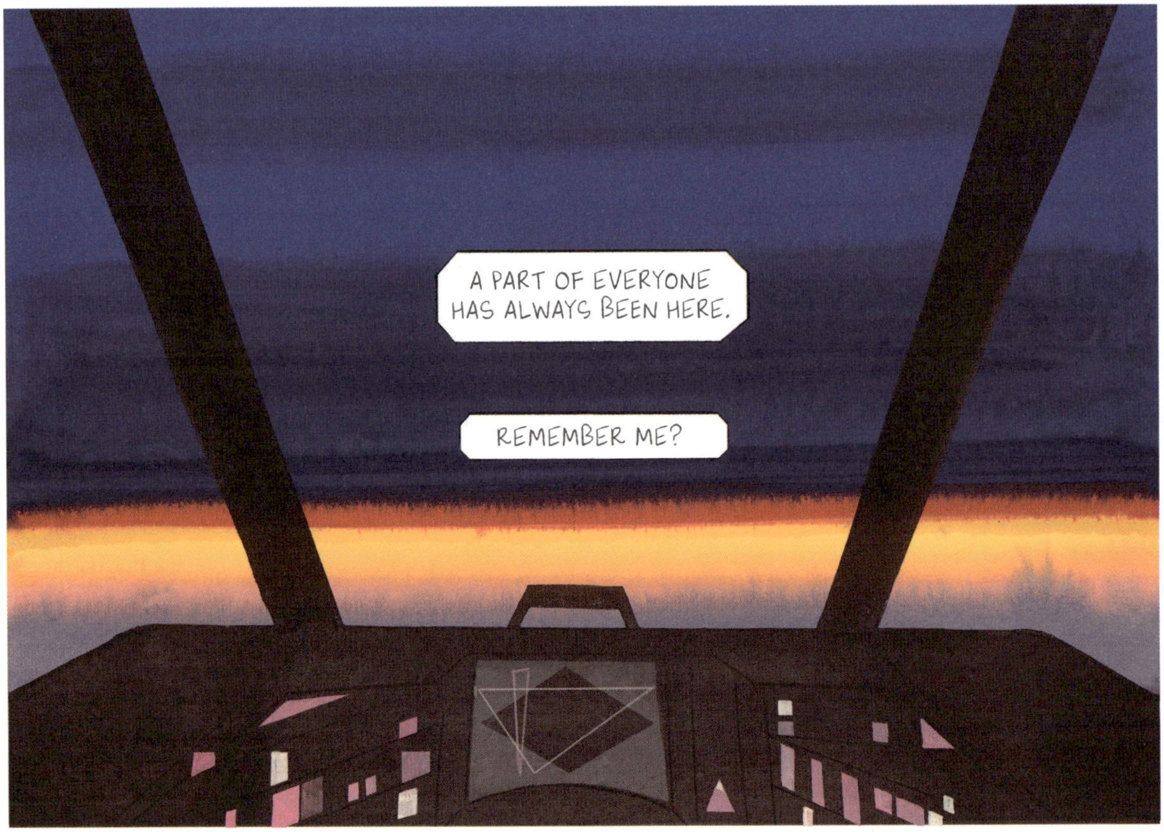
A PART OF EVERYONE HAS ALWAYS BEEN HERE.
REMEMBER ME?

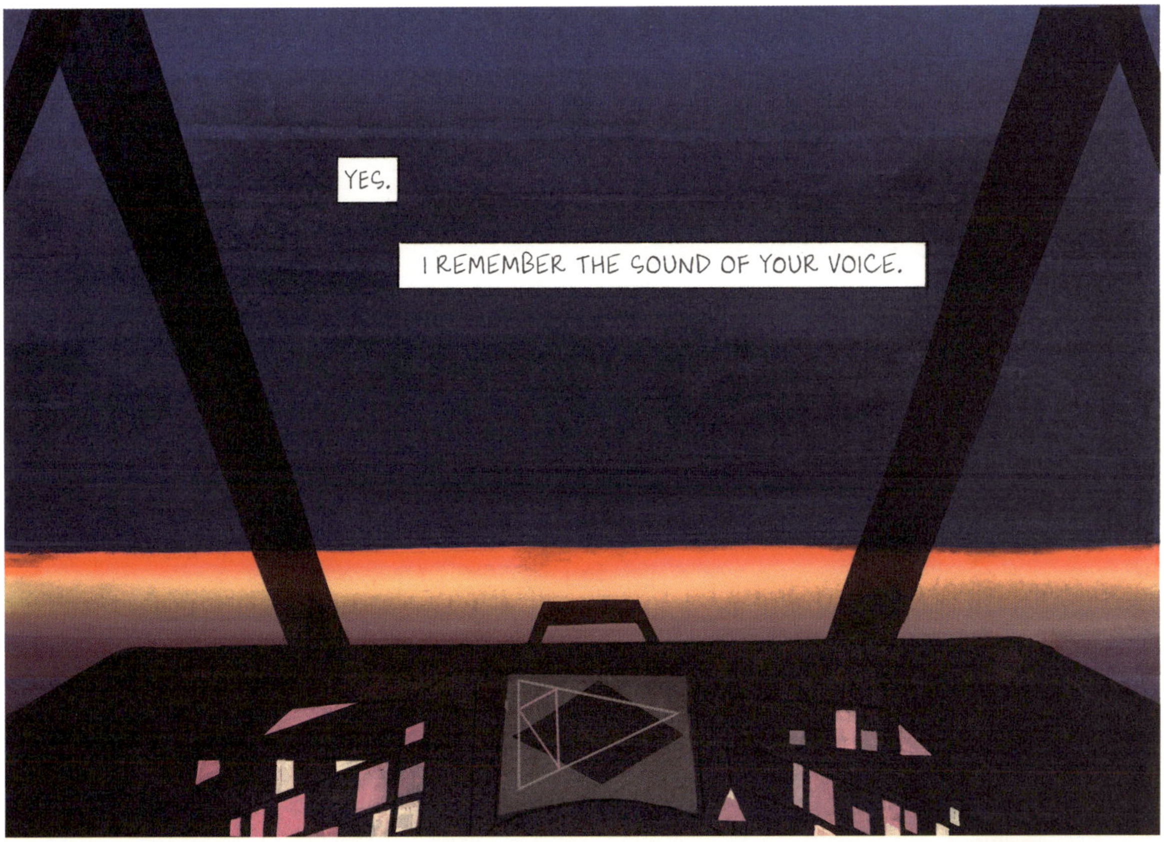
YES.
I REMEMBER THE SOUND OF YOUR VOICE.

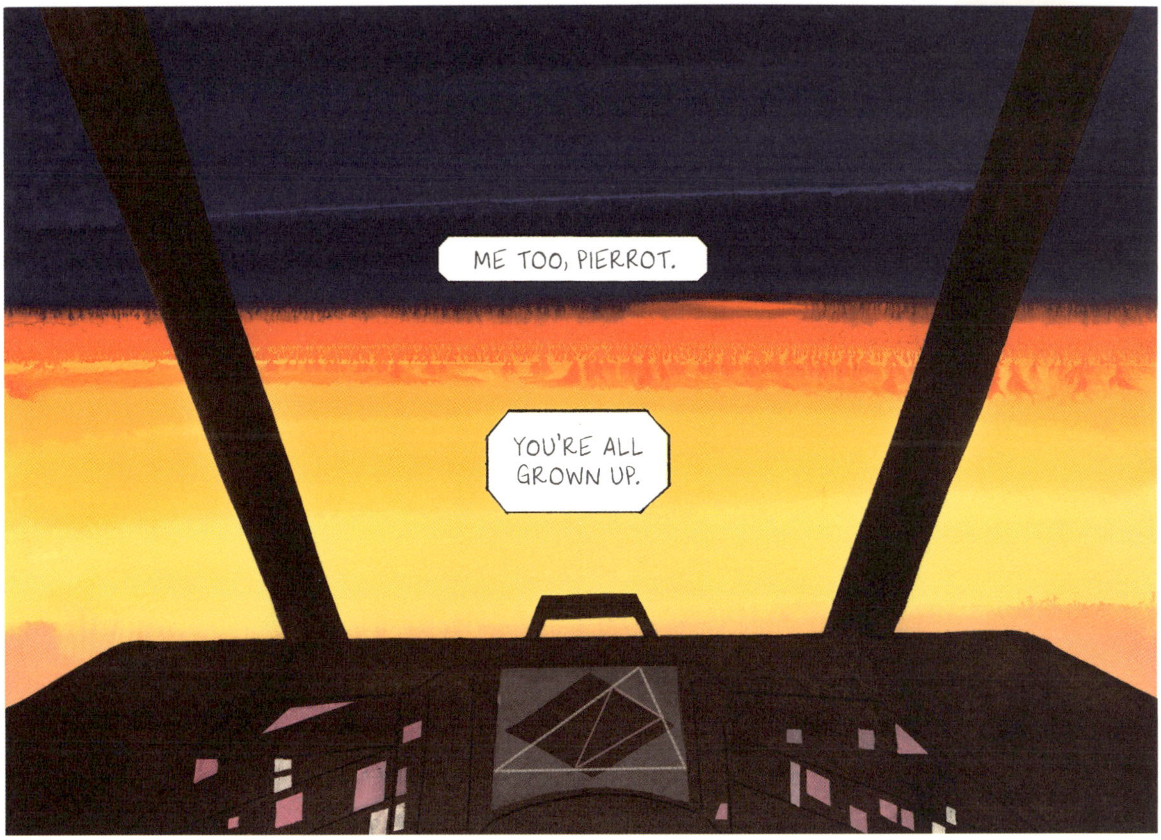
ME TOO, PIERROT.
YOU'RE ALL GROWN UP.

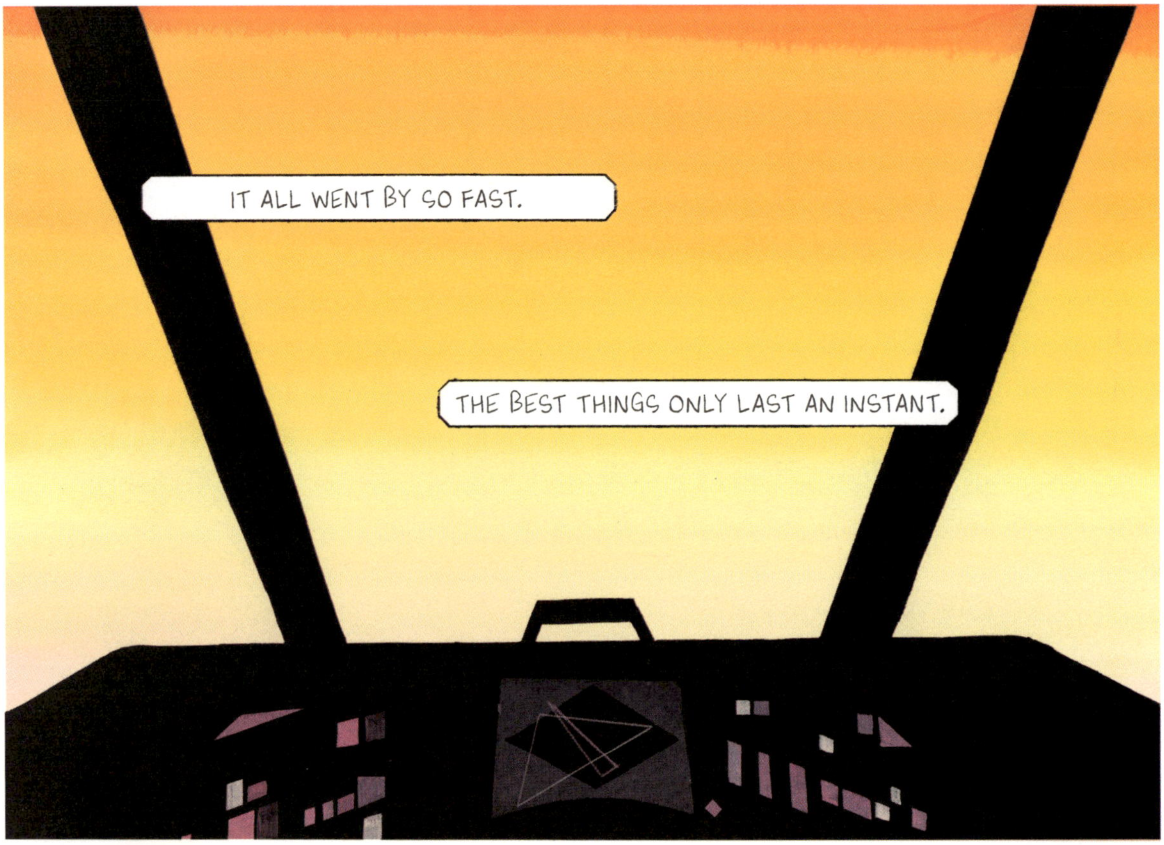
IT ALL WENT BY SO FAST.
THE BEST THINGS ONLY LAST AN INSTANT.

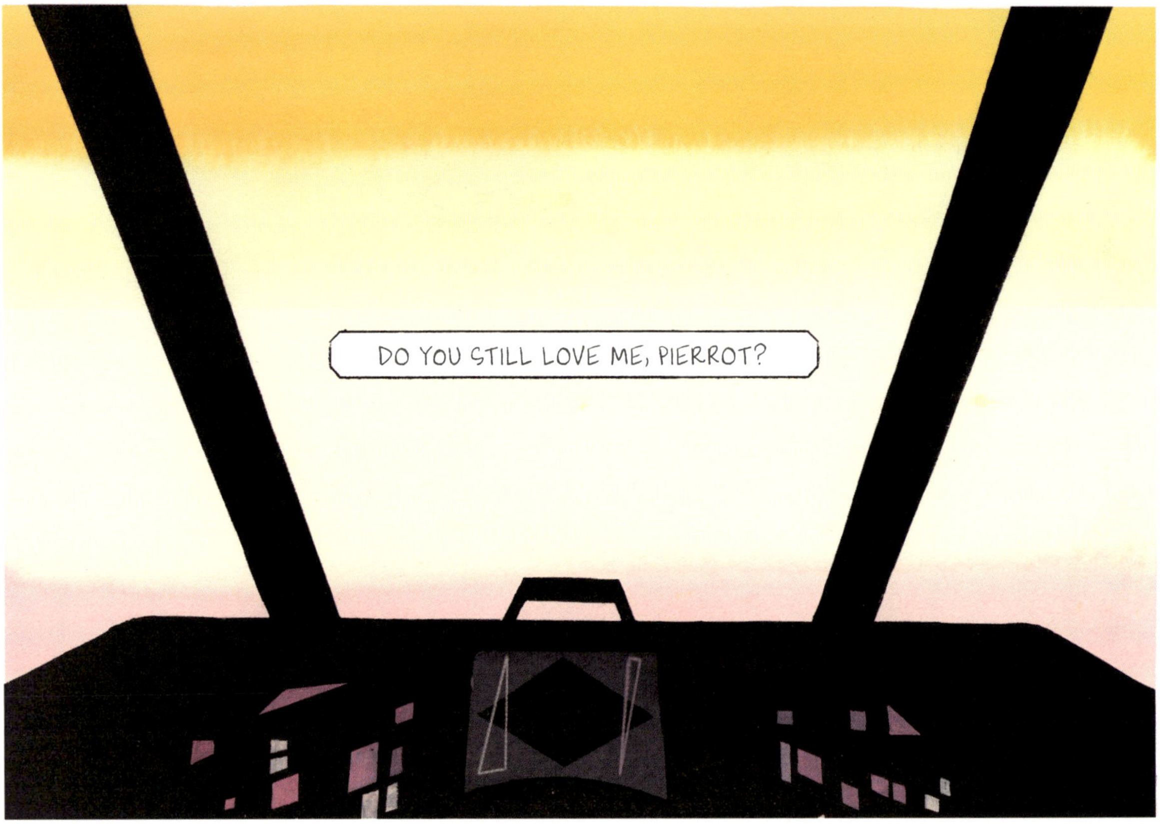
DO YOU STILL LOVE ME, PIERROT?

I DON'T KNOW.

COME CLOSER.

IT'S SO NICE
TO BE TOGETHER
A LITTLE LONGER.

I ALMOST FEEL LIKE
I CAN TOUCH YOU.

AND THAT MILD NAUSEA?

DON'T WORRY, IT'LL GO AWAY SOON.

SO CAN I OPEN MY EYES?

WHENEVER YOU WANT,

MY LITTLE PRODIGY.

MAMMA?

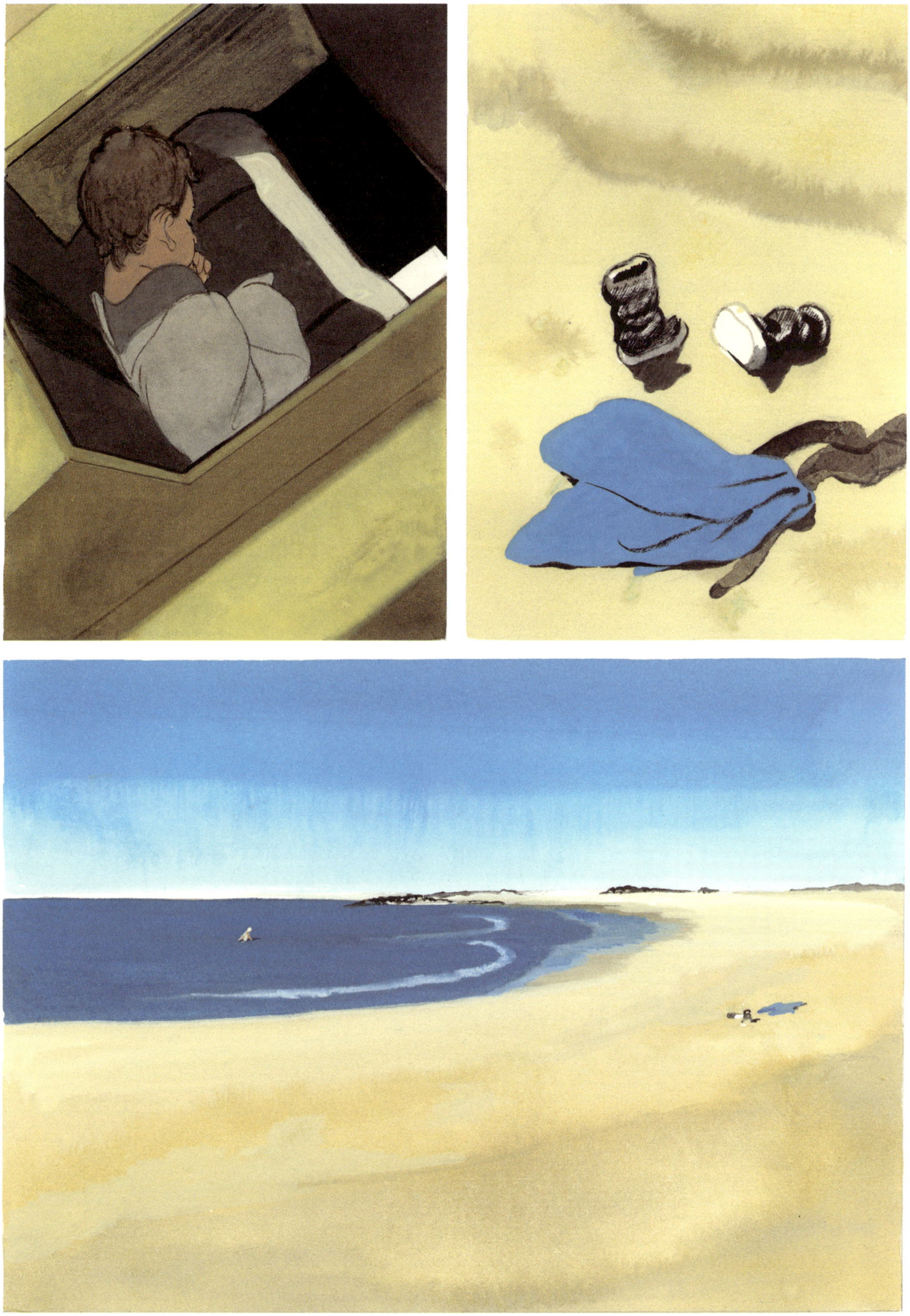

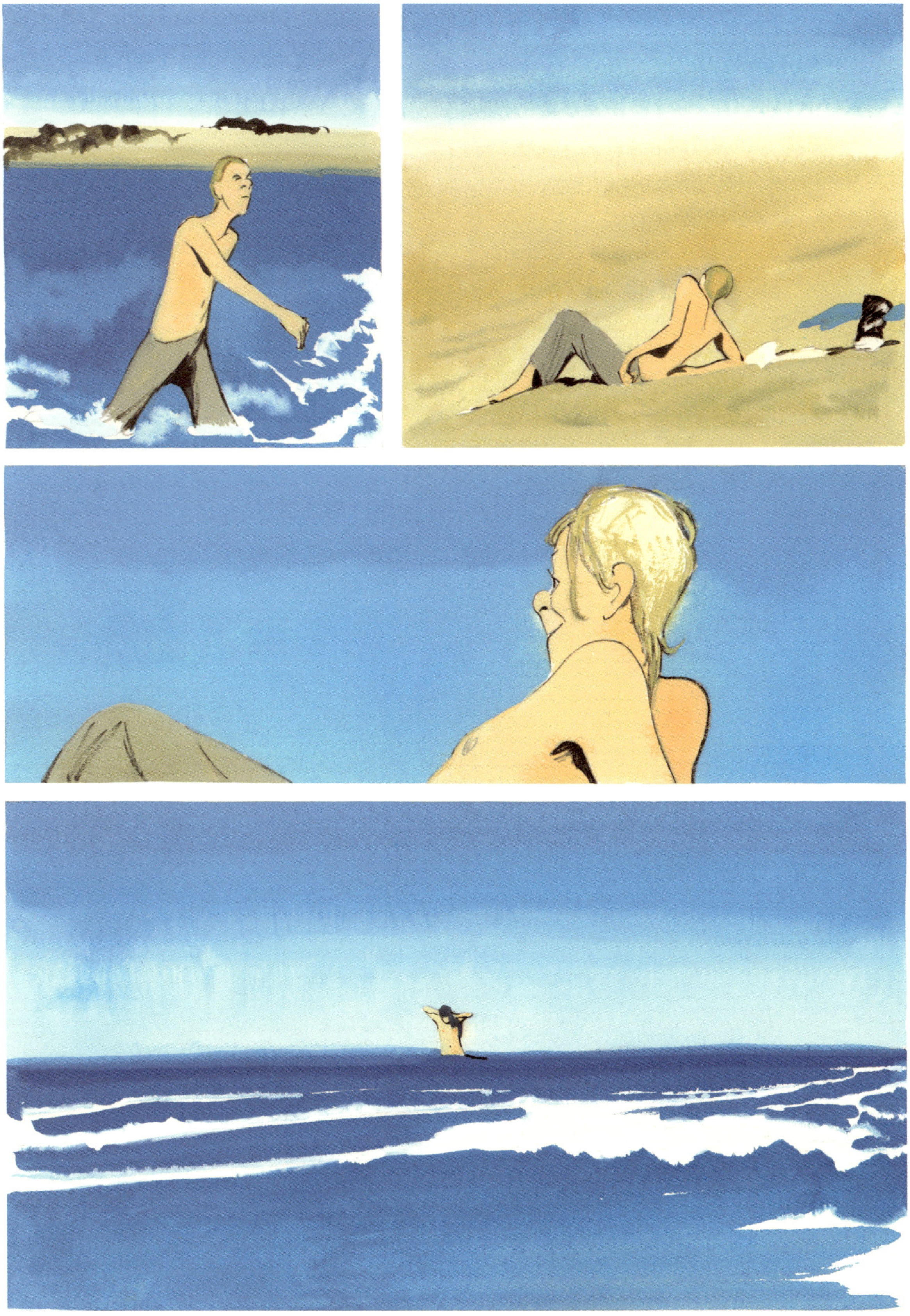

"YOUR HAIR'S A DIFFERENT COLOR."

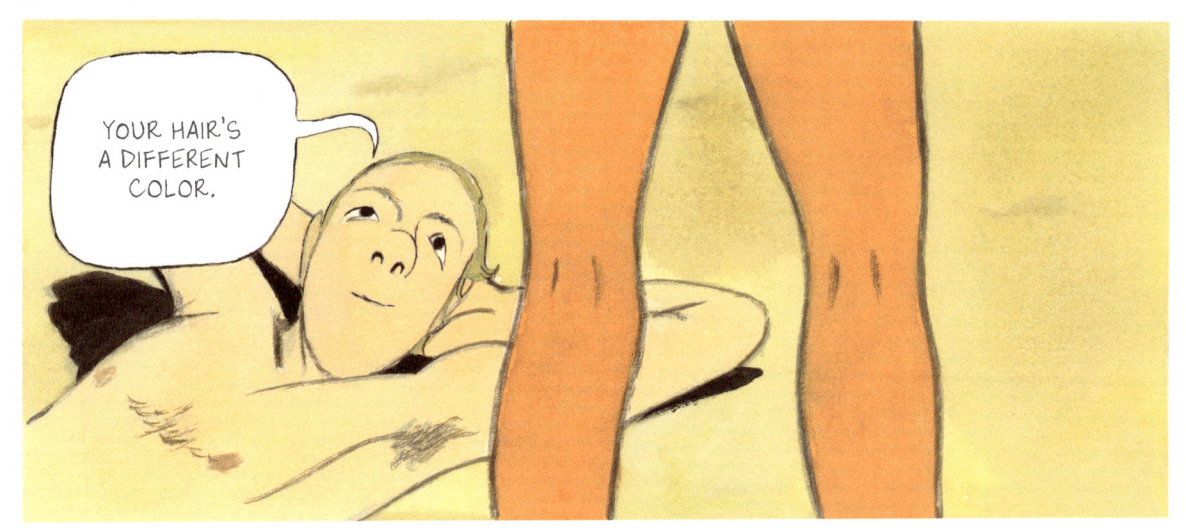

"THIS IS MY NATURAL COLOR."

YOU'RE DIFFERENT, TOO.

I'M NOT QUITE SURE HOW...

YOUR TEAR.

IT WASHED AWAY IN THE WATER.

GIVE ME SOMETHING!

SOME MAKEUP, A MARKER!

A PIECE OF COAL!
HELP ME!
WAIT.
LET ME SEE.
YOU KNOW, YOU DON'T LOOK HALF BAD!!

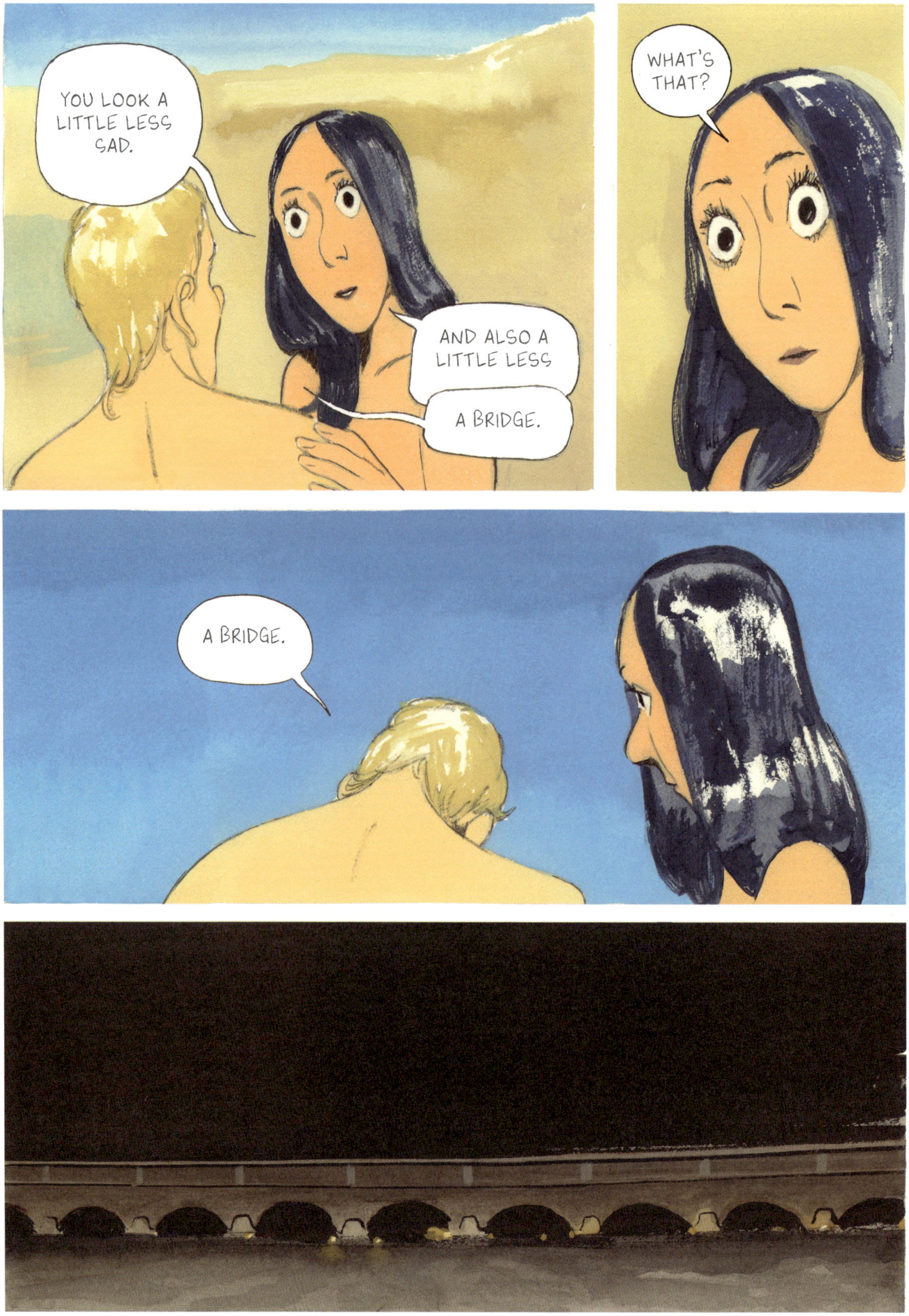
YOU LOOK A LITTLE LESS SAD.
AND ALSO A LITTLE LESS
A BRIDGE.
WHAT'S THAT?
A BRIDGE.

"A FLASH."

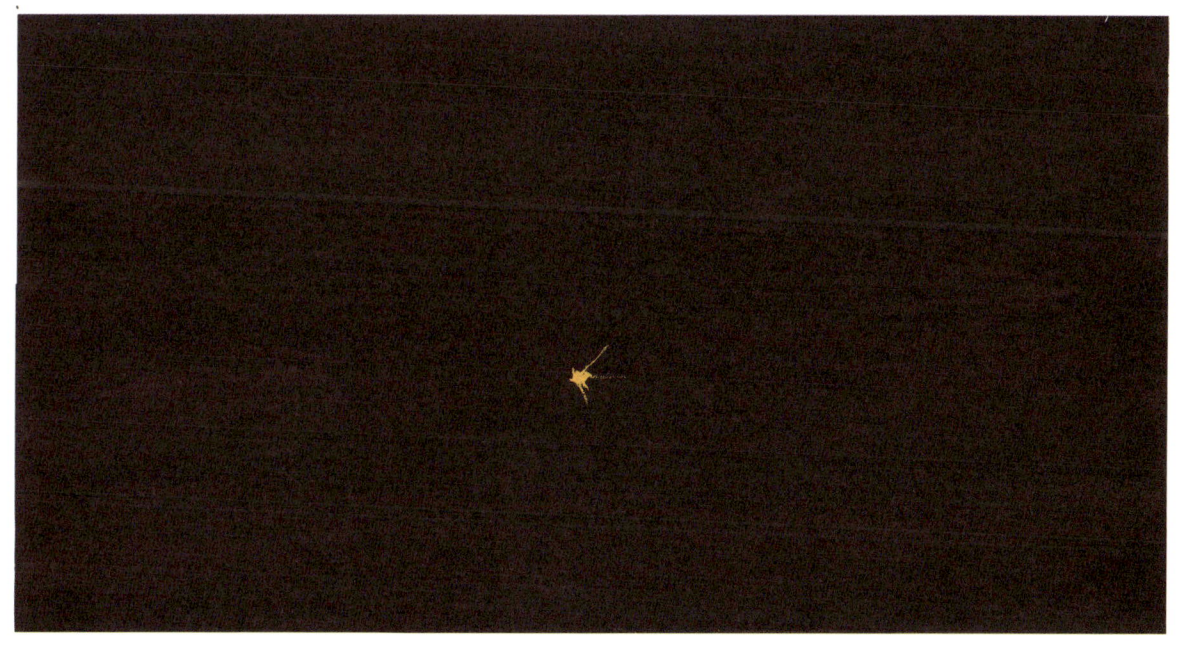

"A BIG EXPLOSION."

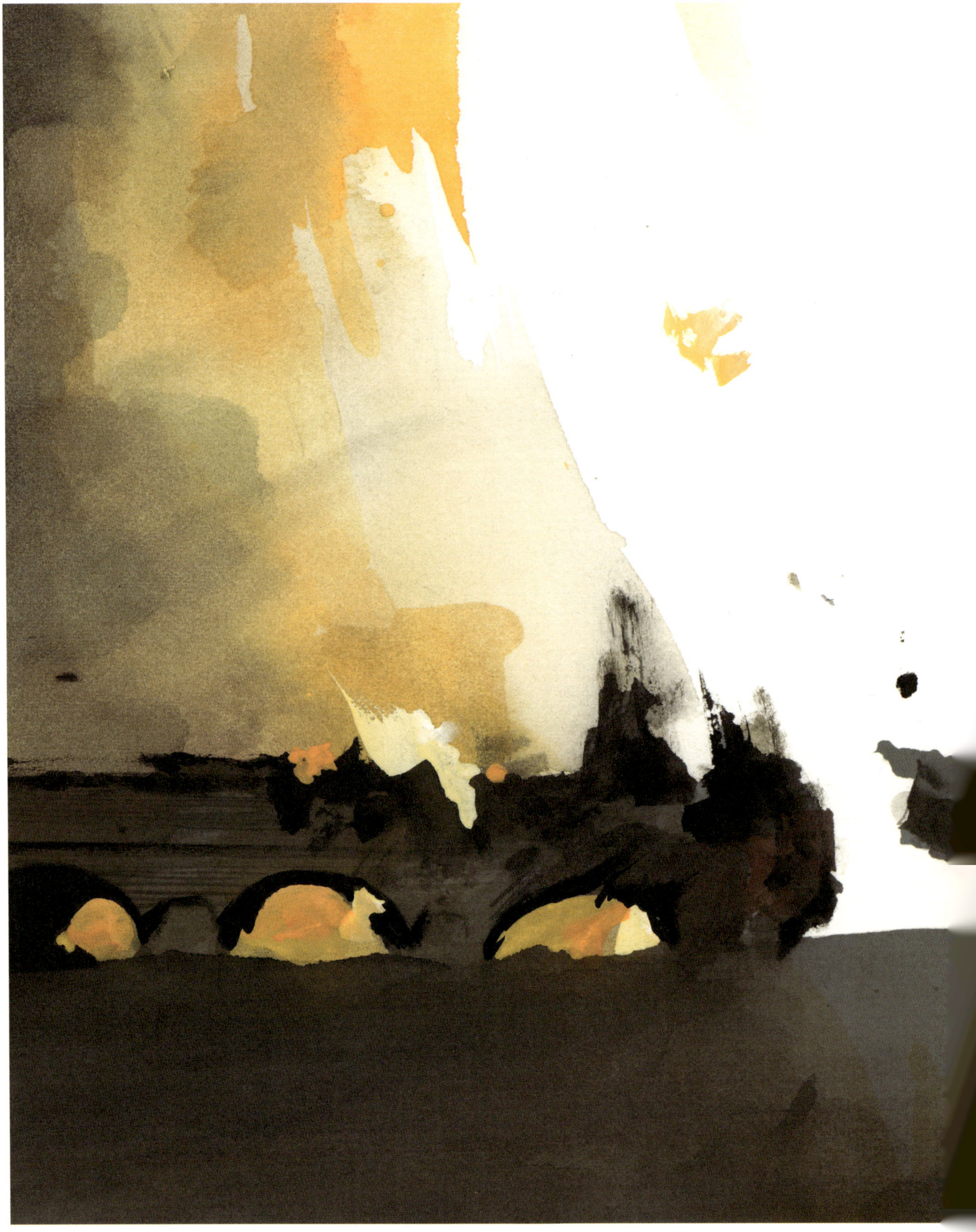

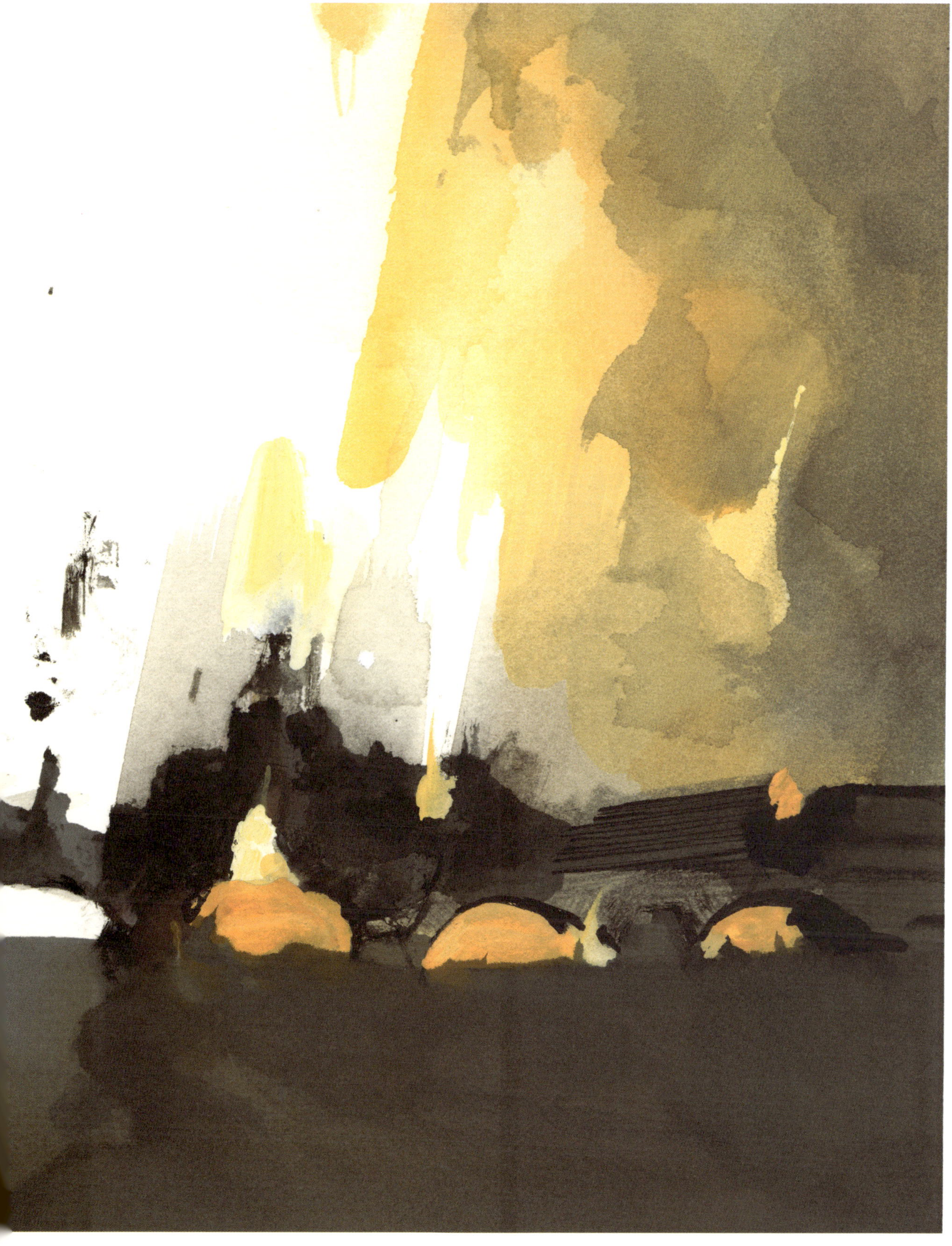

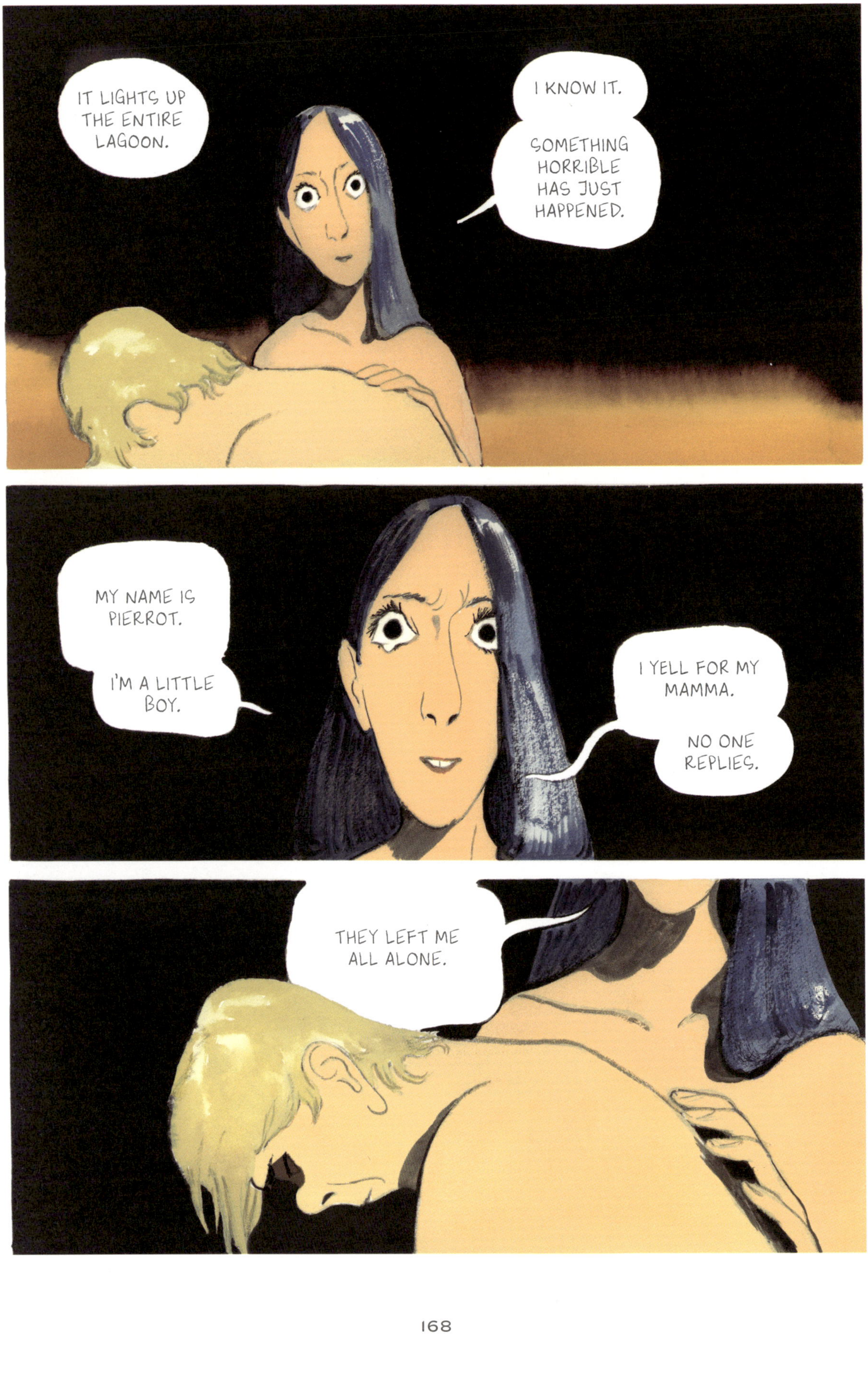
IT LIGHTS UP THE ENTIRE LAGOON.
I KNOW IT.
SOMETHING HORRIBLE HAS JUST HAPPENED.
MY NAME IS PIERROT.
I'M A LITTLE BOY.
I YELL FOR MY MAMMA.
NO ONE REPLIES.
THEY LEFT ME ALL ALONE.

BUT I SAW EVERYTHING.
EVEN WITH MY EYES CLOSED I CAN SEE THINGS.
AS IF I WERE IN SOMEONE ELSE'S MIND.
AM I IN YOURS, MAMMA?
IT'S PIERROT, DO YOU REMEMBER?

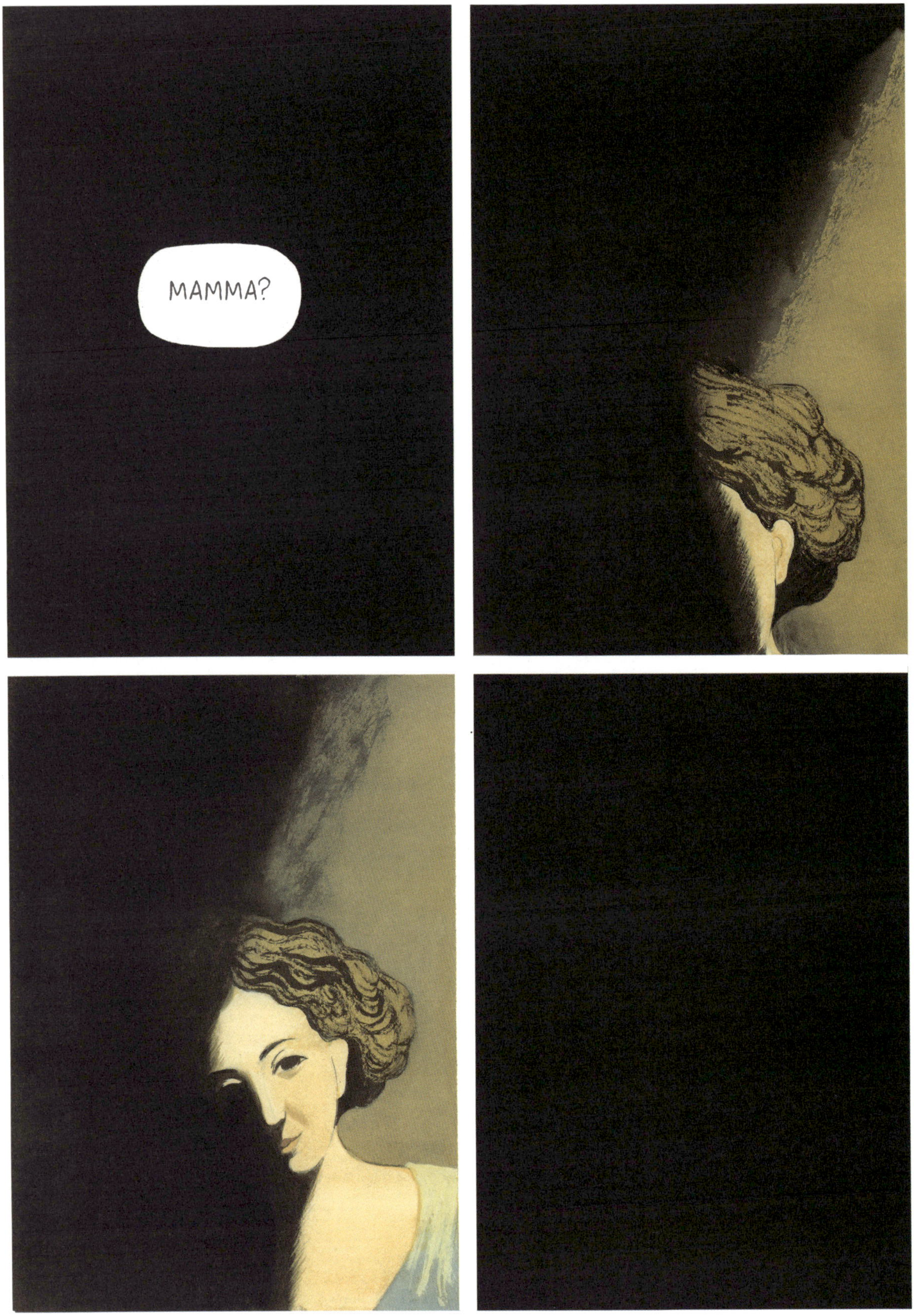
MAMMA?

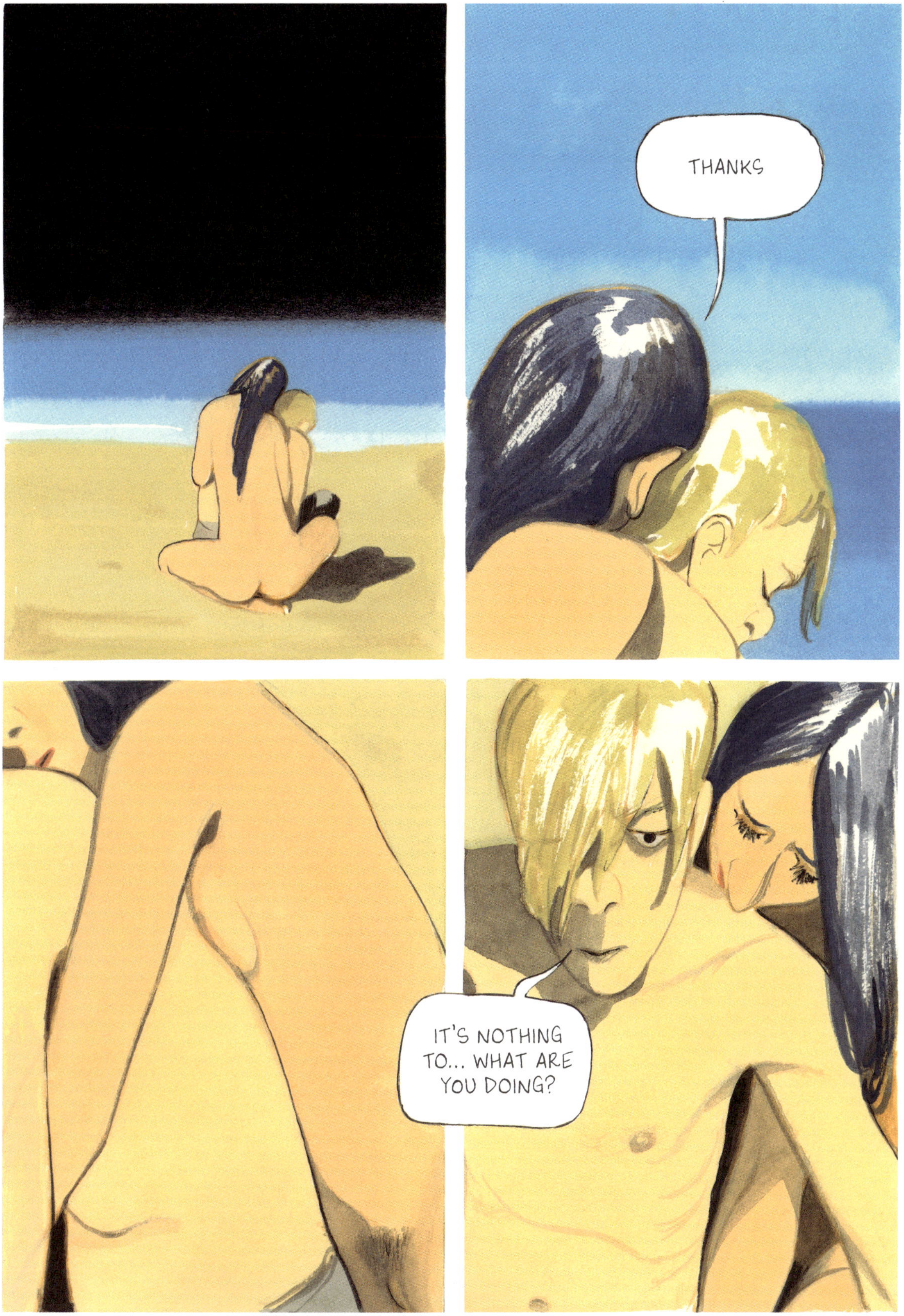
THANKS
IT'S NOTHING TO... WHAT ARE YOU DOING?

WHAT DO YOU THINK?

I'VE TRIED, I'M INCAPABLE.

DO YOU WANT TO TRY AGAIN?

ALL RIGHT.

JUST THIS ONCE.

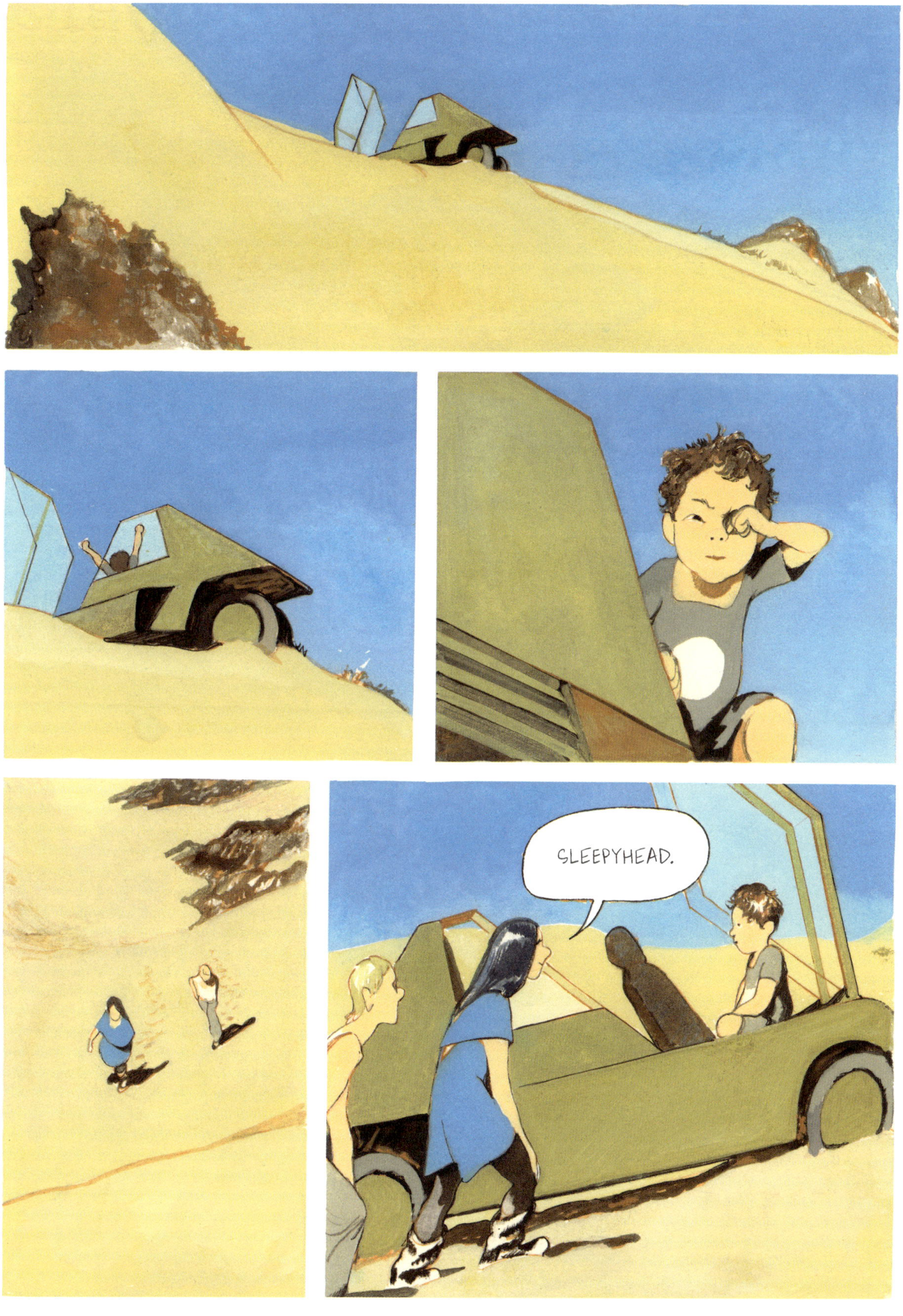
SLEEPYHEAD.

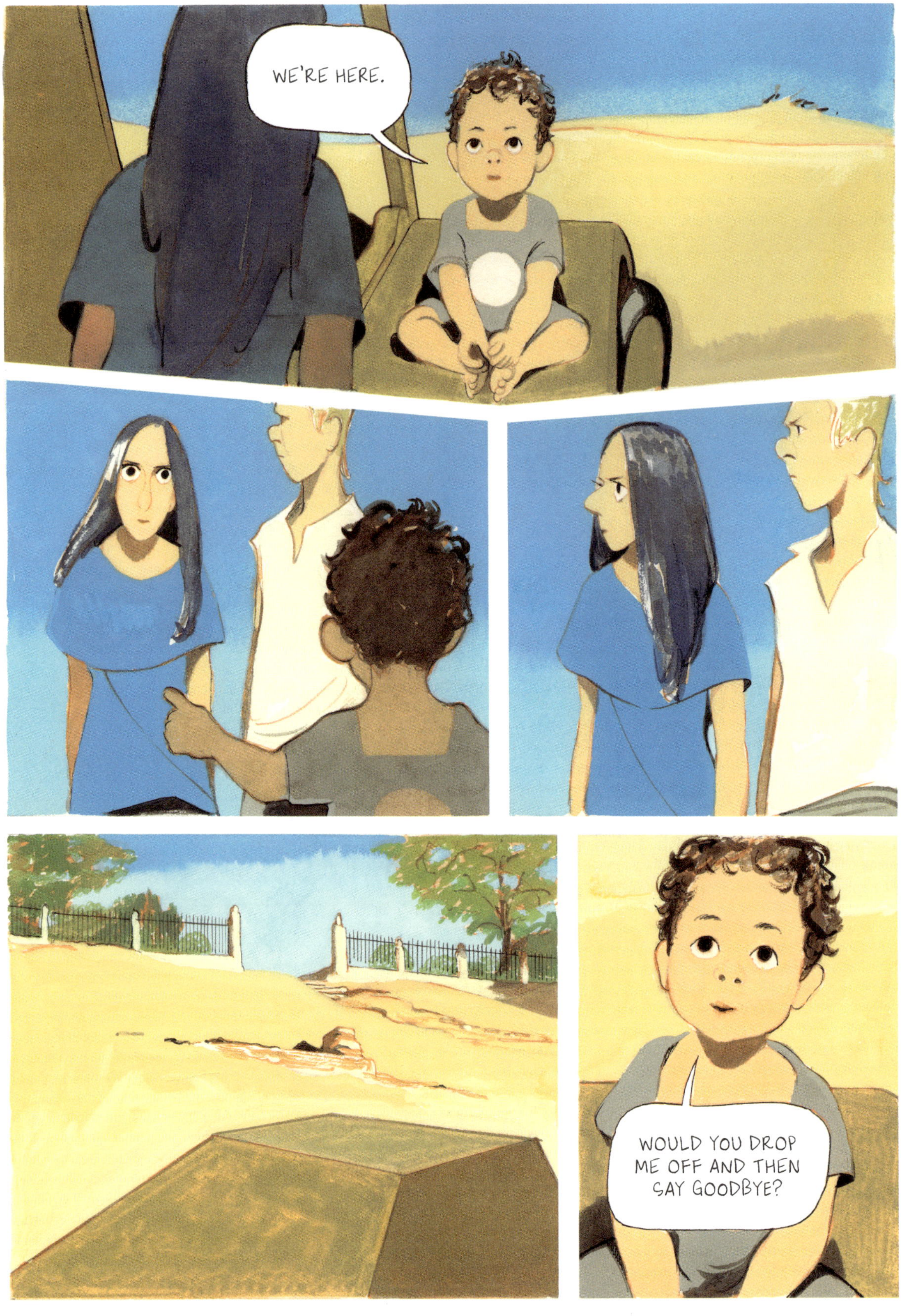
WE'RE HERE.
WOULD YOU DROP ME OFF AND THEN SAY GOODBYE?

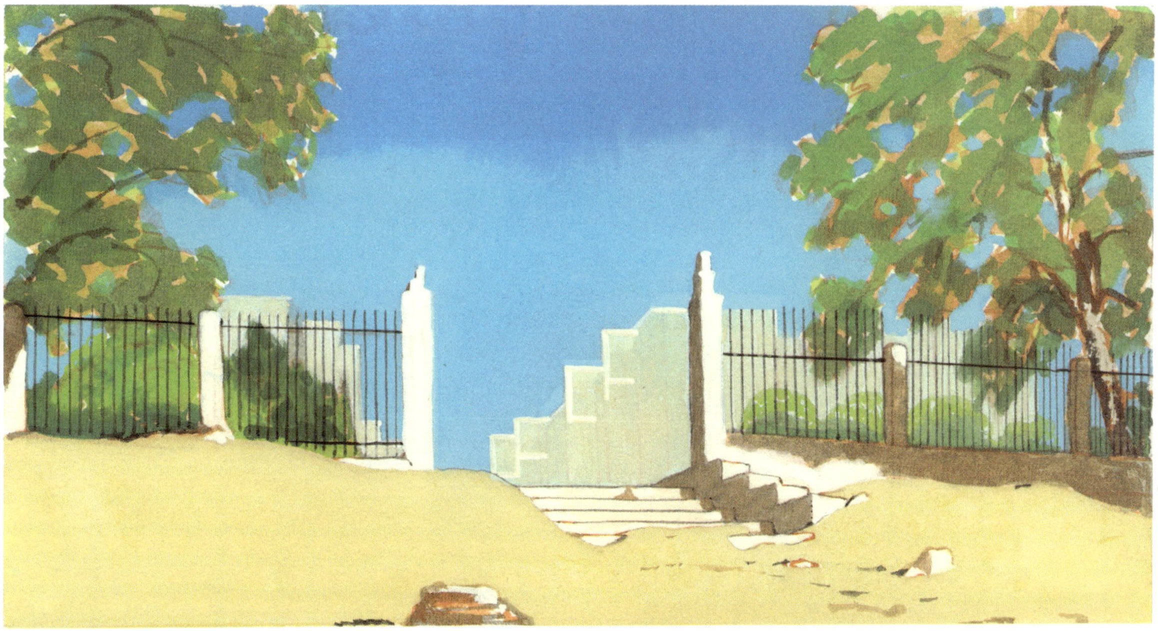

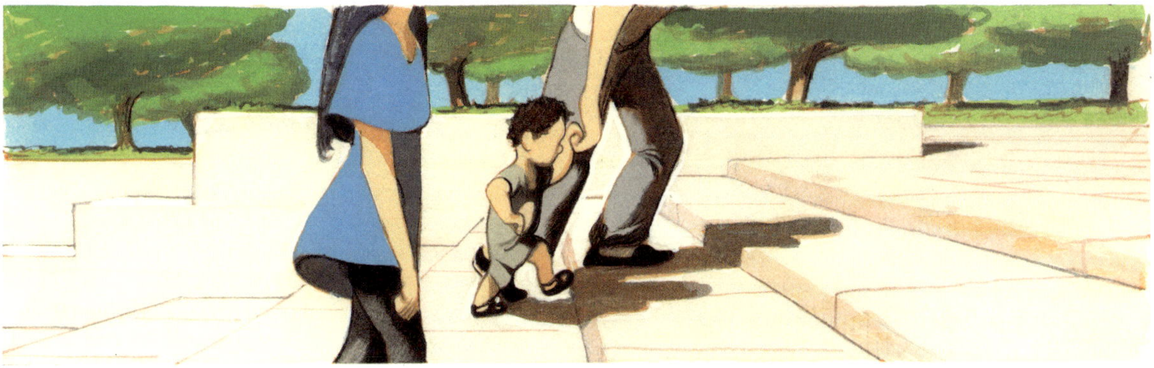

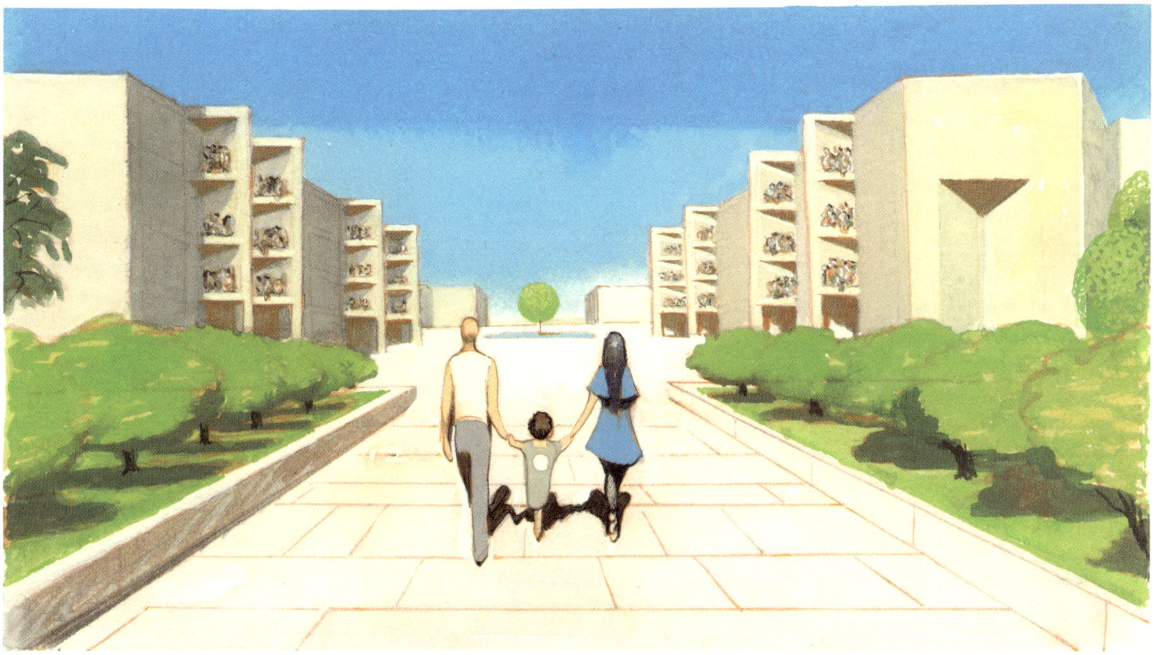

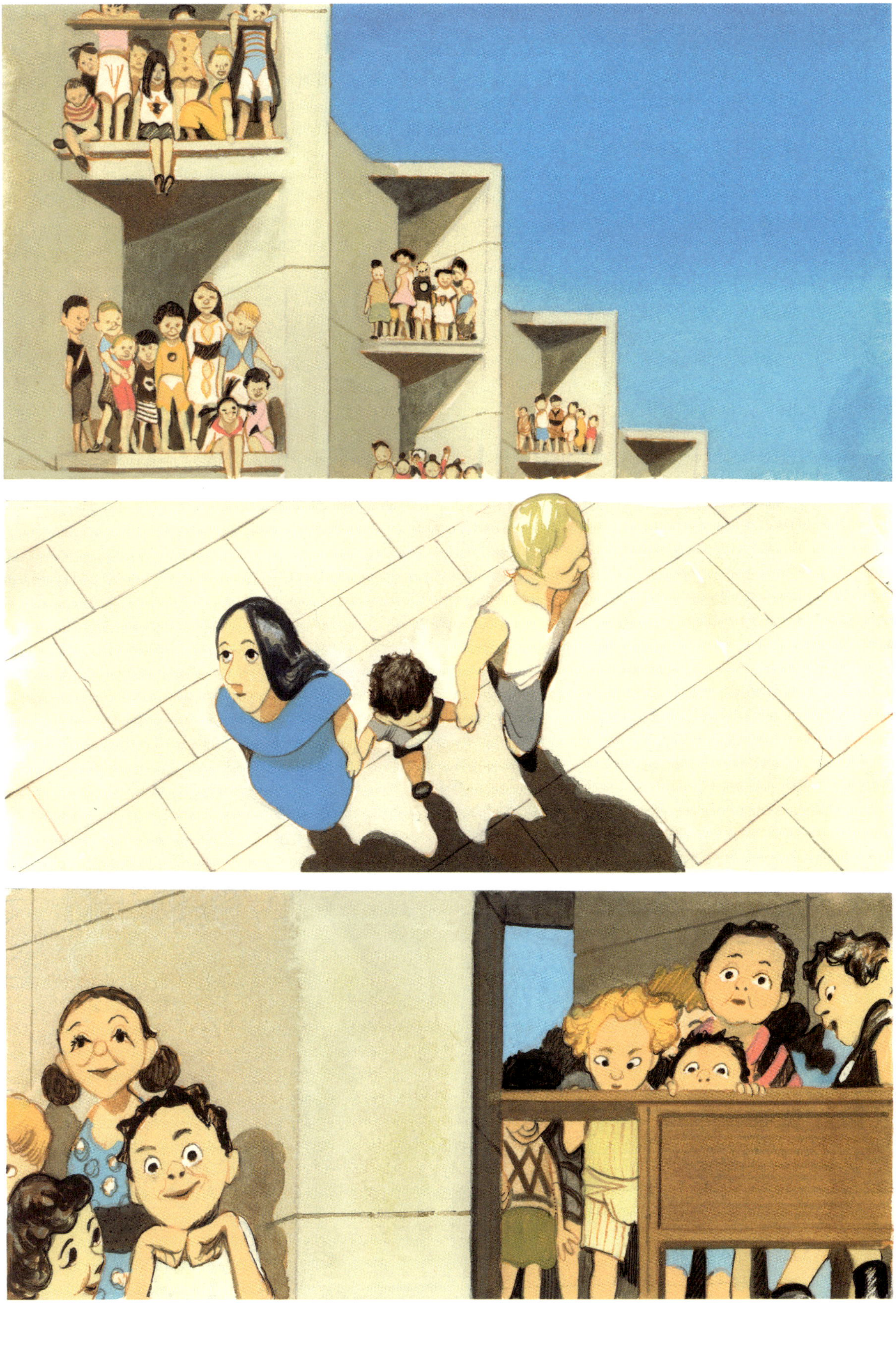

TOOK YOU LONG ENOUGH.
I HAD A LOT TO DO.
I KNOW. WE'RE ALL DOING OUR BEST.

"WE TAKE CARE OF THE PEOPLE WHO STAYED ON THE MAINLAND."

"BUT YOU DON'T SEEM LIKE YOU'RE FROM HERE."

"WELCOME TO THE NURSERY."

"THE NURSERY WANTS TO CELEBRATE OUR MEMBER'S RETURN."

"WOULD YOU BE OUR GUESTS FOR THE NIGHT?"

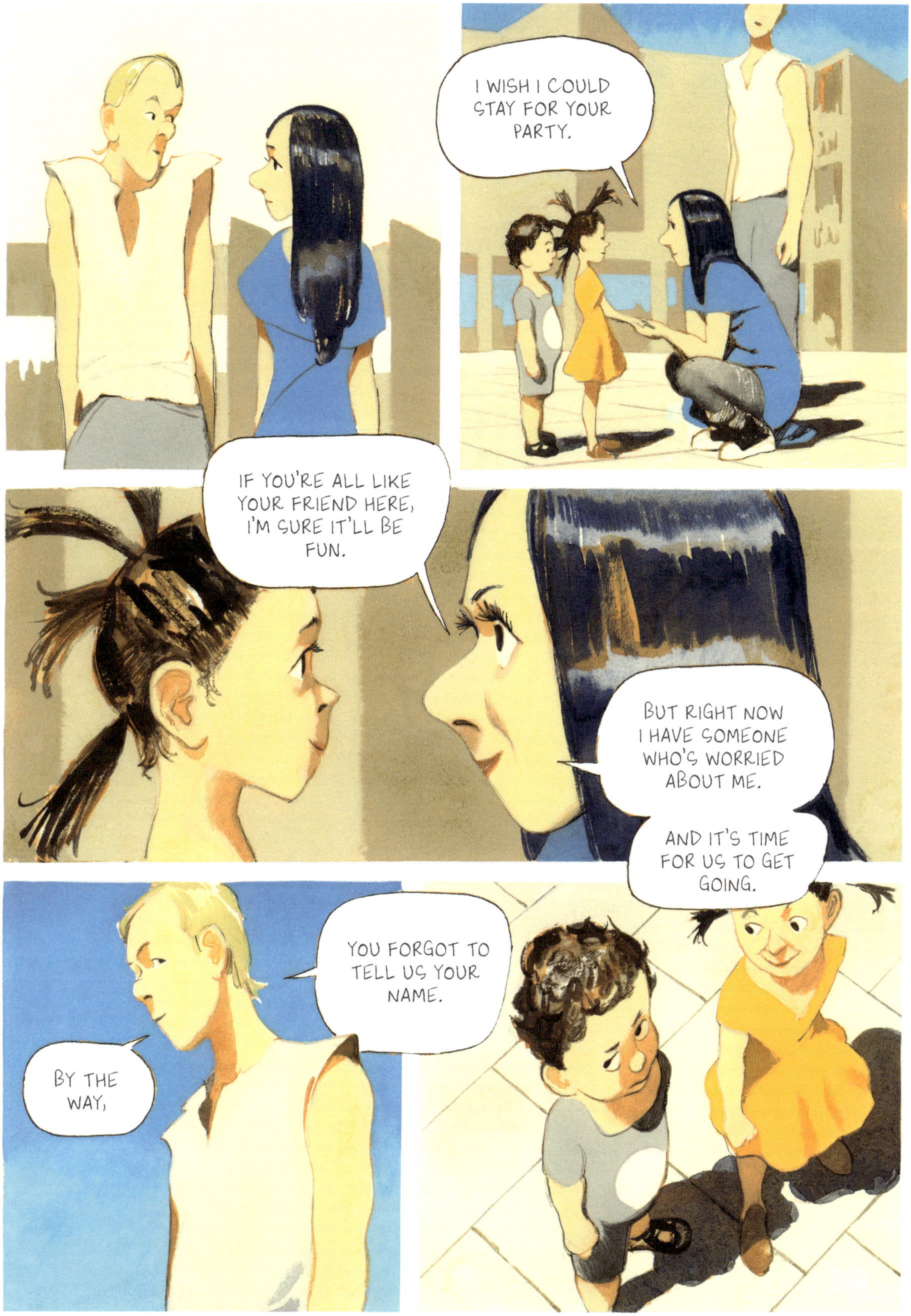
I WISH I COULD STAY FOR YOUR PARTY.
IF YOU'RE ALL LIKE YOUR FRIEND HERE, I'M SURE IT'LL BE FUN.
BUT RIGHT NOW I HAVE SOMEONE WHO'S WORRIED ABOUT ME.
AND IT'S TIME FOR US TO GET GOING.
BY THE WAY,
YOU FORGOT TO TELL US YOUR NAME.

MY NAME IS CHILD.
IN THE FUTURE I WILL BE CALLED MAN.
AND OTHER NAMES TOO, SOME OF WHICH HAVEN'T BEEN INVENTED YET.
A FORGOTTEN LANGUAGE WILL SPREAD FROM THESE CASTLES THROUGHOUT THE MAINLAND.

FROM CELESTIA TO ALBIREO, TO MEROPE, TO GALA...

AND EVEN FURTHER BEYOND THOSE WALLS.

UNTIL IT SCATTERS IN THE WIND.

LIKE AN ANCIENT SOUND.

A MORNING SONG.

A GREETING.

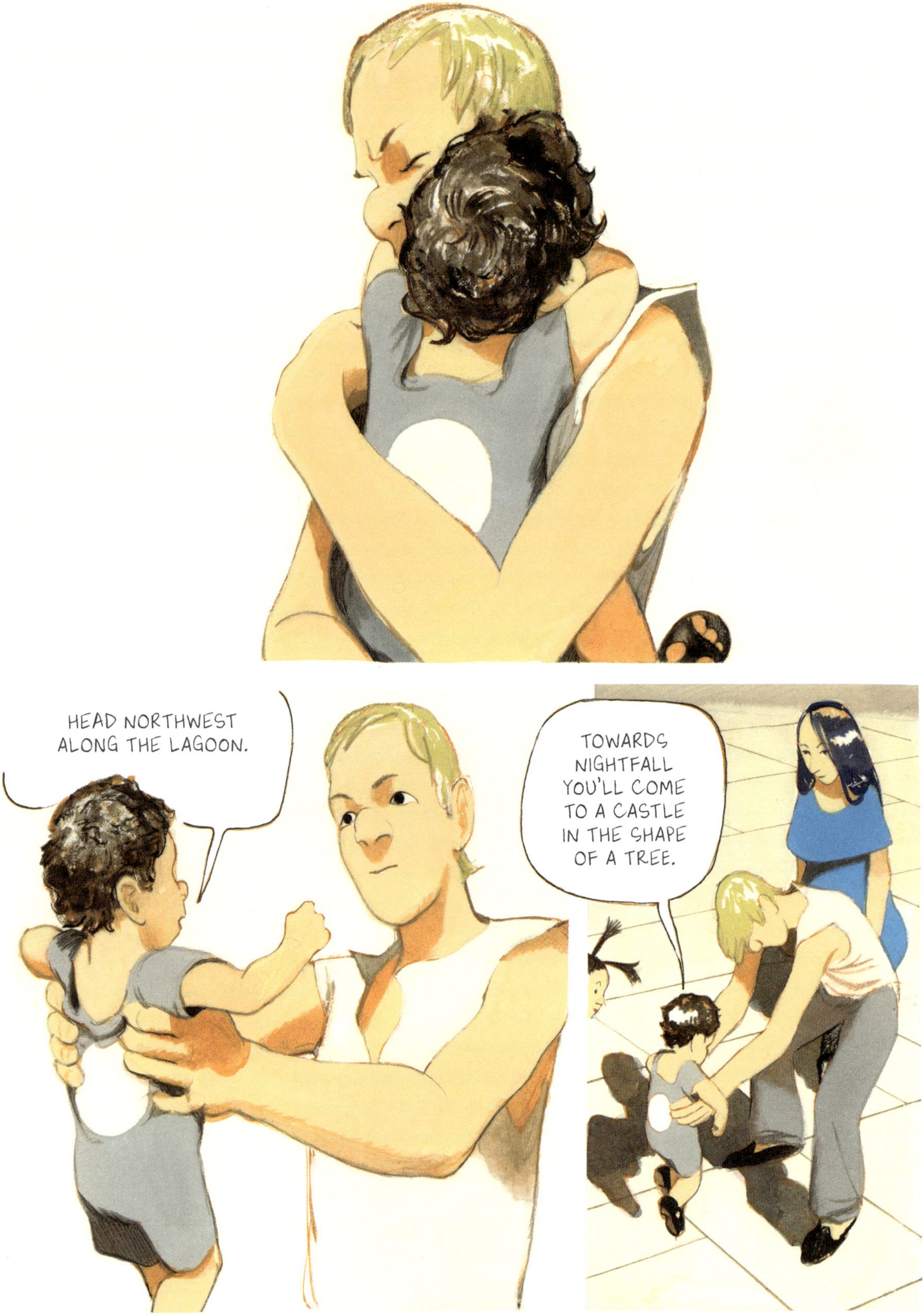
HEAD NORTHWEST ALONG THE LAGOON.
TOWARDS NIGHTFALL YOU'LL COME TO A CASTLE IN THE SHAPE OF A TREE.

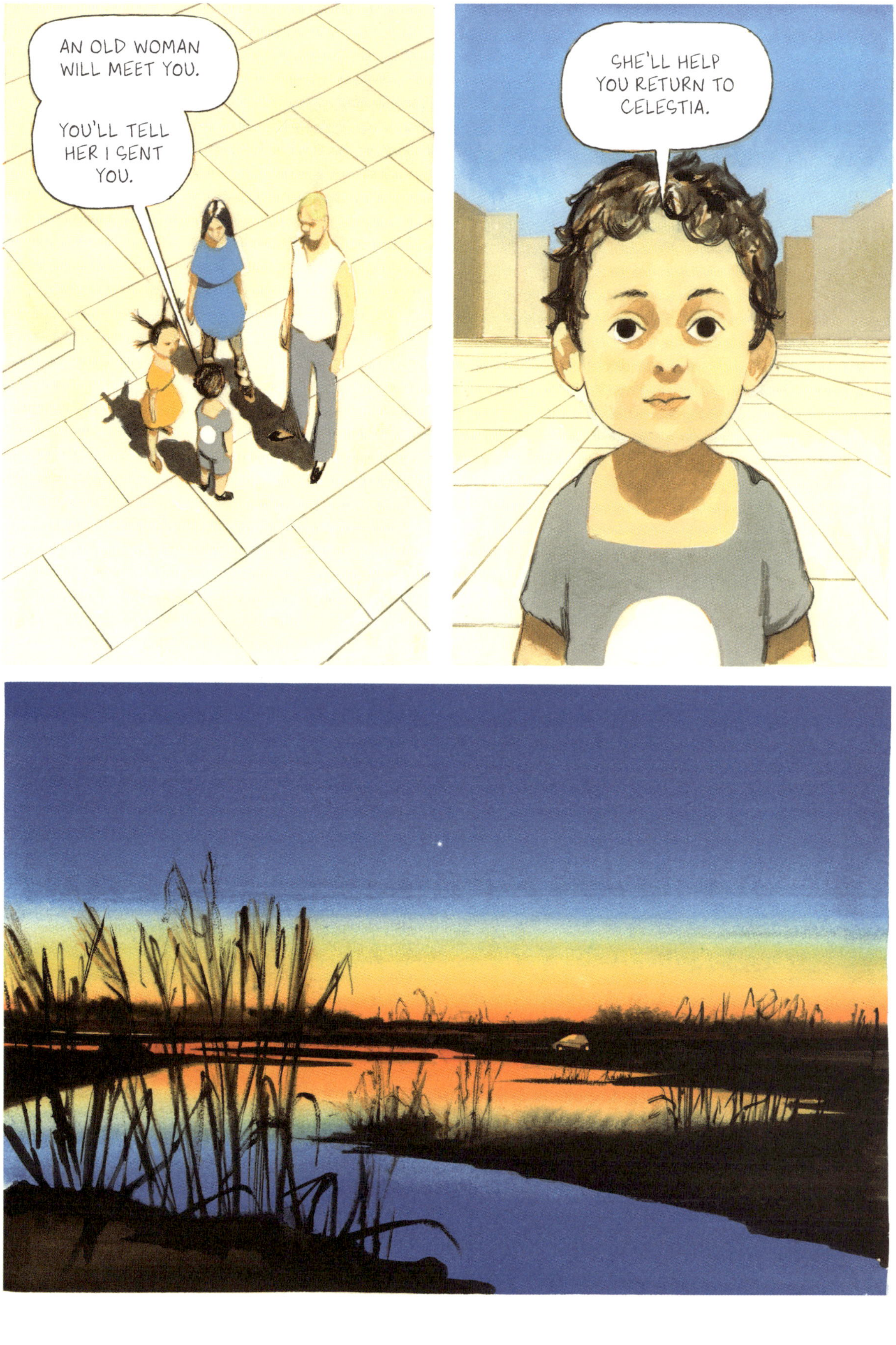
AN OLD WOMAN WILL MEET YOU.
YOU'LL TELL HER I SENT YOU.
SHE'LL HELP YOU RETURN TO CELESTIA.

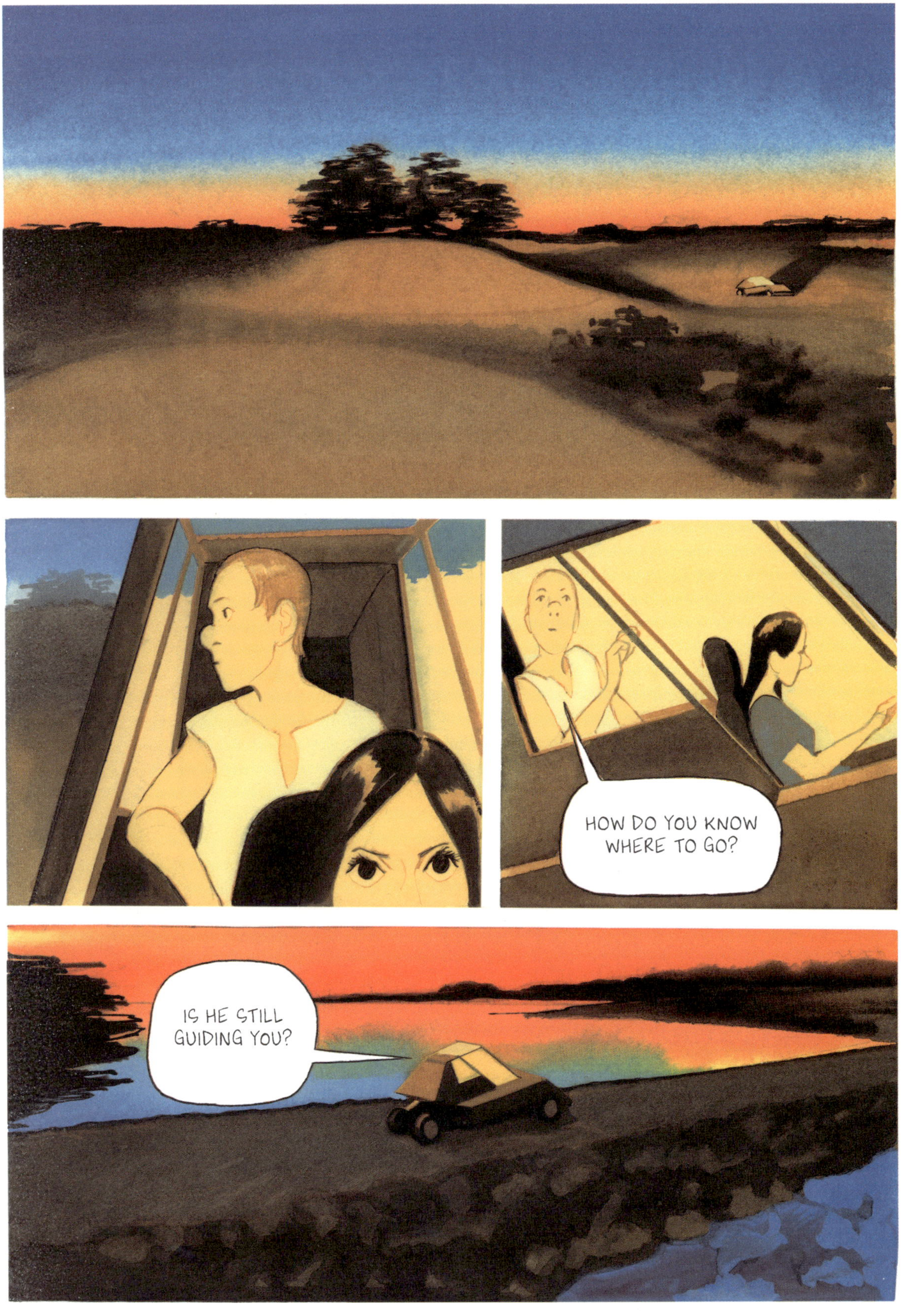
HOW DO YOU KNOW WHERE TO GO?
IS HE STILL GUIDING YOU?

I MISS HIM ALREADY.
YOU'LL SEE EACH OTHER AGAIN.
HOW DO YOU KNOW?
HE JUST TOLD ME.

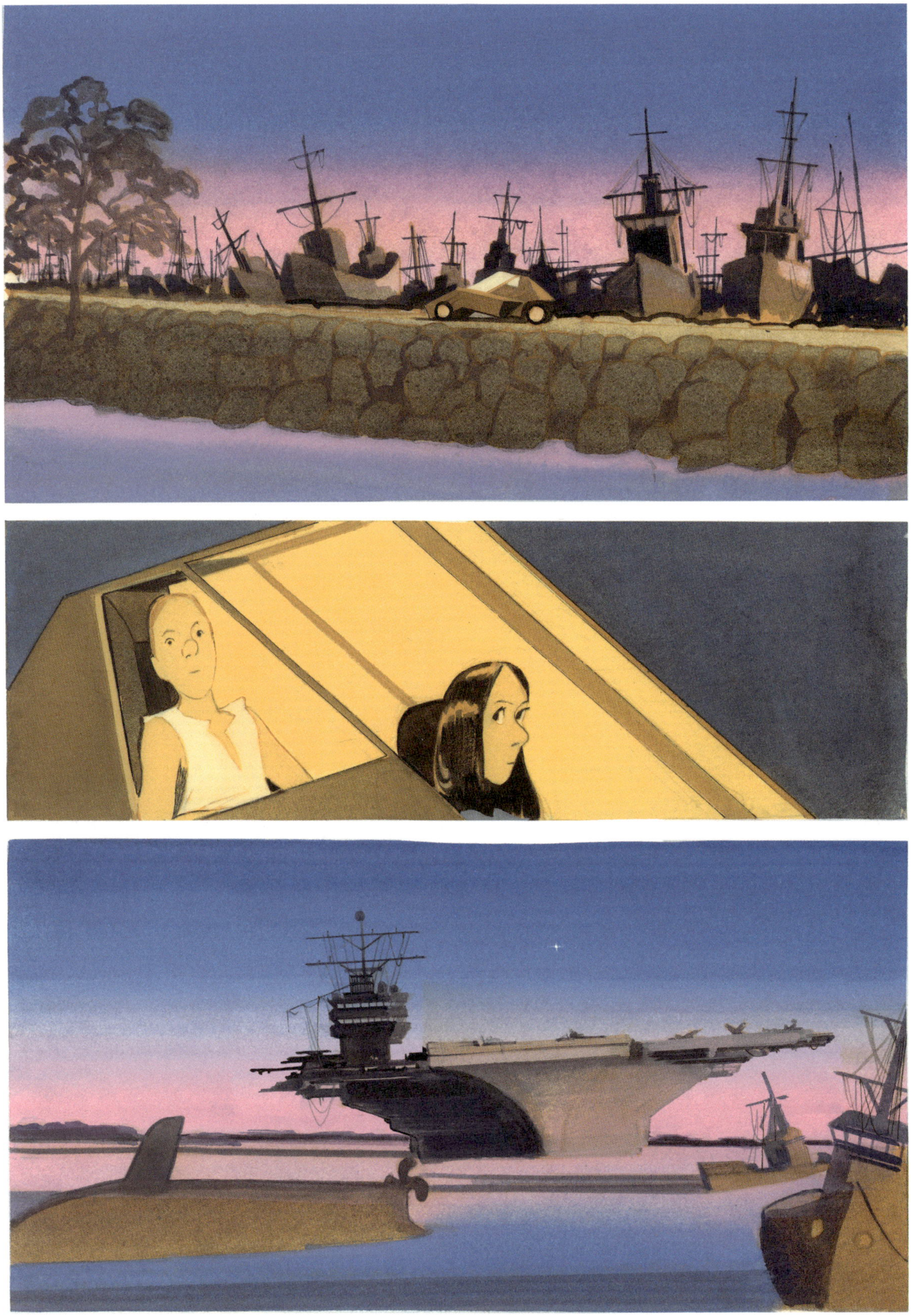

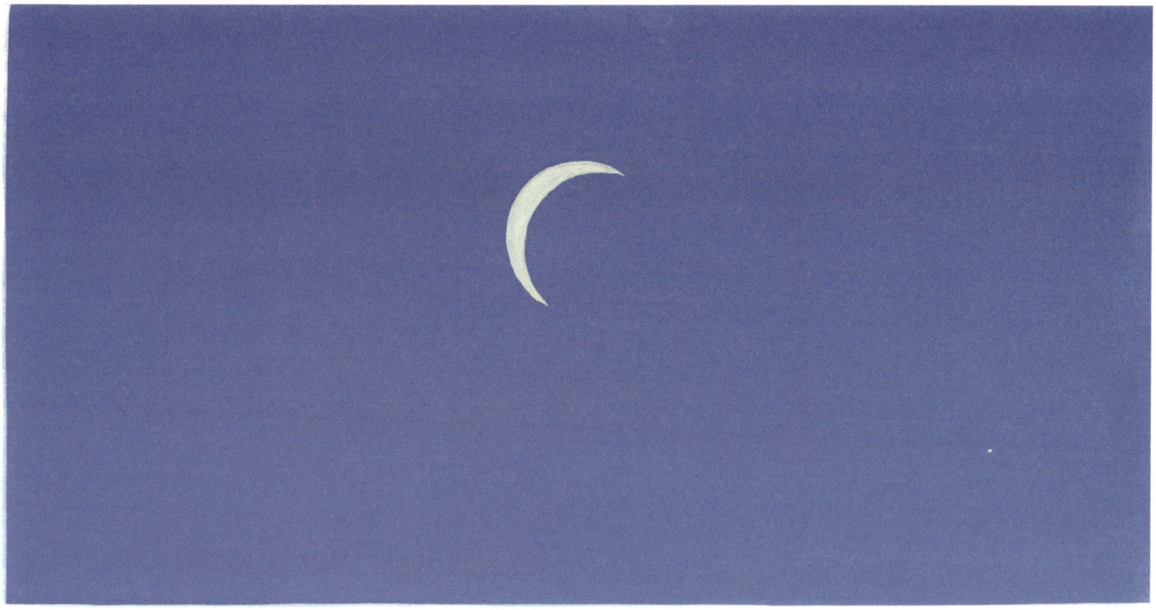

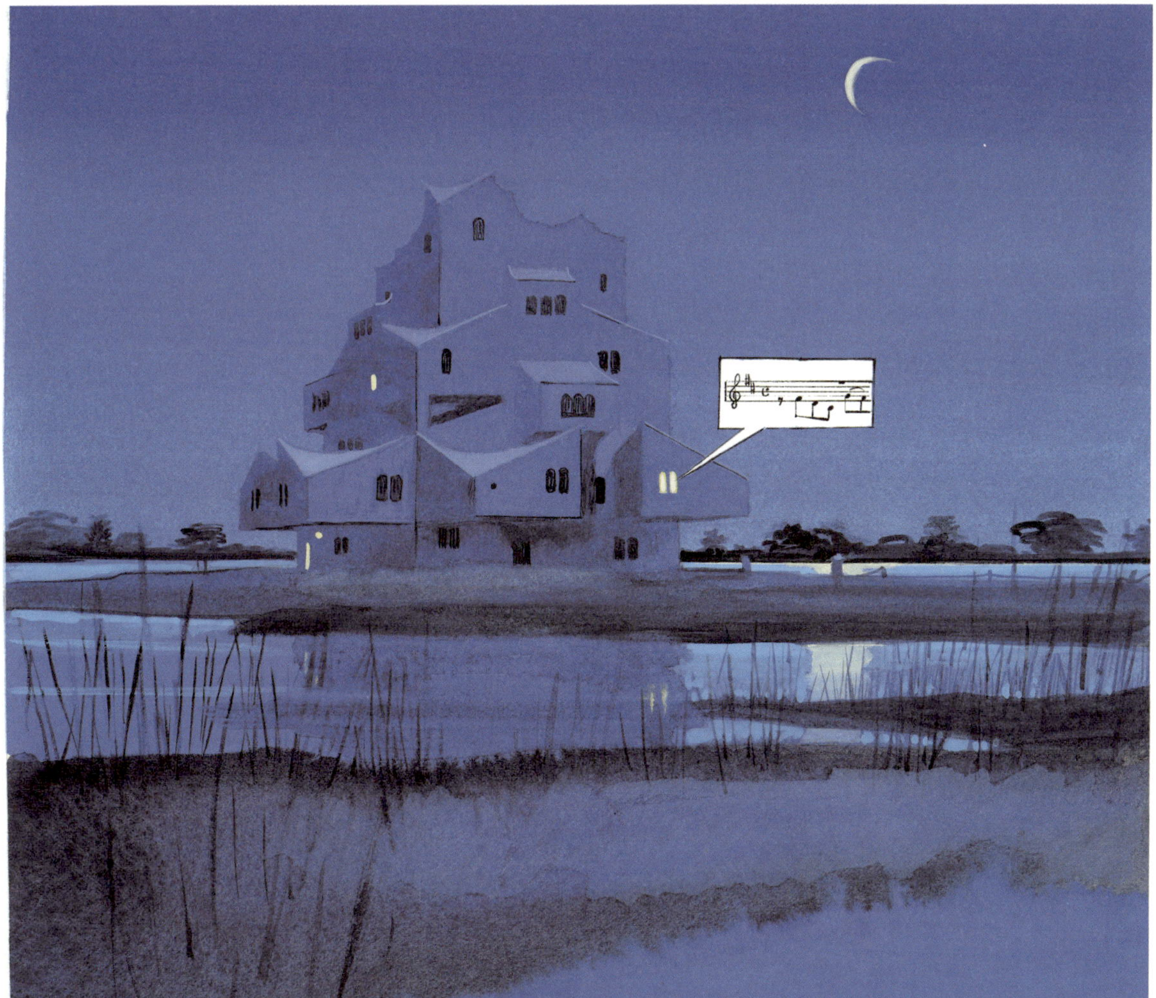

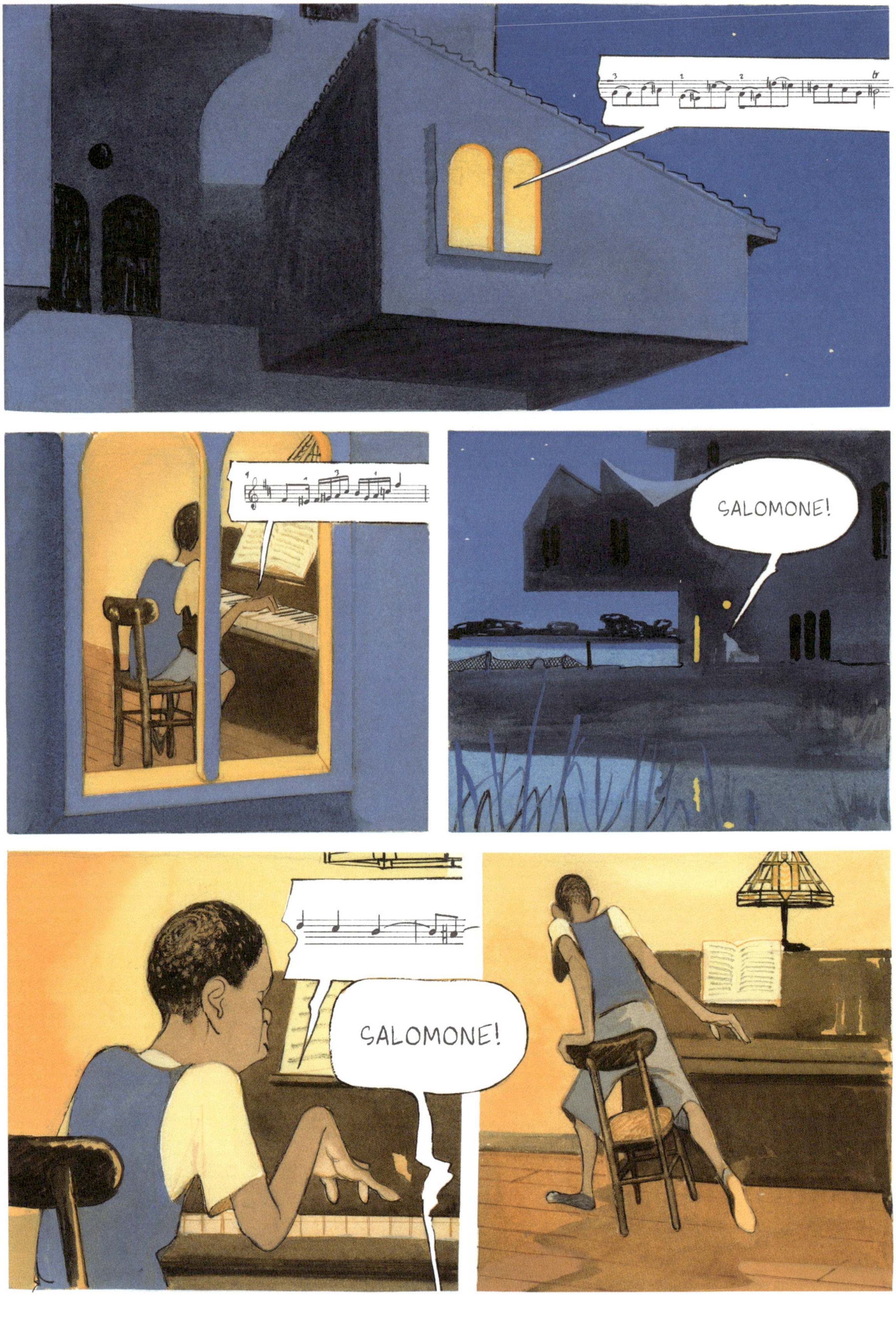
SALOMONE!
SALOMONE!

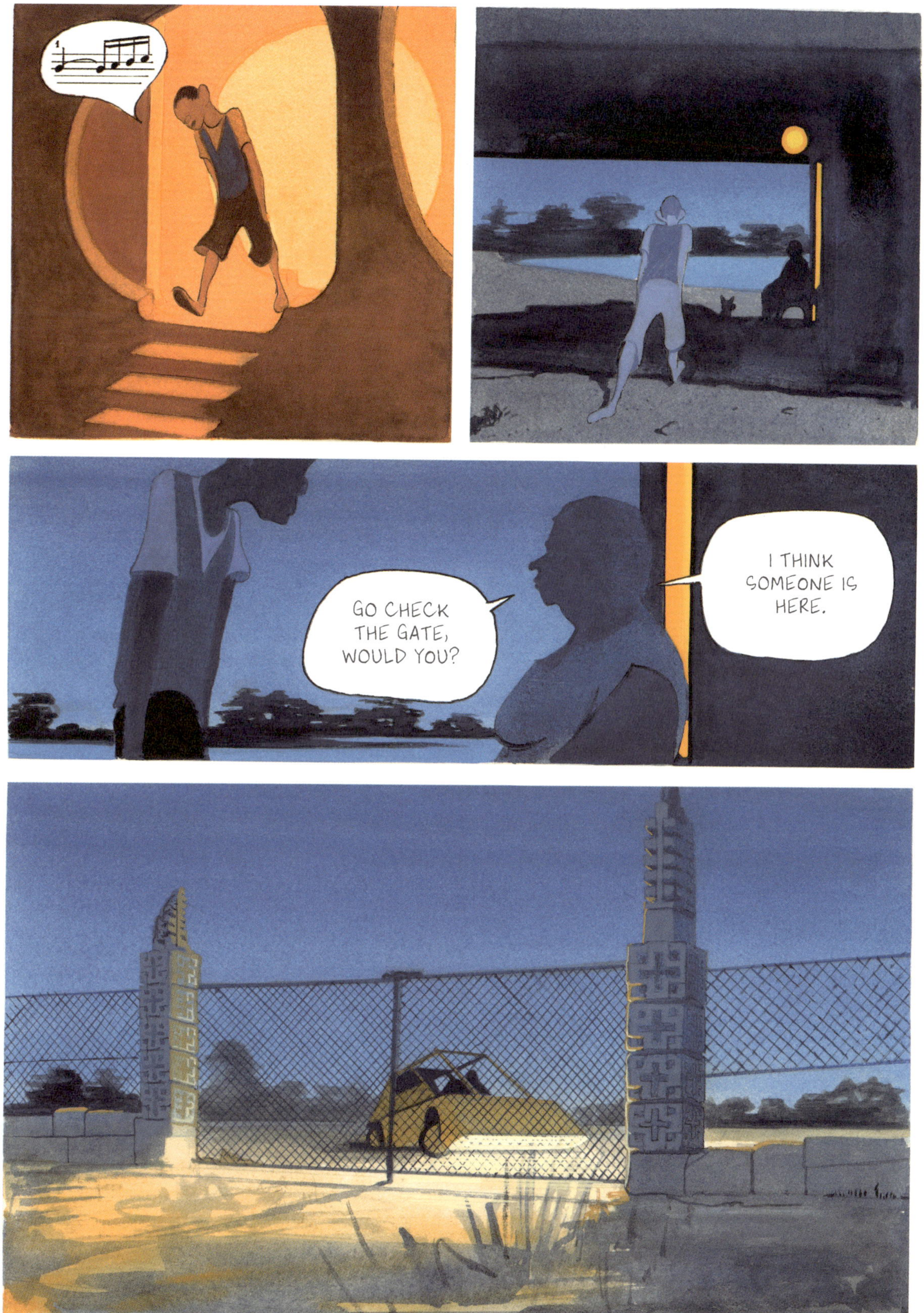
I THINK SOMEONE IS HERE.
GO CHECK THE GATE, WOULD YOU?

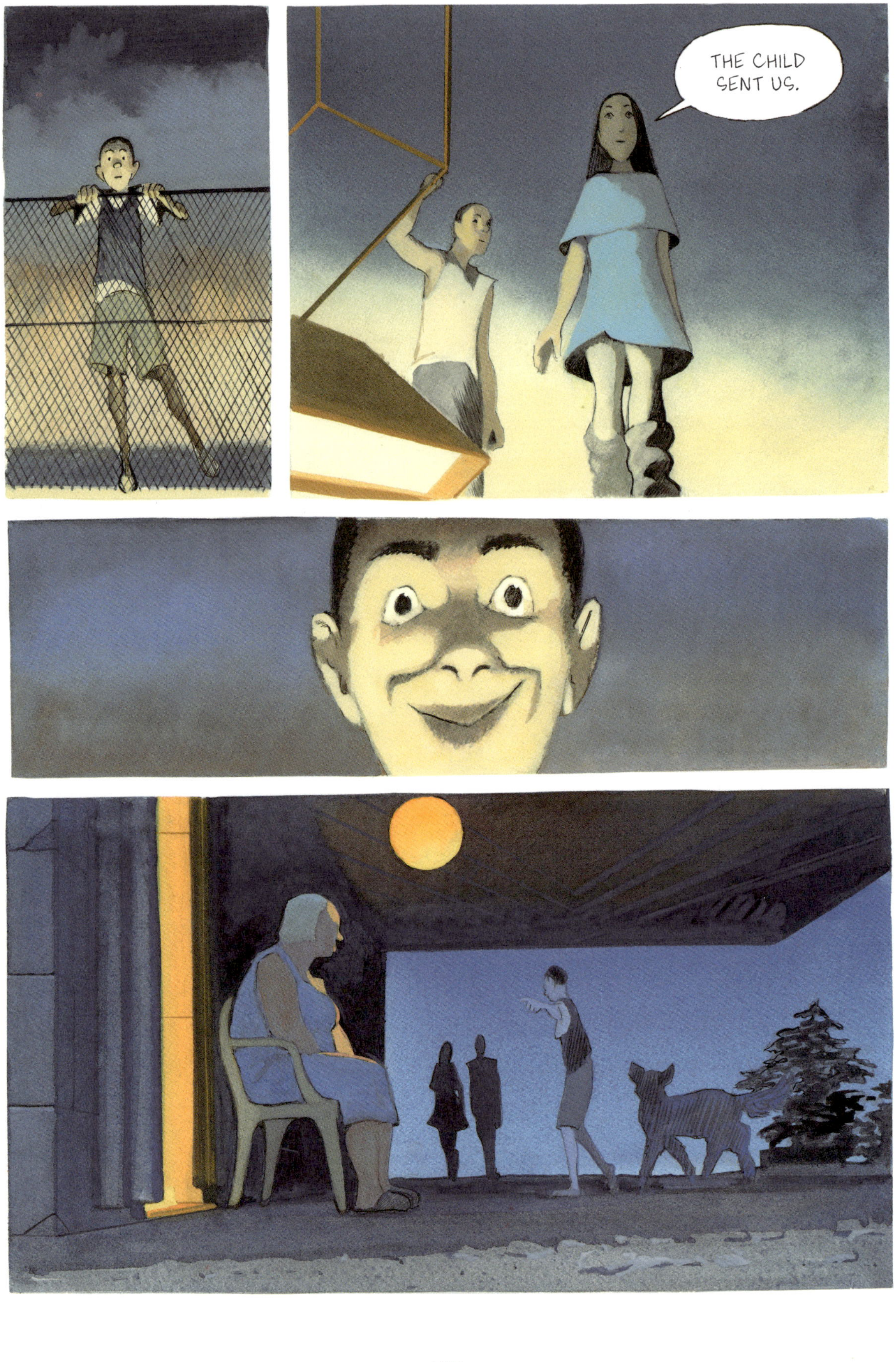
THE CHILD
SENT US.

"GOOD EVENING, MA'AM."

"SALOMONE, BRING US SOME CHAIRS."

"WOULD YOU LIKE A DRINK?"

"AN APERITIF?"

"SALOMONE, LOOK IN THE FRIDGE, THERE'S SOME BEER!"

"HE'S A BIG HELP"

"IF IT WEREN'T FOR HIM..."

"THERE'D BE NO REASON TO GO ON."

— HAVE YOU LIVED HERE LONG?

— FOREVER.

SINCE THEY BUILT THE CASTLE.

— MY HUSBAND BROUGHT ME HERE, THE SAINT.

TO DEFEND US FROM THE INVASION.

THEY'D BUILT THE CASTLES.

BUT THEN WE SAW THEM COMING...
THERE WERE MILLIONS.
THEY RAZED EVERYTHING IN THEIR PATH...
AND NEVER LOOKED BACK.
FORTU-NATELY, SALOMONE WAS SPARED.
WHEN I DIE, THIS HOUSE WILL GO TO HIM.

AND HE AND HIS CHILDREN WILL MAKE IT THE LOVELIEST PLACE ON EARTH.
SATISFIED?
I'VE NEVER EATEN SO MUCH IN MY LIFE.
YOU NEED TO BE IN GOOD SHAPE FOR THE RETURN TRIP.
YOU REALLY KNOW ALL ABOUT US, DON'T YOU?

"I DON'T EVEN KNOW YOUR NAMES."

"BUT THE CHILDREN..."

"NOWADAYS THEY CAN COMMUNICATE EVEN FROM FAR AWAY..."

"AT TIMES I HAVE STRANGE DREAMS..."

"IT'S LIKE I'M REMEMBERING THINGS."

"IT'S THEIR WAY OF TELLING ME THINGS."

"LOOKING AFTER THE ONES LEFT BEHIND."

SALOMONE WILL TAKE YOU BACK TO CELESTIA TONIGHT.
IT'S PEAK TIDE. BEST NOT TO WAIT ANY LONGER.
GIVE GRANNY A KISS NOW.
PUT ON SOME SPRAY, IT'S FULL OF MOSQUITOES OUT THERE.
THERE ARE TWO WOOL BLANKETS.
SEND A THOUGHT MY WAY ONCE YOU ARRIVE.
SALOMONE WILL MAKE SURE I GET IT.

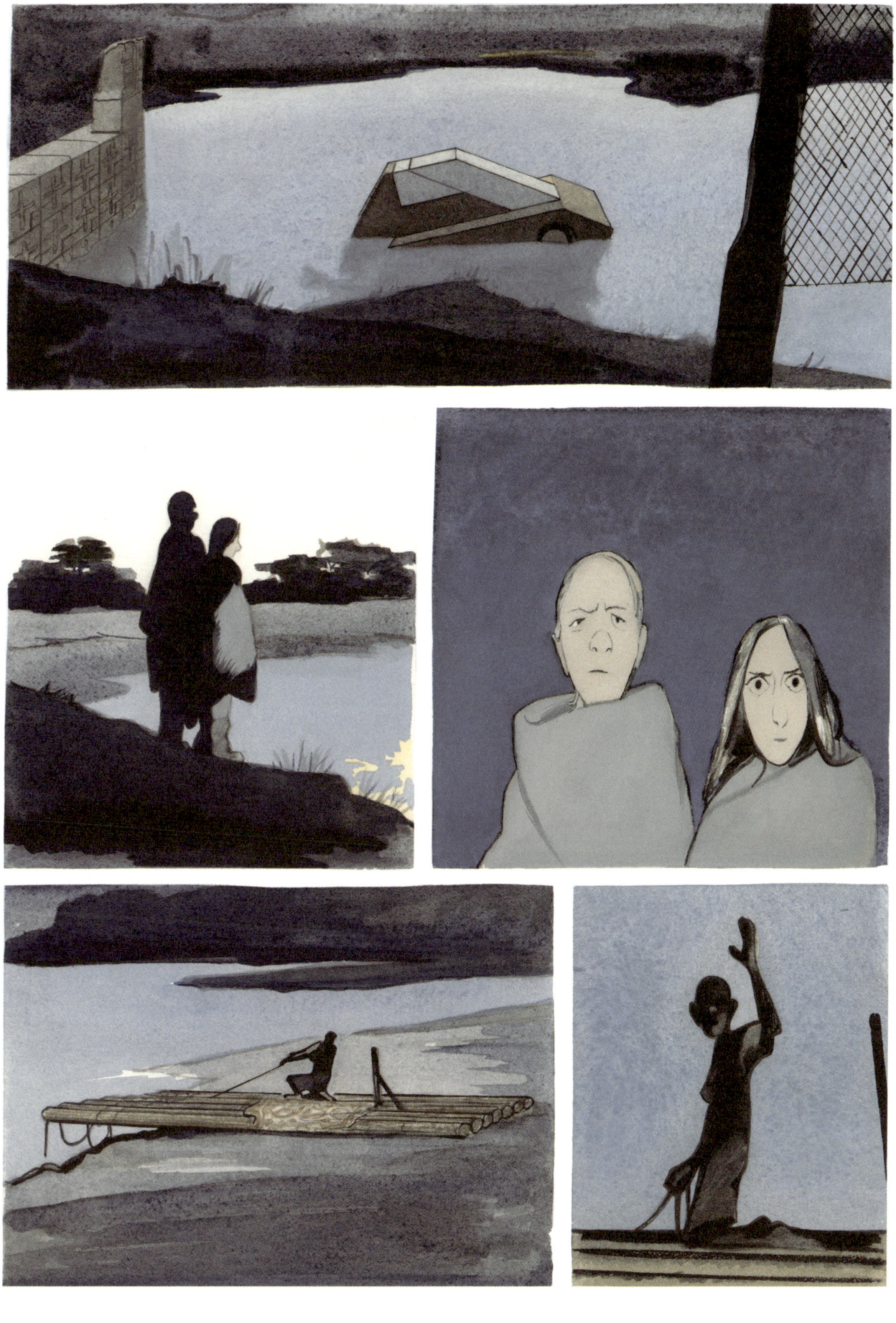

THAT'S A RAFT.
ARE WE SUPPOSED TO LIE ON THAT RUG?
LET'S AT LEAST TAKE OUR SHOES OFF.
BUT I DON'T UNDERSTAND HOW YOU'LL GET US TO CELESTIA.

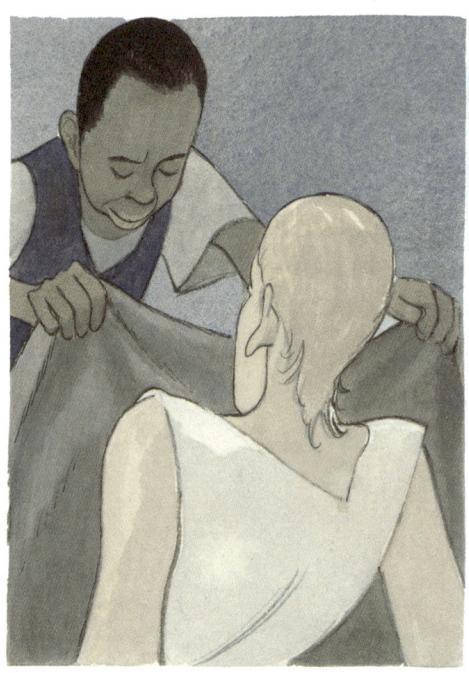

"THERE'S NOT EVEN A PUFF OF WIND AND THIS RAFT HAS ONLY ONE OAR."

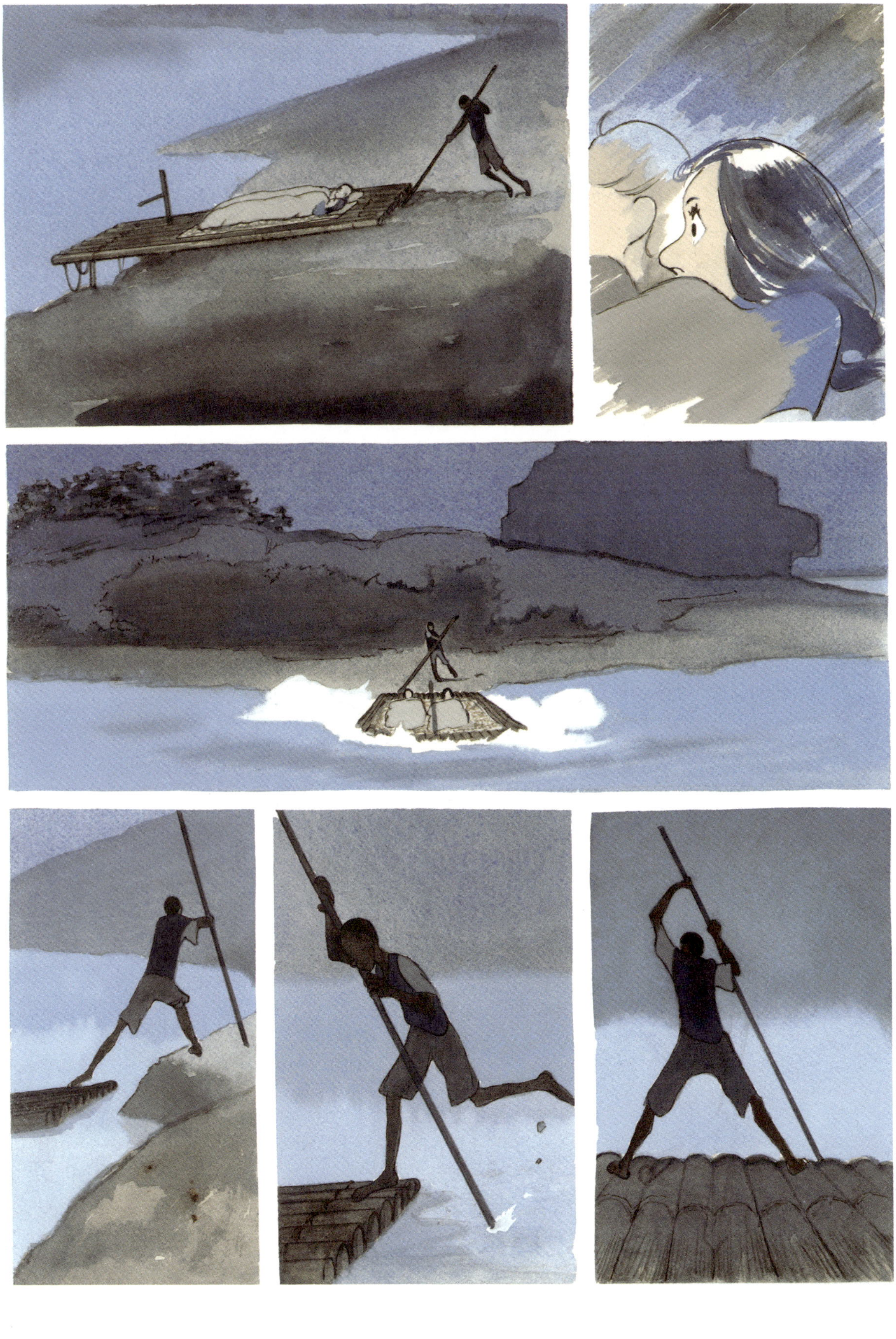

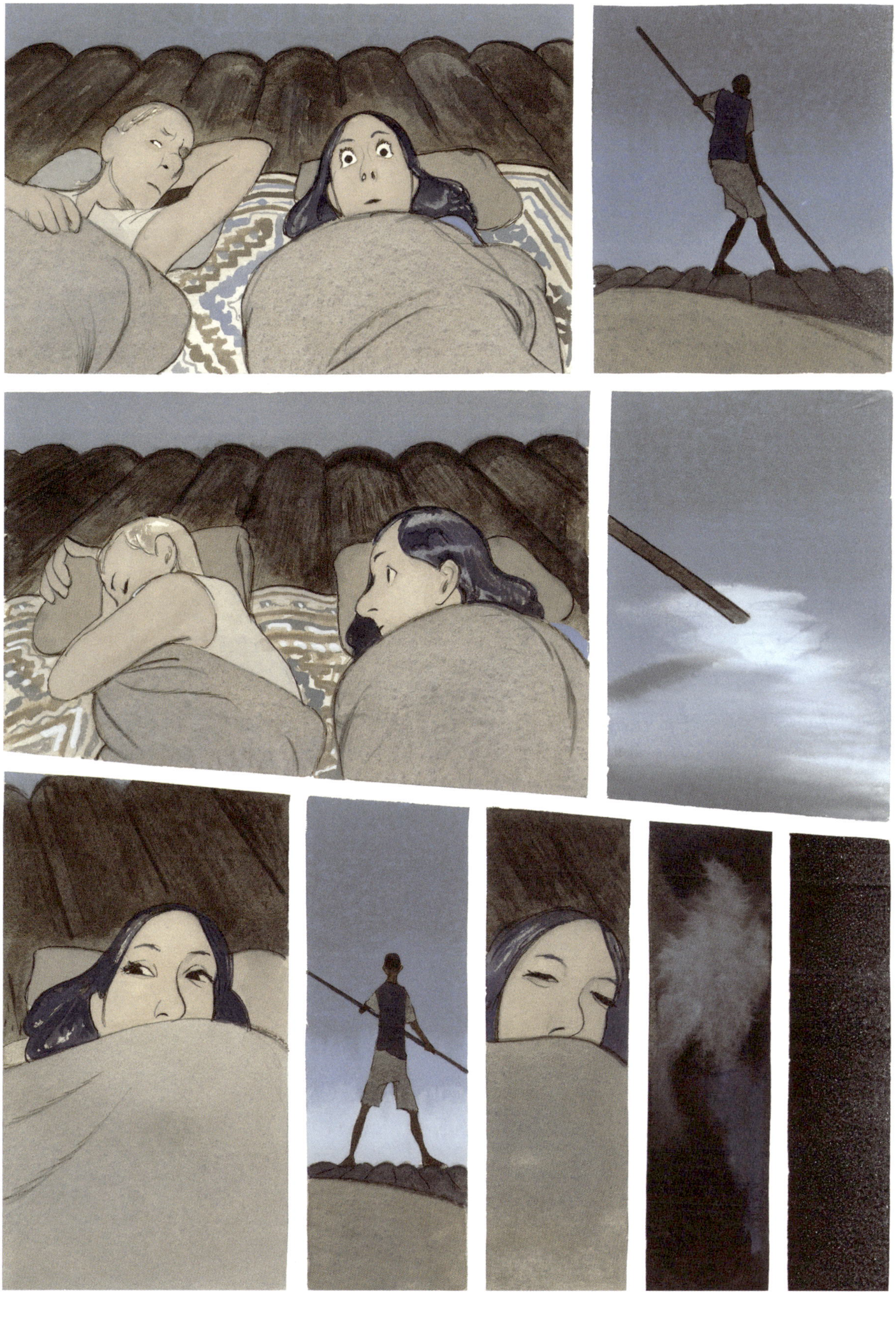

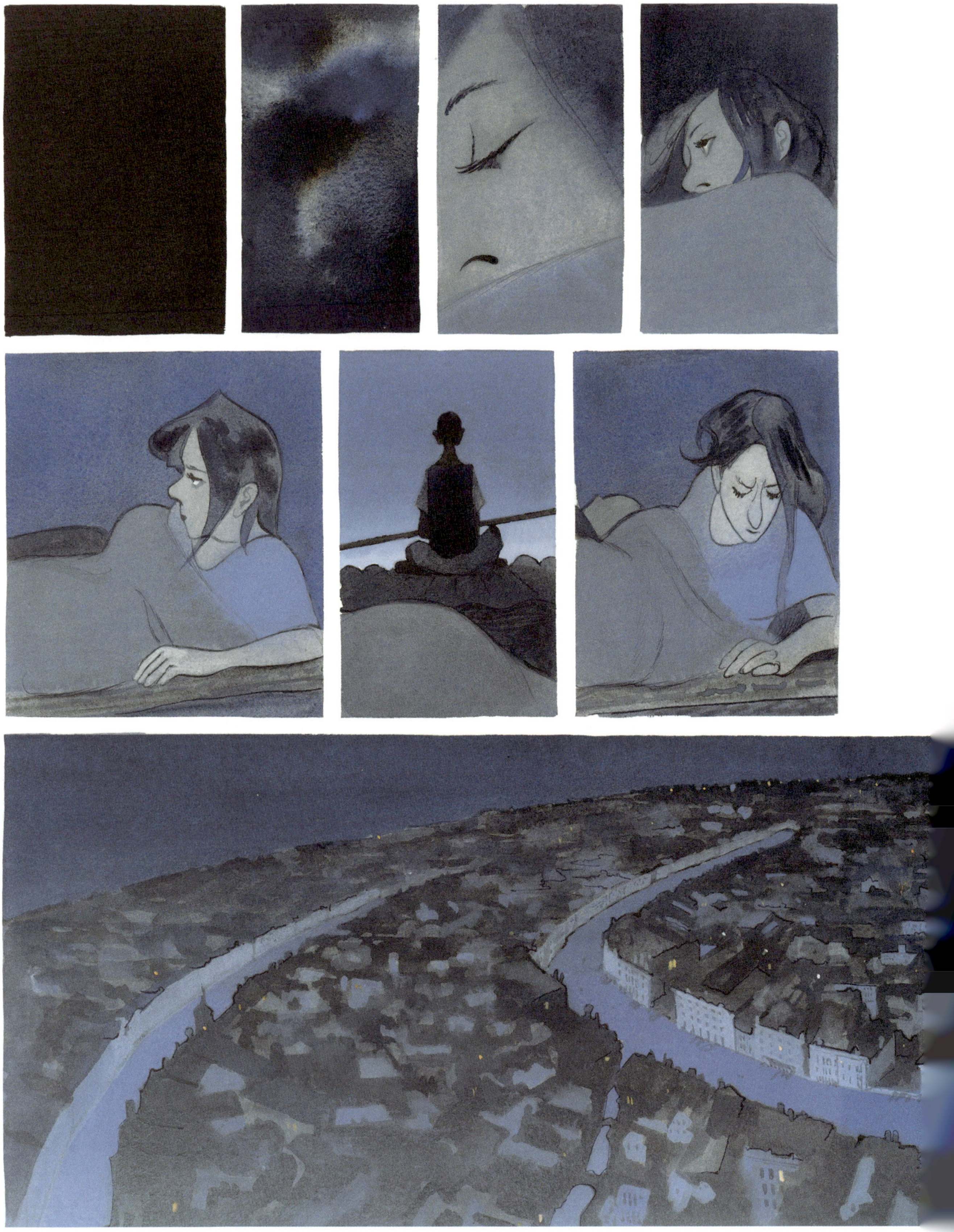

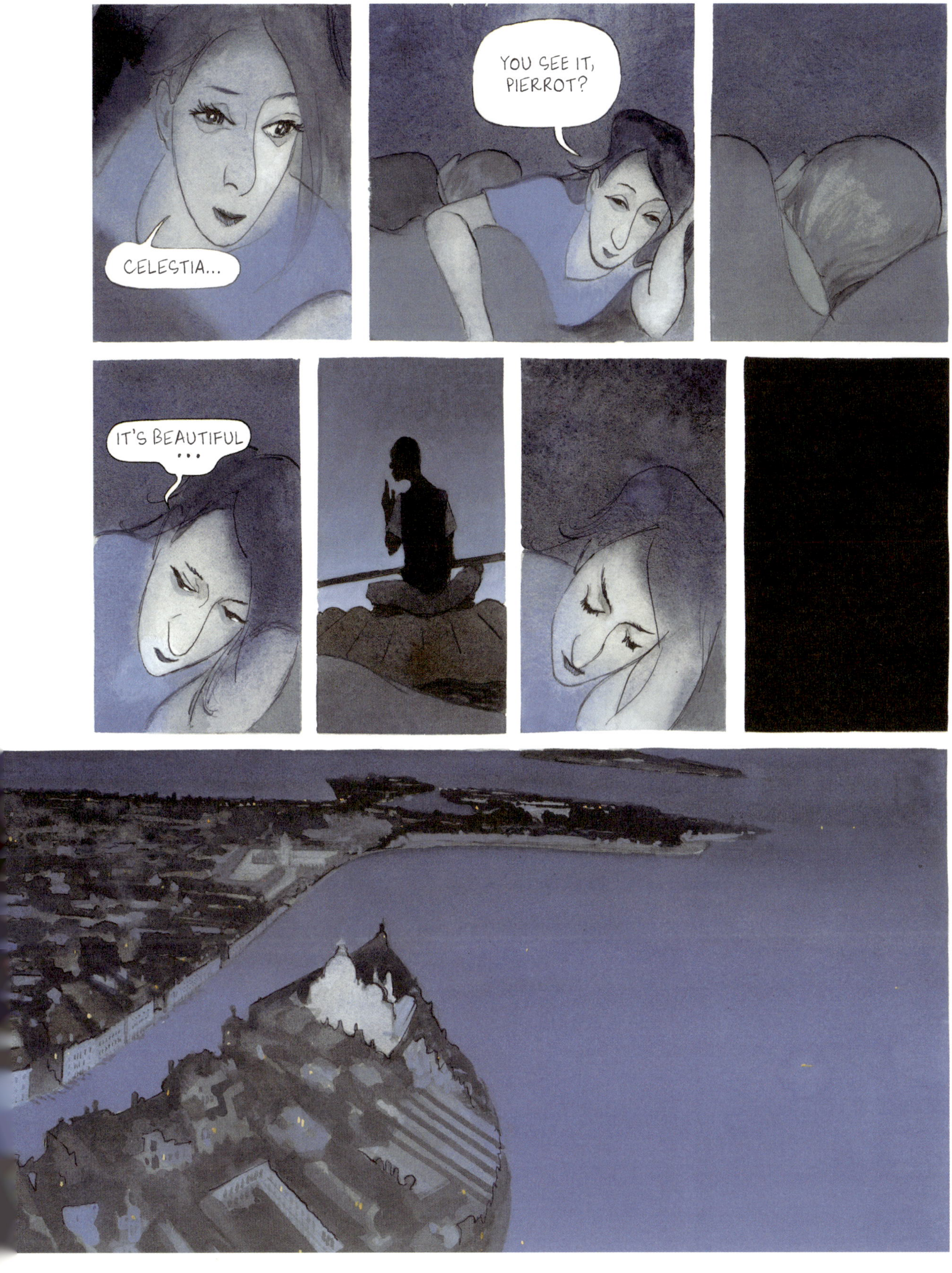
CELESTIA...
YOU SEE IT, PIERROT?
IT'S BEAUTIFUL ...

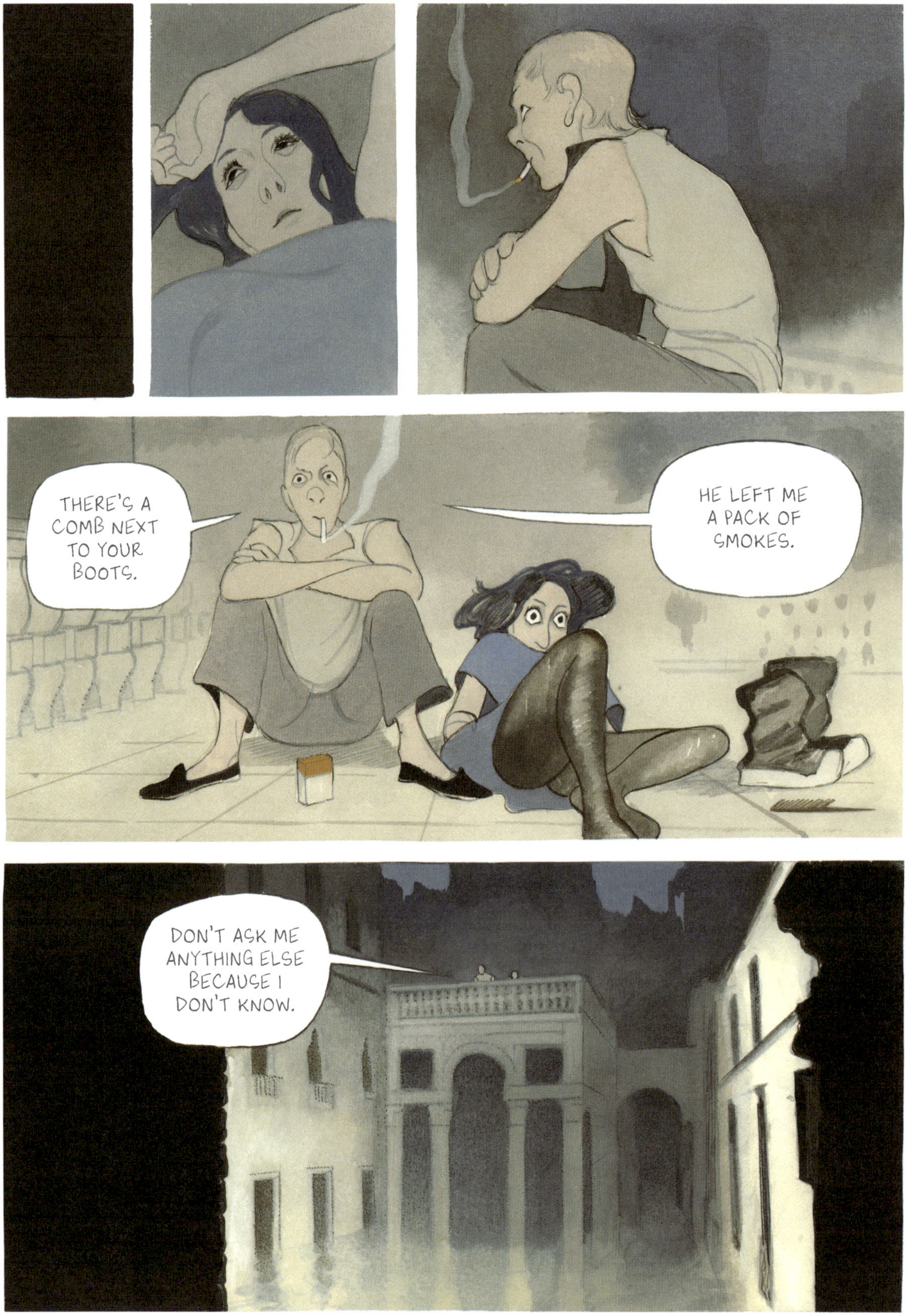
THERE'S A COMB NEXT TO YOUR BOOTS.
HE LEFT ME A PACK OF SMOKES.
DON'T ASK ME ANYTHING ELSE BECAUSE I DON'T KNOW.

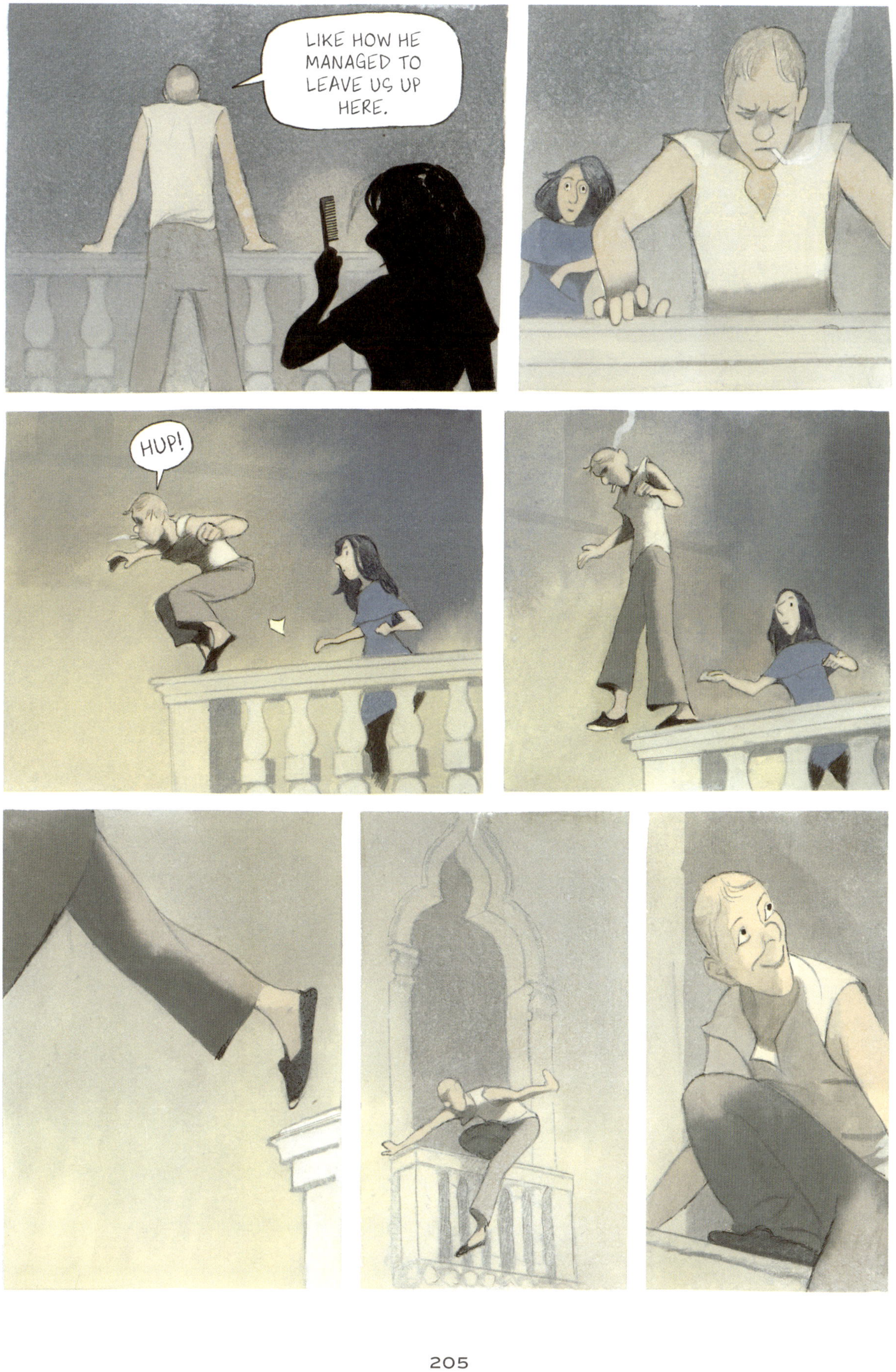
LIKE HOW HE MANAGED TO LEAVE US UP HERE.
HUP!

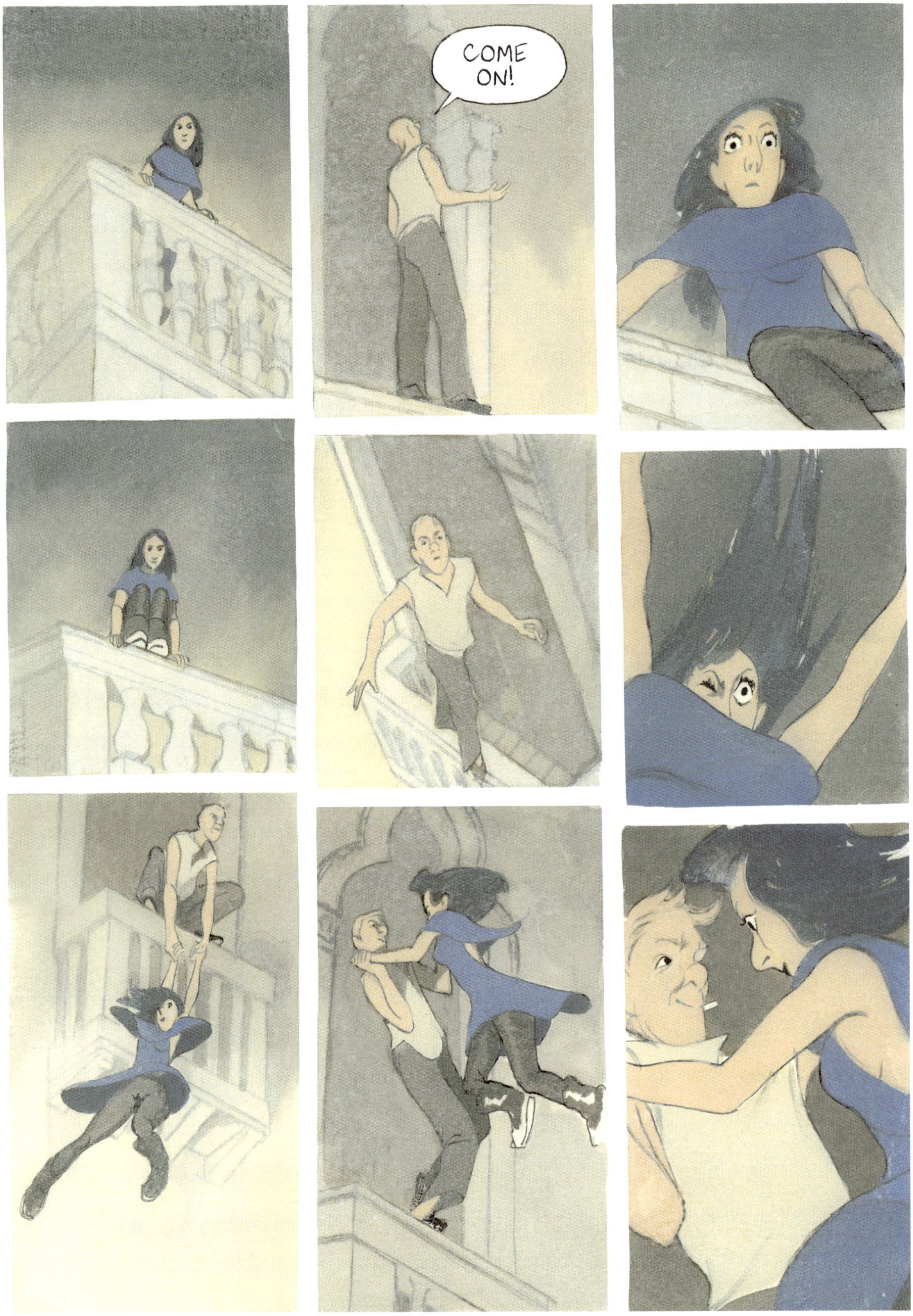
COME ON!

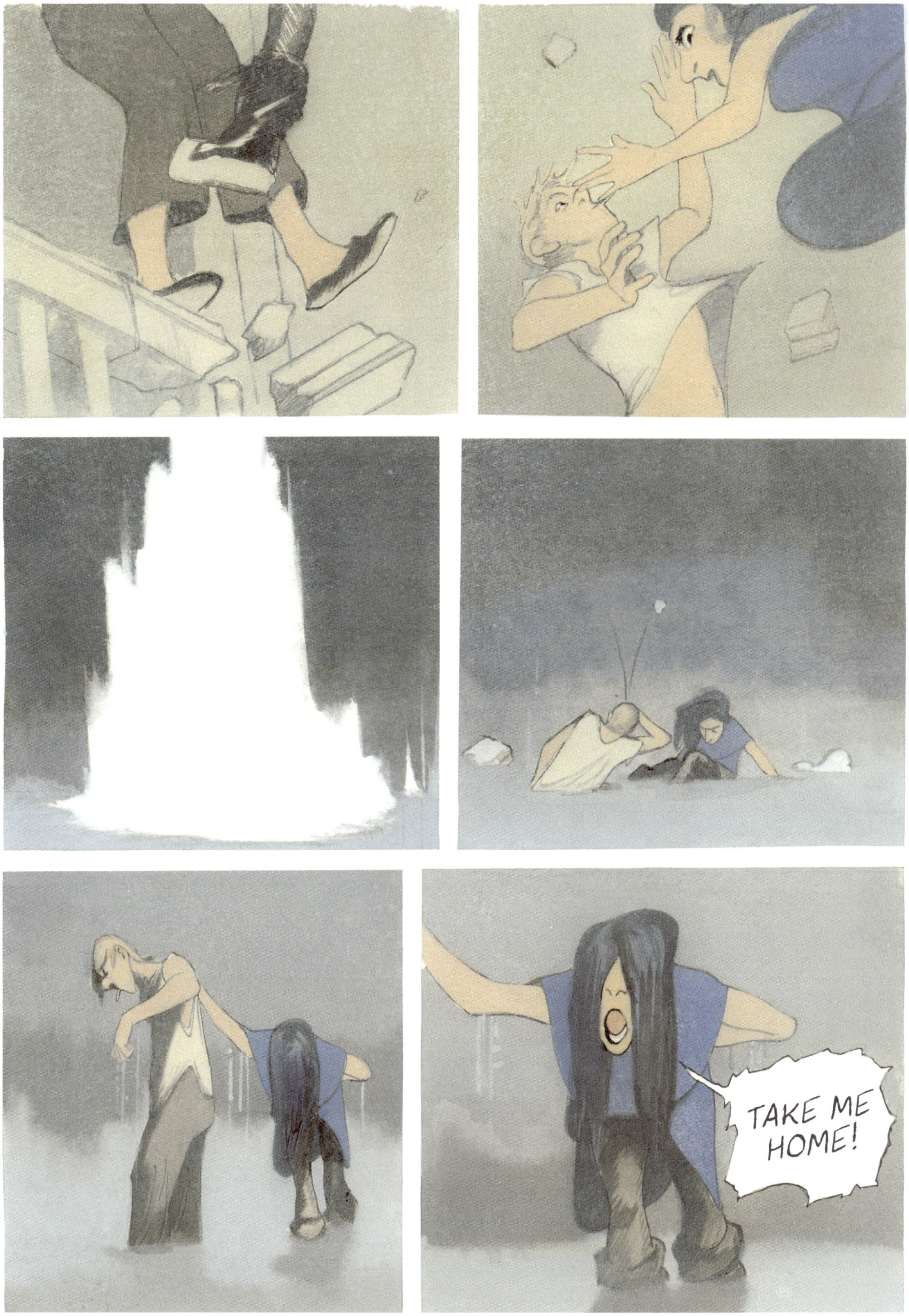
TAKE ME HOME!

Panel 1:
"DON'T YELL!"
"THERE ARE STILL PEOPLE AROUND HERE WHO WANT MY HIDE!"

Panel 2:
"TAKE ME TO YOUR FATHER."
"PLEASE."
"FINE."

Panel 3:
"AND THEN STAY WITH ME?"
"WITH YOU?"

Panel 4:
"AFTER ALL WE'RE NOT SO BAD TOGETHER."

Panel 5:
"YOU SMELL THAT?"
"COOKIES... BAICOLI JUST OUT OF THE OVEN..."
"DON'T CHANGE THE SUBJECT, PIERROT."

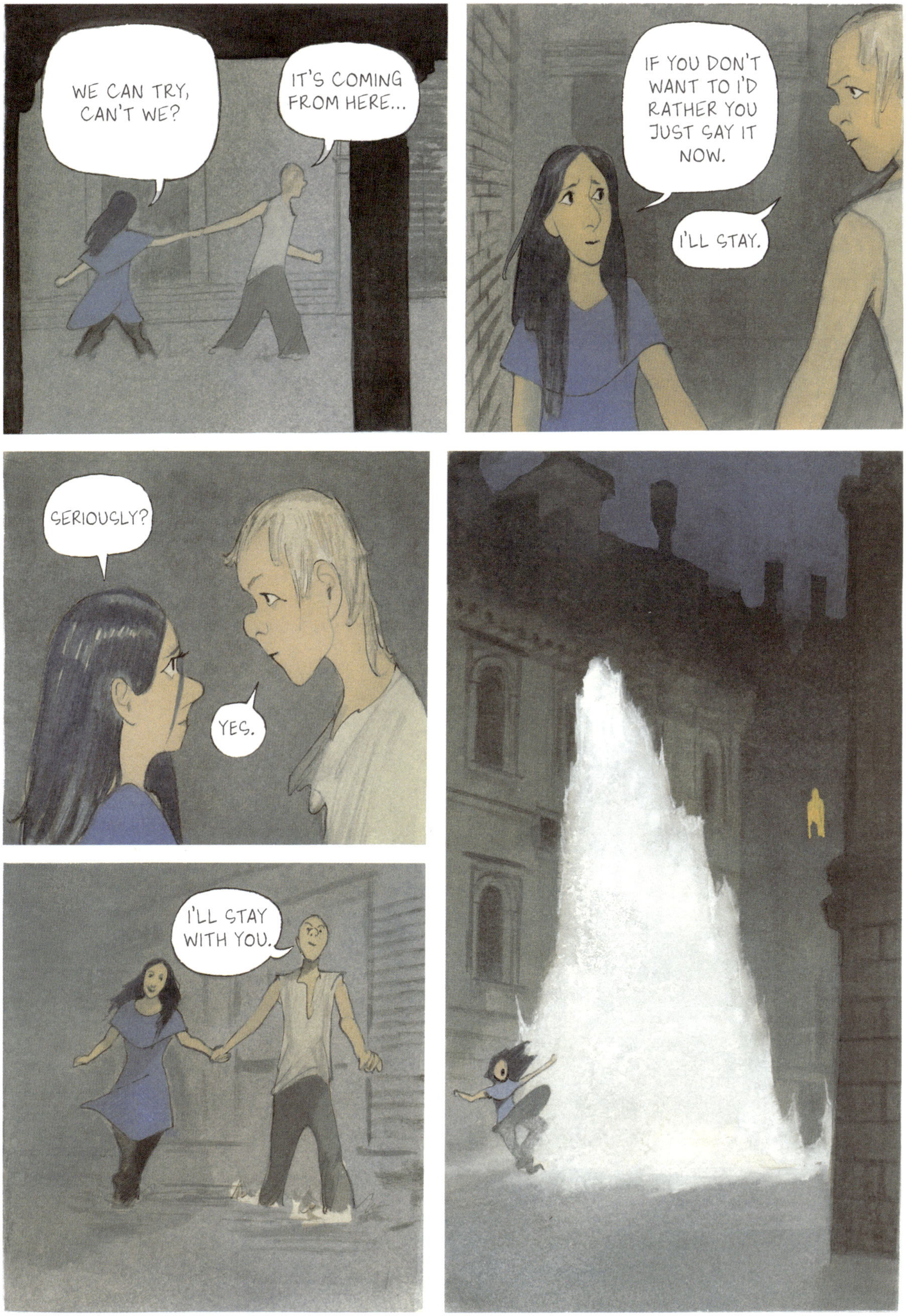
WE CAN TRY, CAN'T WE?
IT'S COMING FROM HERE...
IF YOU DON'T WANT TO I'D RATHER YOU JUST SAY IT NOW.
I'LL STAY.
SERIOUSLY?
YES.
I'LL STAY WITH YOU.

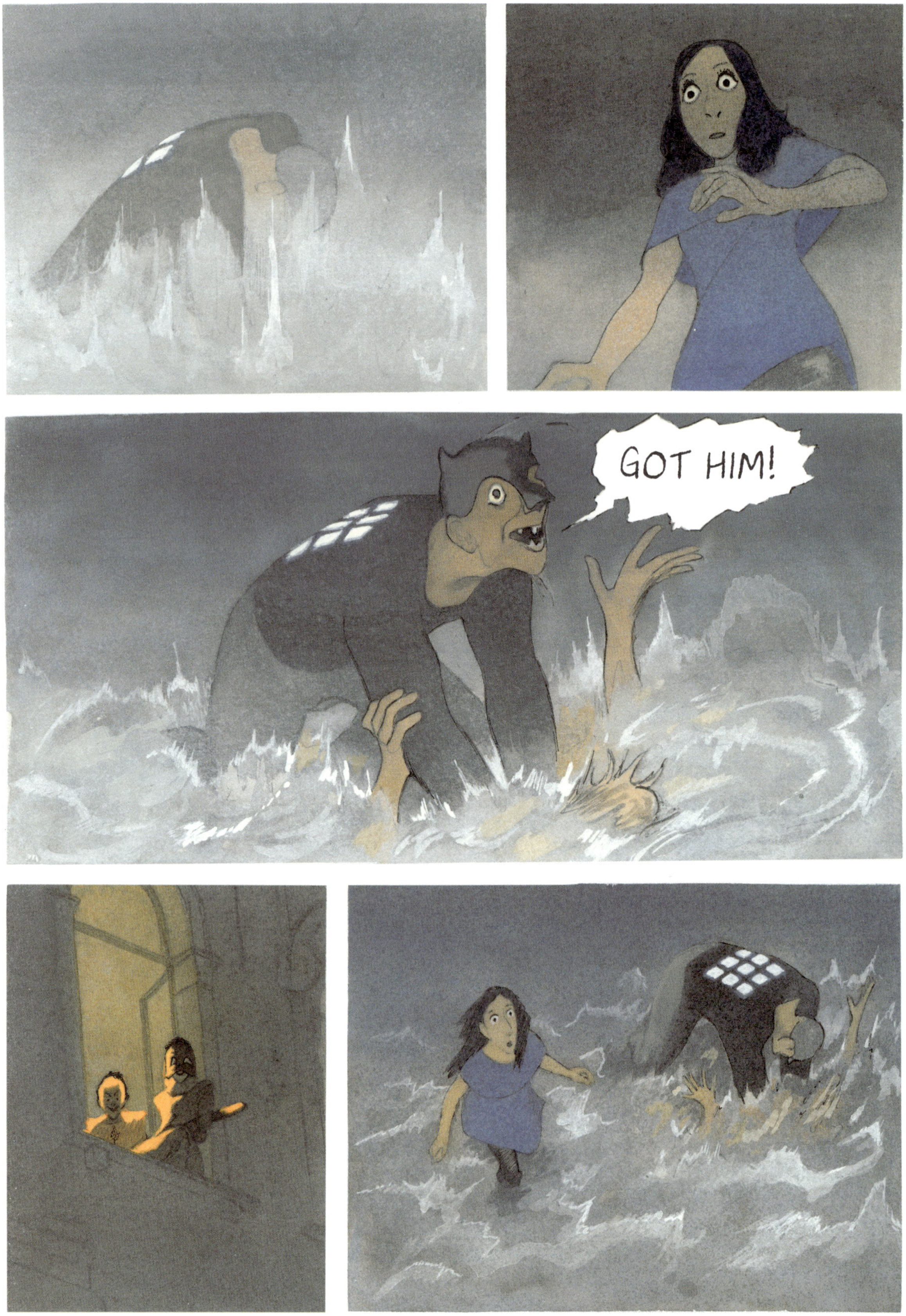
GOT HIM!

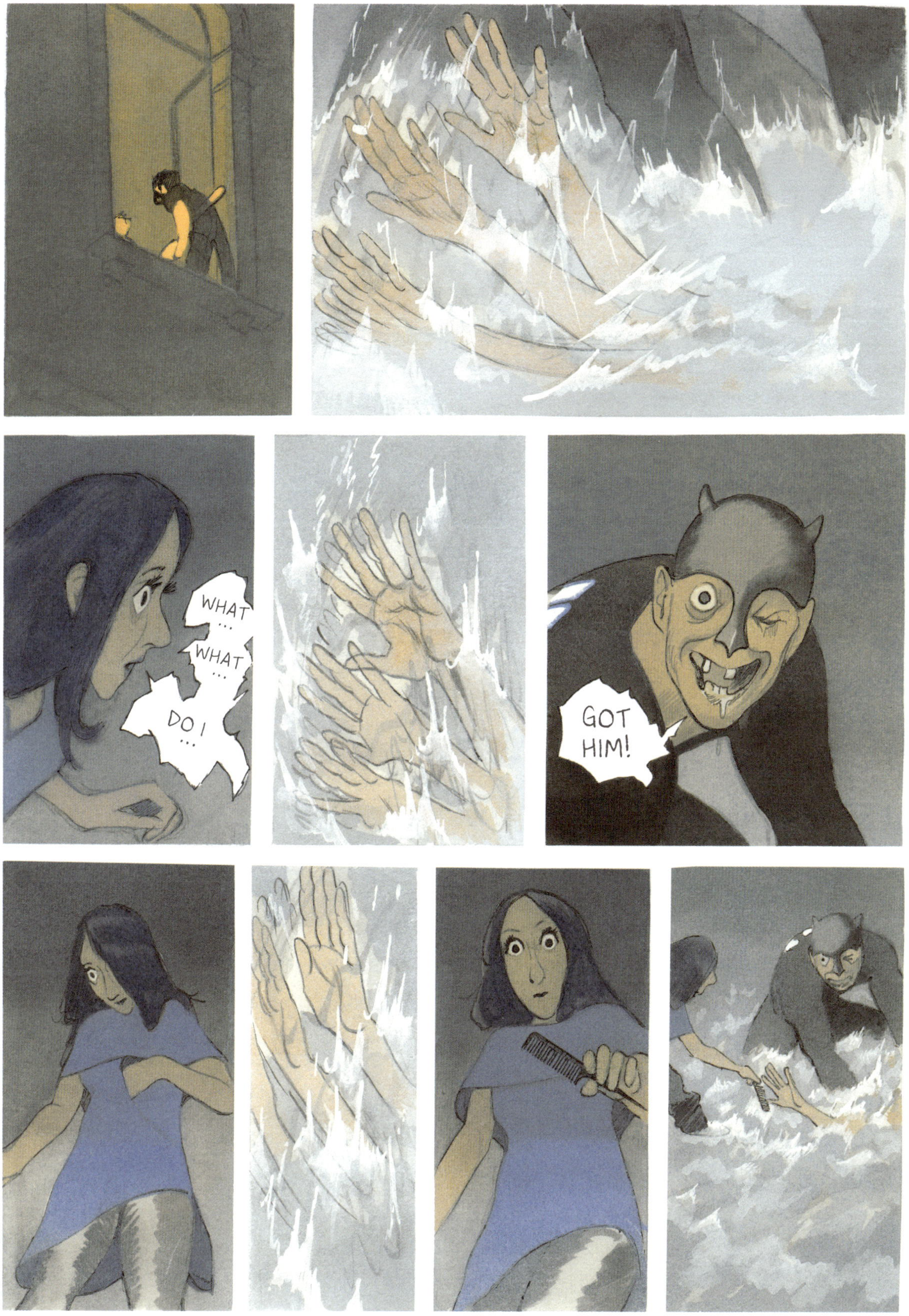
WHAT ...
WHAT ...
DO I ...
GOT HIM!

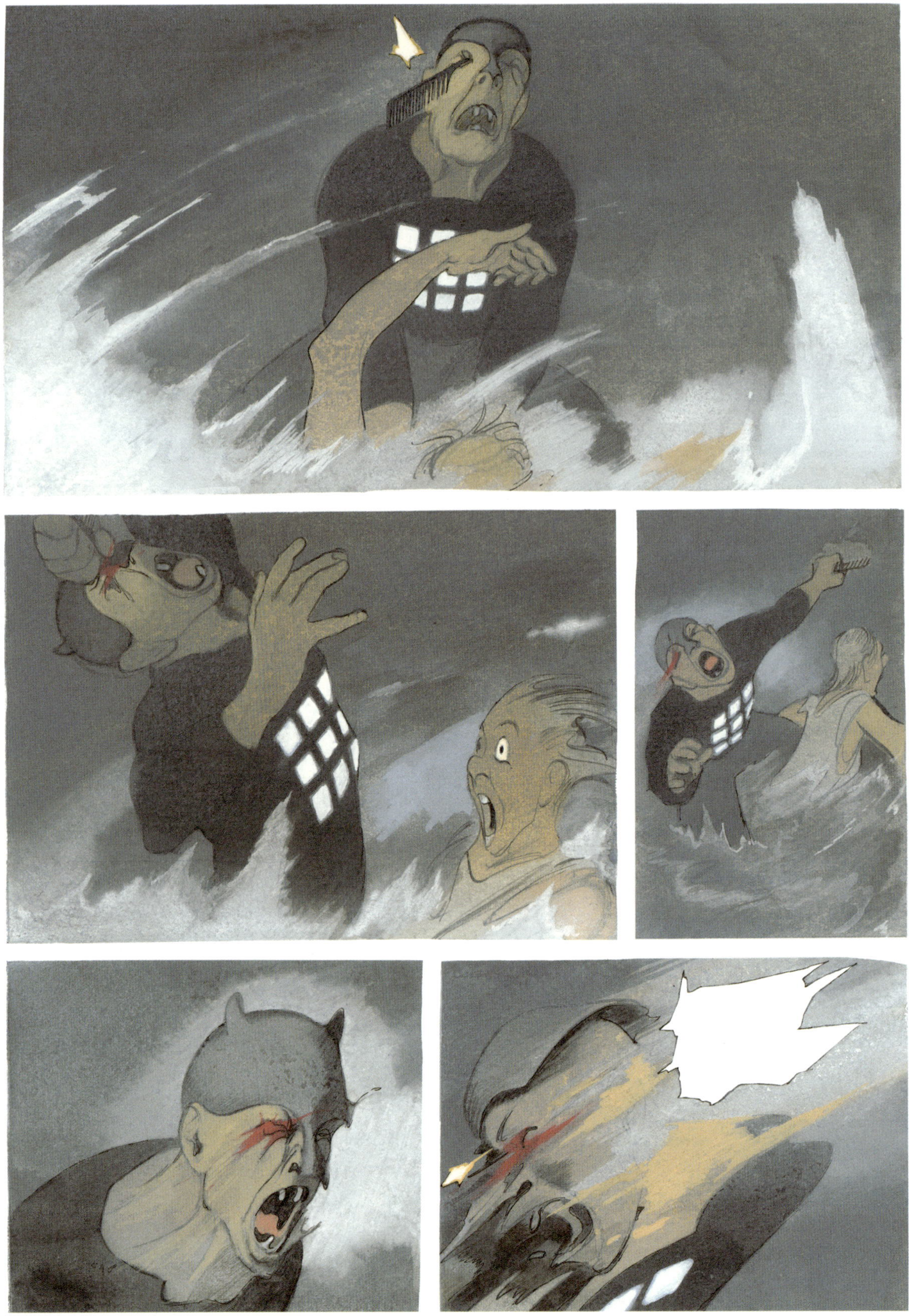

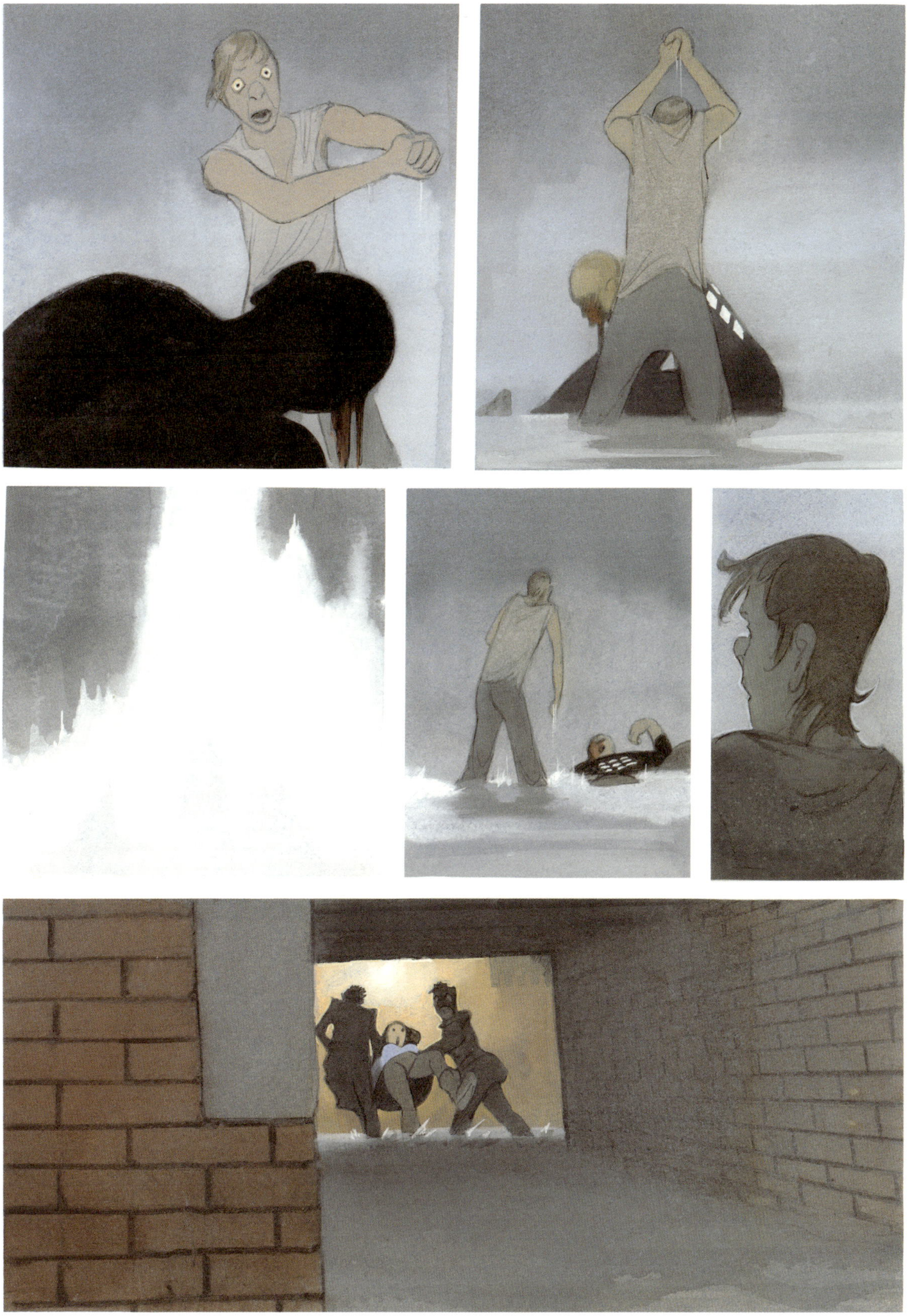

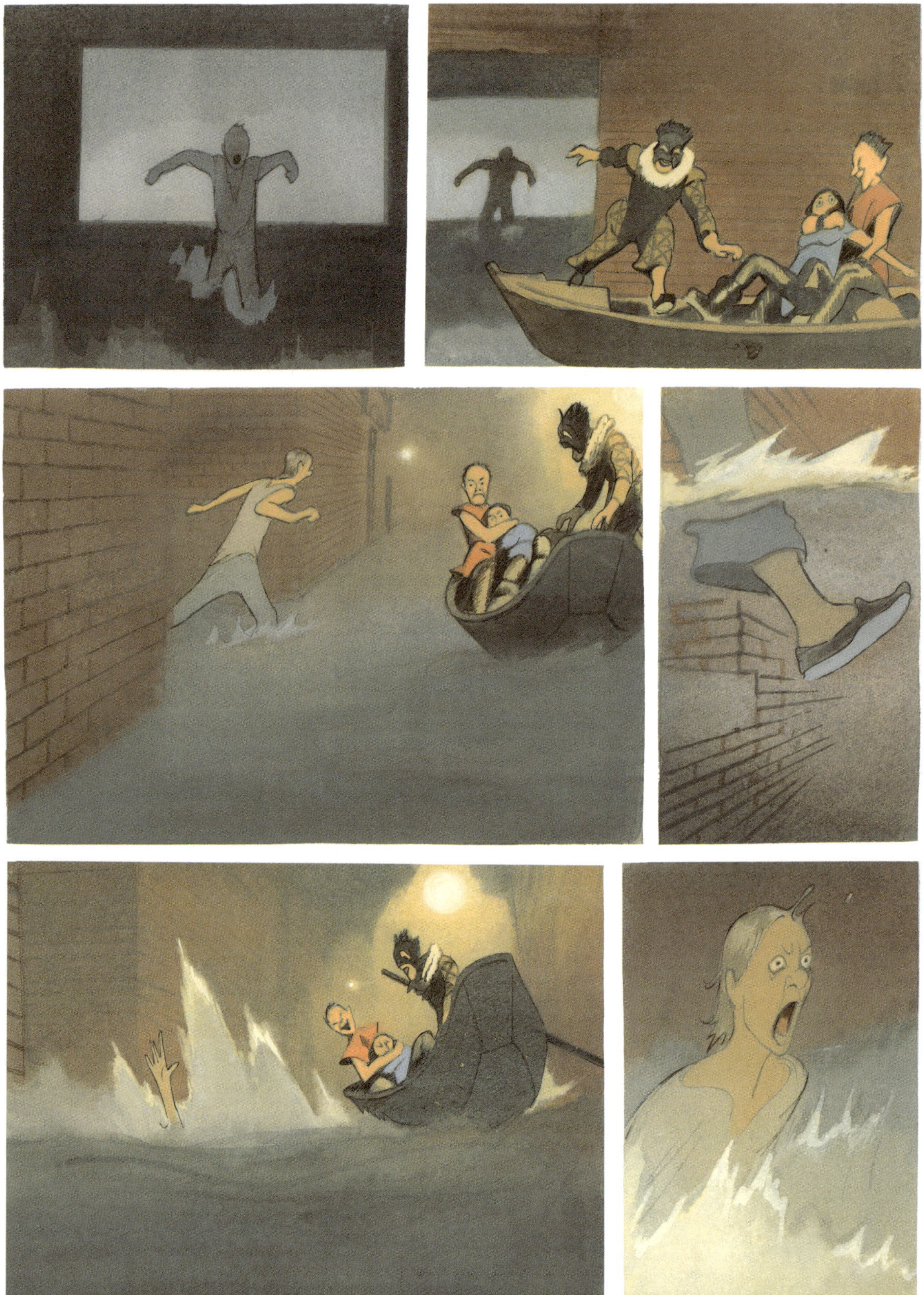

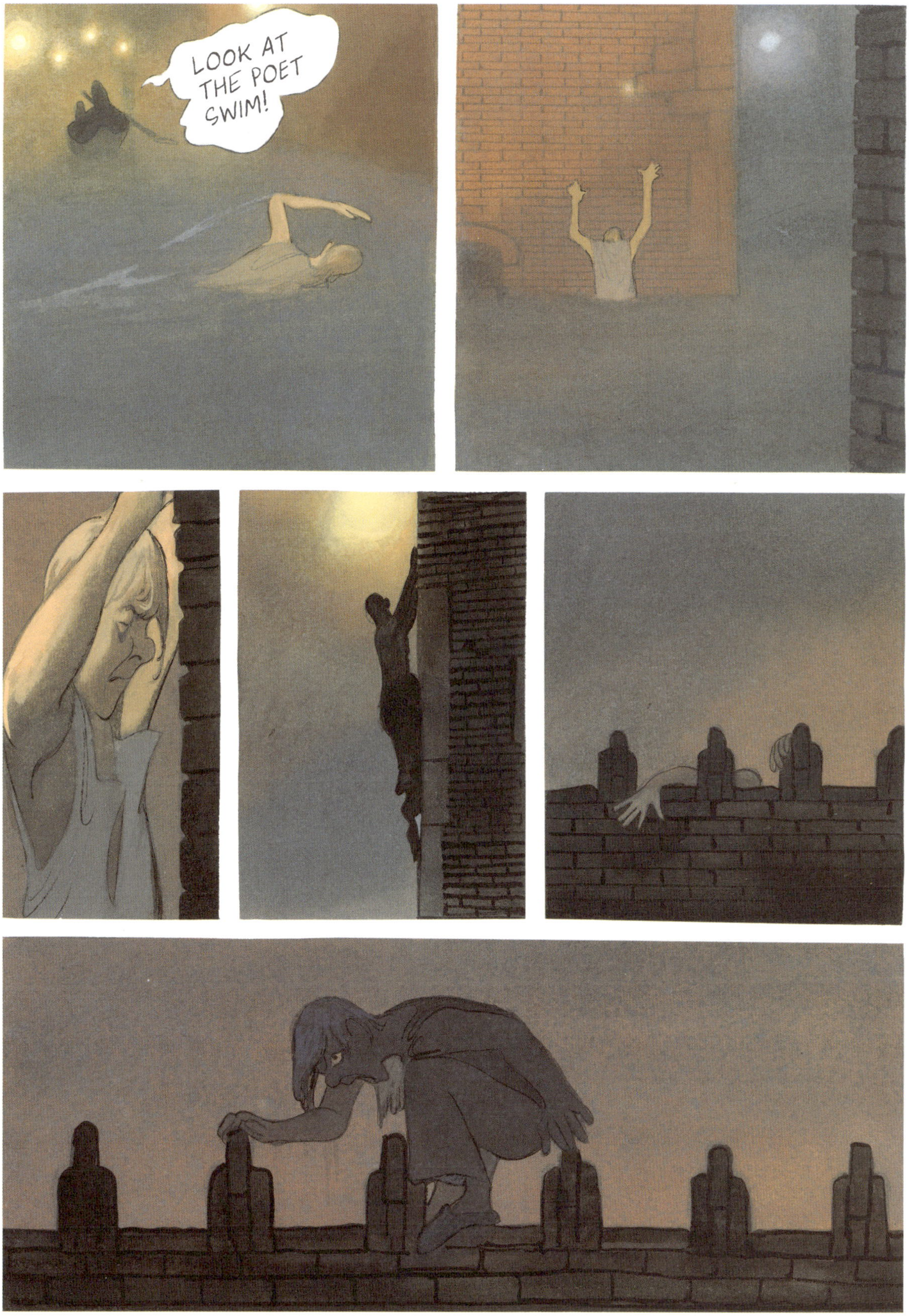
LOOK AT THE POET SWIM!

HURRY UP, I KEN BARELY KEEP 'ER DOWN'!

WHY YOU GO MIXING UP YOUR LIFE WITH THAT NUT?!

A PURTY LITTLE THING LIKE YOU...

...ASIDES HER NOSE!

AH HA HA HA...

SHE IS REAL PURTY...

ANYWAY, YOU SHOULDA THOUGHT TWICE.

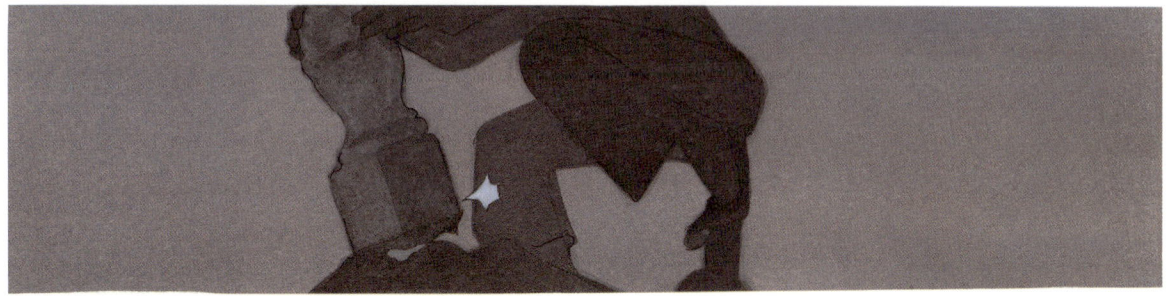

'CAUSE NOW YOU'RE ALL OURS...

AND WE'RE EVEN NUTTIER THAN HIM! AH HA HA!

PULL UP THAT DRESS, LET'S SEE WHAT WE GOT.

SHE'S NOT EVEN RESISTING.

THAT MEANS SHE LIKES IT.

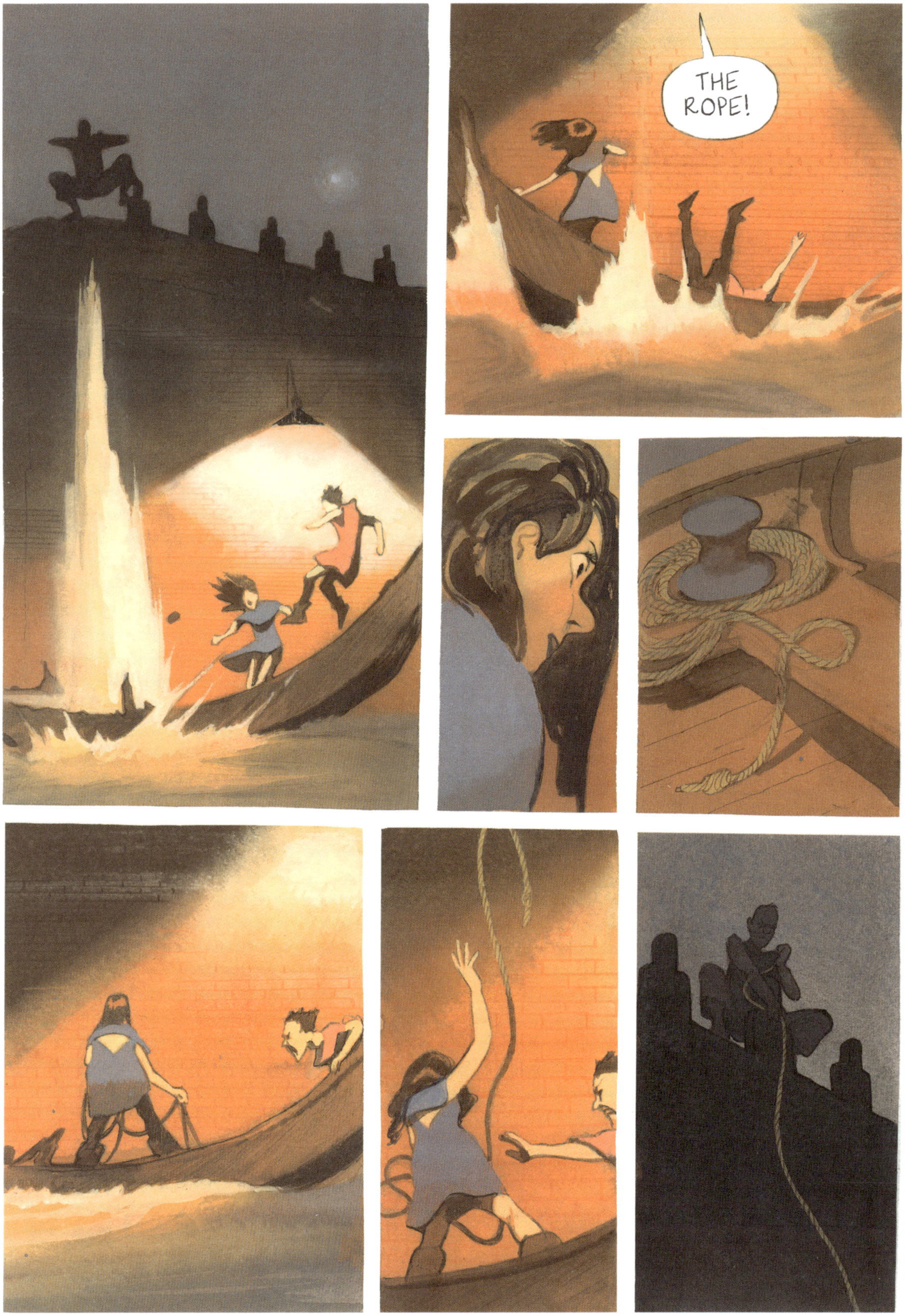
THE ROPE!

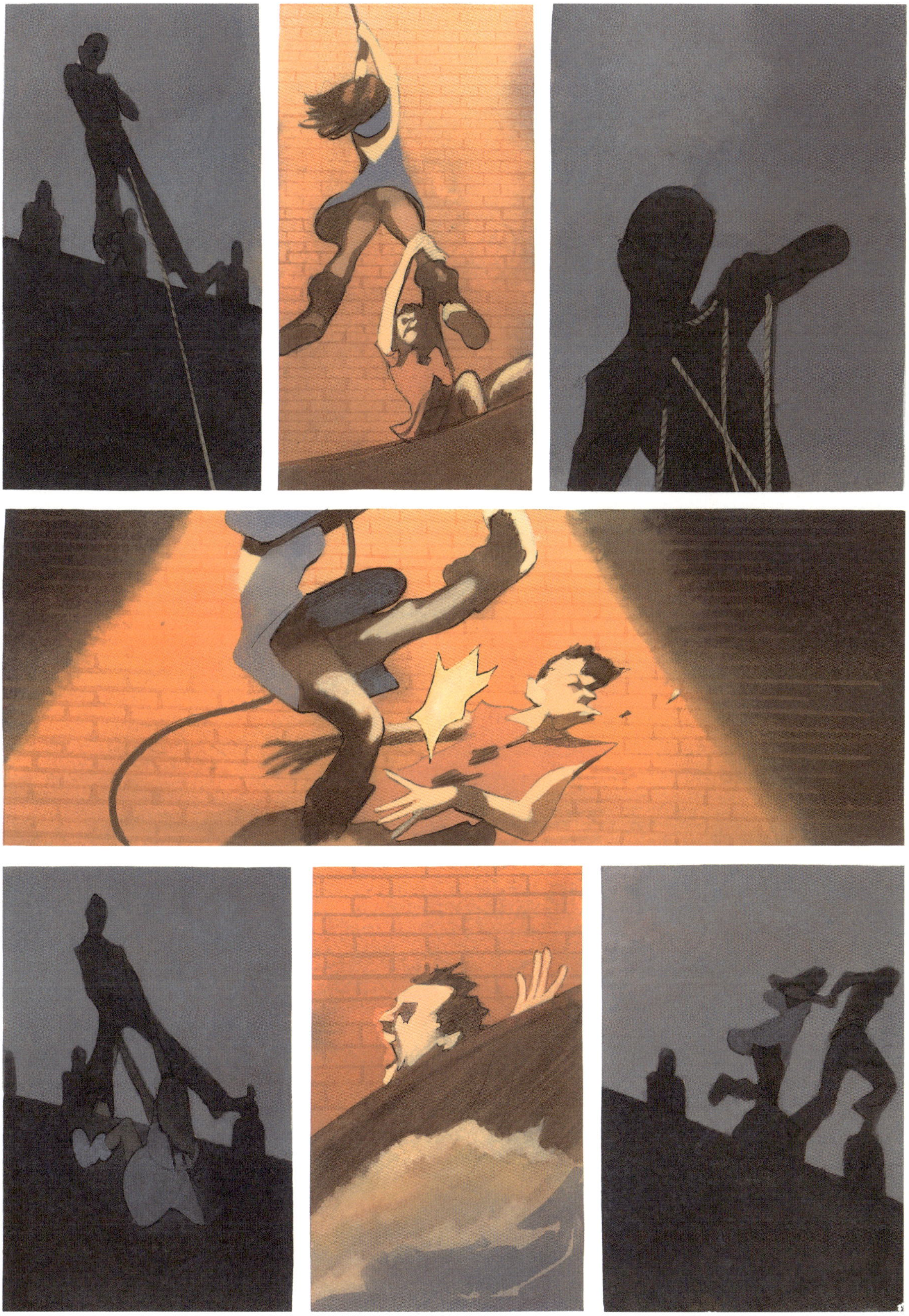

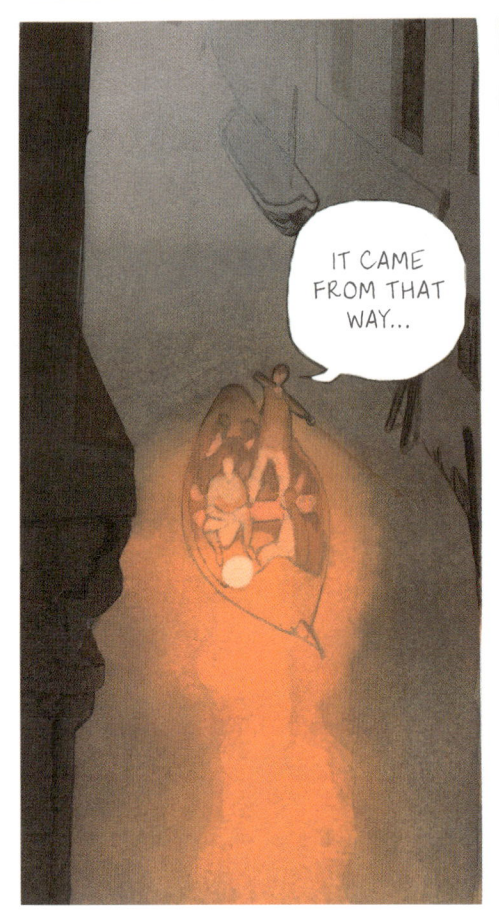

"HEAR THAT?"

"IT CAME FROM THAT WAY..."

"WHAT'S WRONG, ROSSELLA?"

"JUST A LITTLE NAUSEA."

ONE DÉJÀ VU AFTER ANOTHER...
I CAN'T MAKE SENSE OF THEM...
IT'S DORA.
SHE'S SCARED.
SHE CAN'T BE TOO FAR NOW.
TRY TO KEEP A CLEAR HEAD, DEAR.
WHAT DO YOU TWO FEEL?
NOTHING UNUSUAL, AT THE MOMENT.
SCATTER ACROSS THE AREA.

> YOUR REACTIONS WILL TELL US HOW SHE'S MOVING.

> THE CITY IS SO QUIET IN THE FOG.

> JUST SHOUT AND WE CAN LOCATE YOU.

> HOW DO YOU FEEL NOW?

> I'VE STOPPED BEING ABLE TO DISTINGUISH SPACES OF THOUGHT FROM FRAGMENTS OF TIME...

> WHAT EXTRAORDINARY POWER.

> DON'T FIGHT IT.

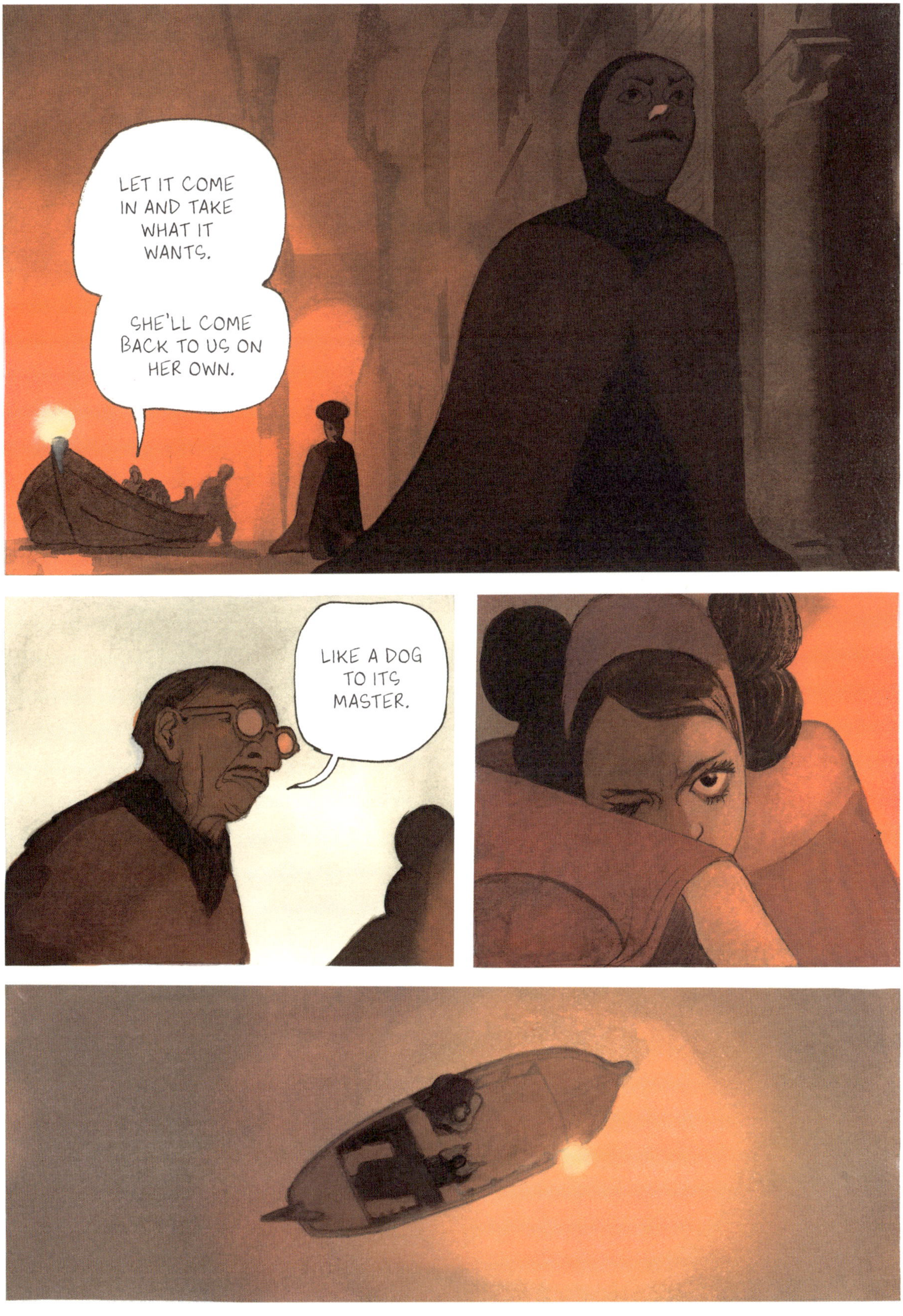
LET IT COME IN AND TAKE WHAT IT WANTS.
SHE'LL COME BACK TO US ON HER OWN.
LIKE A DOG TO ITS MASTER.

UUUUHHH...

AAAAAAH...!

WHAT HAPPENED TO THE OTHERS?

WE'RE REALLY SCREWED, MISTER...

MONA LOST ANOTHER EYE AND ARLECCHINO IS M.I.A.

WARN THEM IN THE GHETTO.

SEND THEM ALL HERE.

THEY RAN OFF BEHIND THE ARSENAL...

NOW GET MOVING OR I'LL BASH YOUR HEAD IN.

BEHIND THE ARSENAL.

HE'S ASKING FOR IT.

IS THAT BETTER?

BETTER, YEAH.

ROSSELLA IS CLOSE BY, PIERROT.

I JUST HEARD ONE OF HER THOUGHTS.

OH, DEAR ROSSELLA...

I KNOW I'M HURTING YOU

BUT PLEASE, STAY WITH ME...

ROSSELLA, WHERE DID YOU GO?
I LOST HER.
CAN'T YOU TRY A LITTLE HARDER?!
FAILURES.
ROSSELLA...
HUF
HUF
HUF
I'M SO SCARED...
HUF
HUF

WAIT.

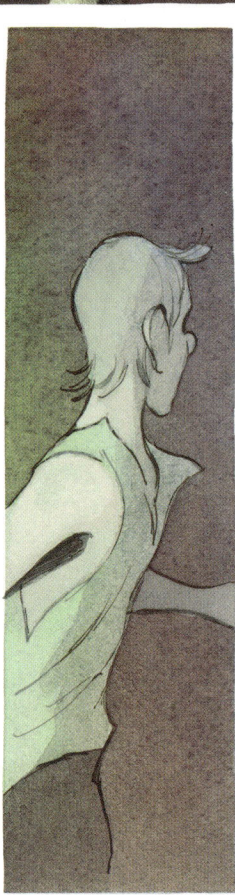

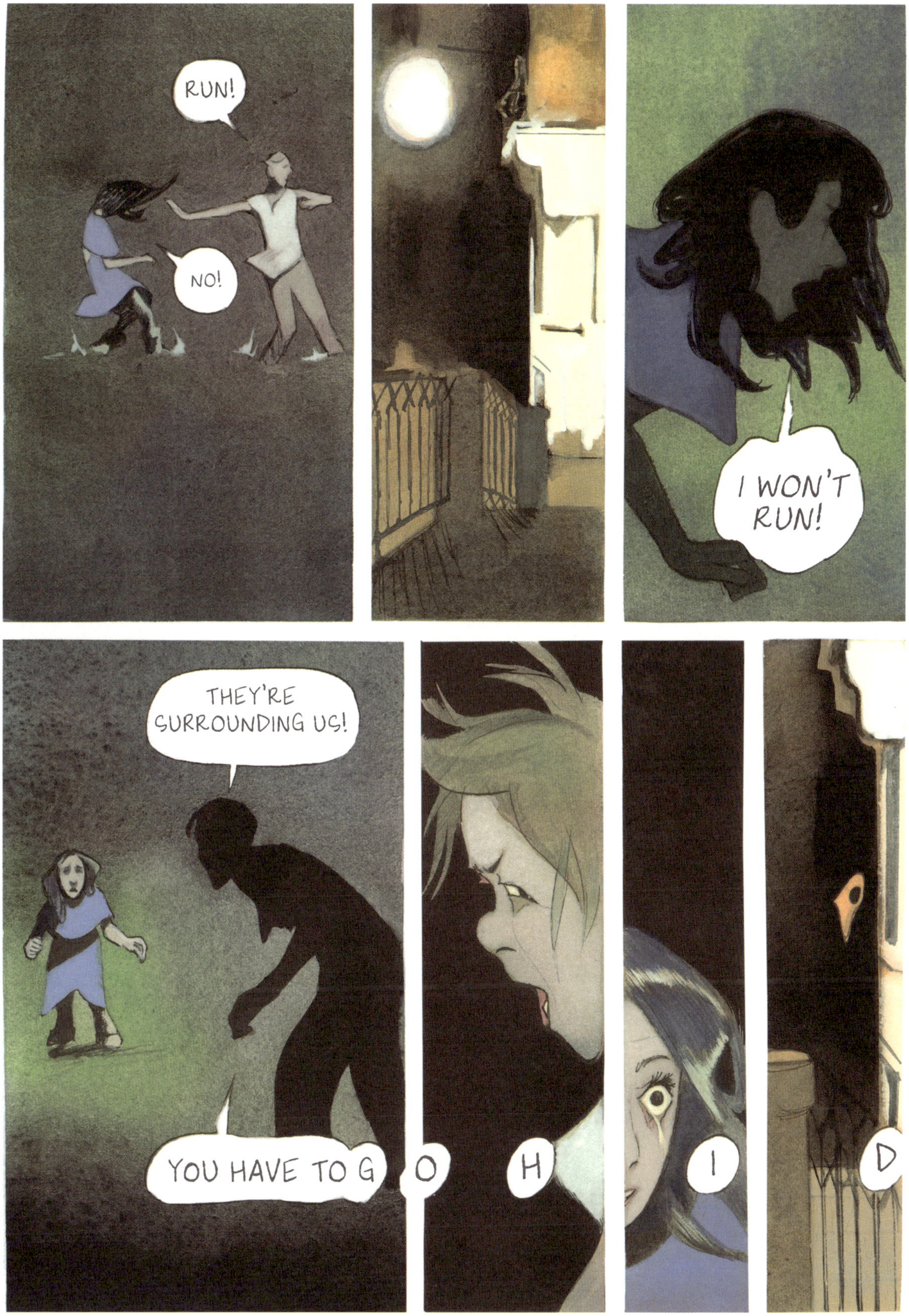
RUN!
NO!
I WON'T RUN!
THEY'RE SURROUNDING US!
YOU HAVE TO G
O
H
I
D

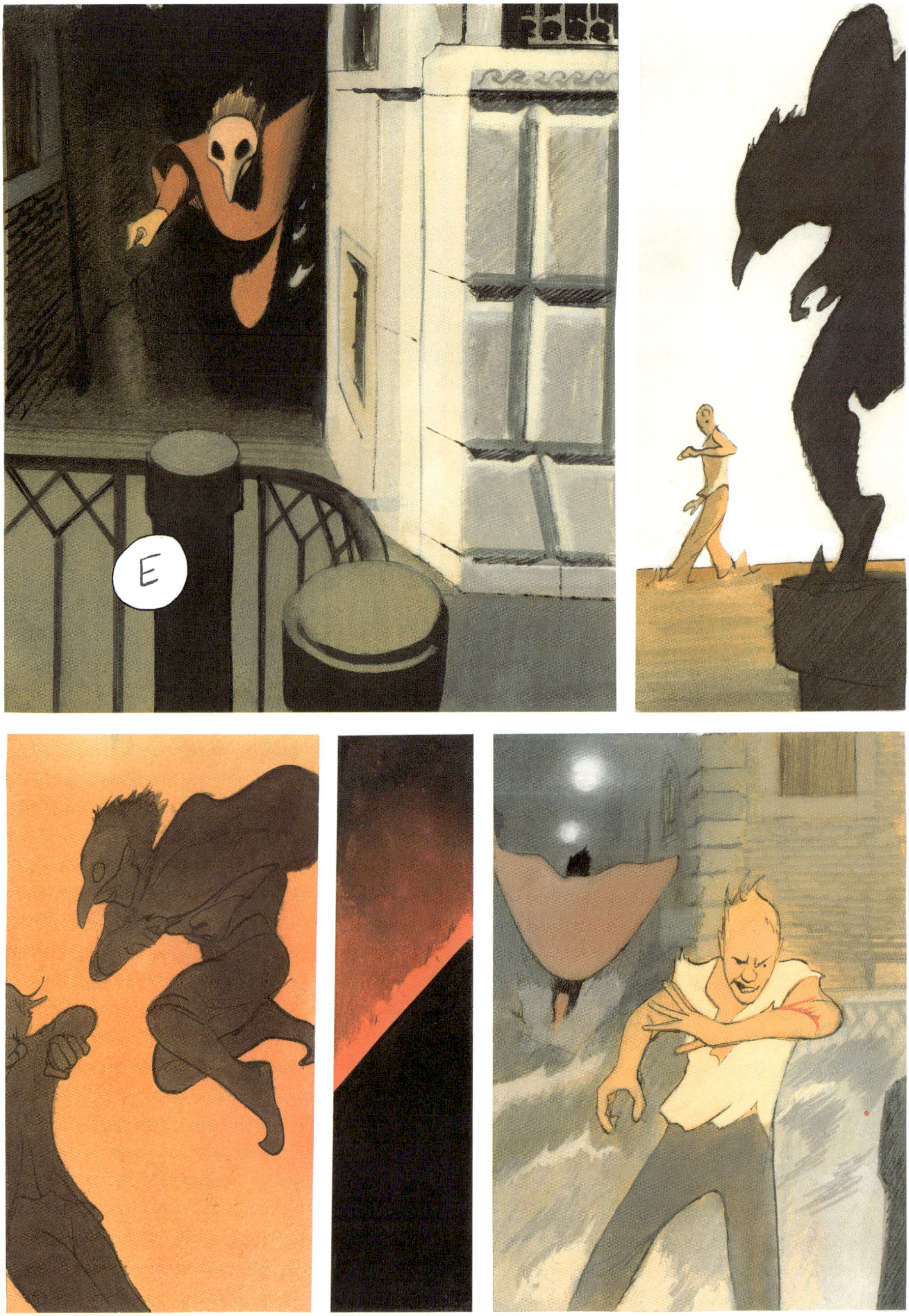
E

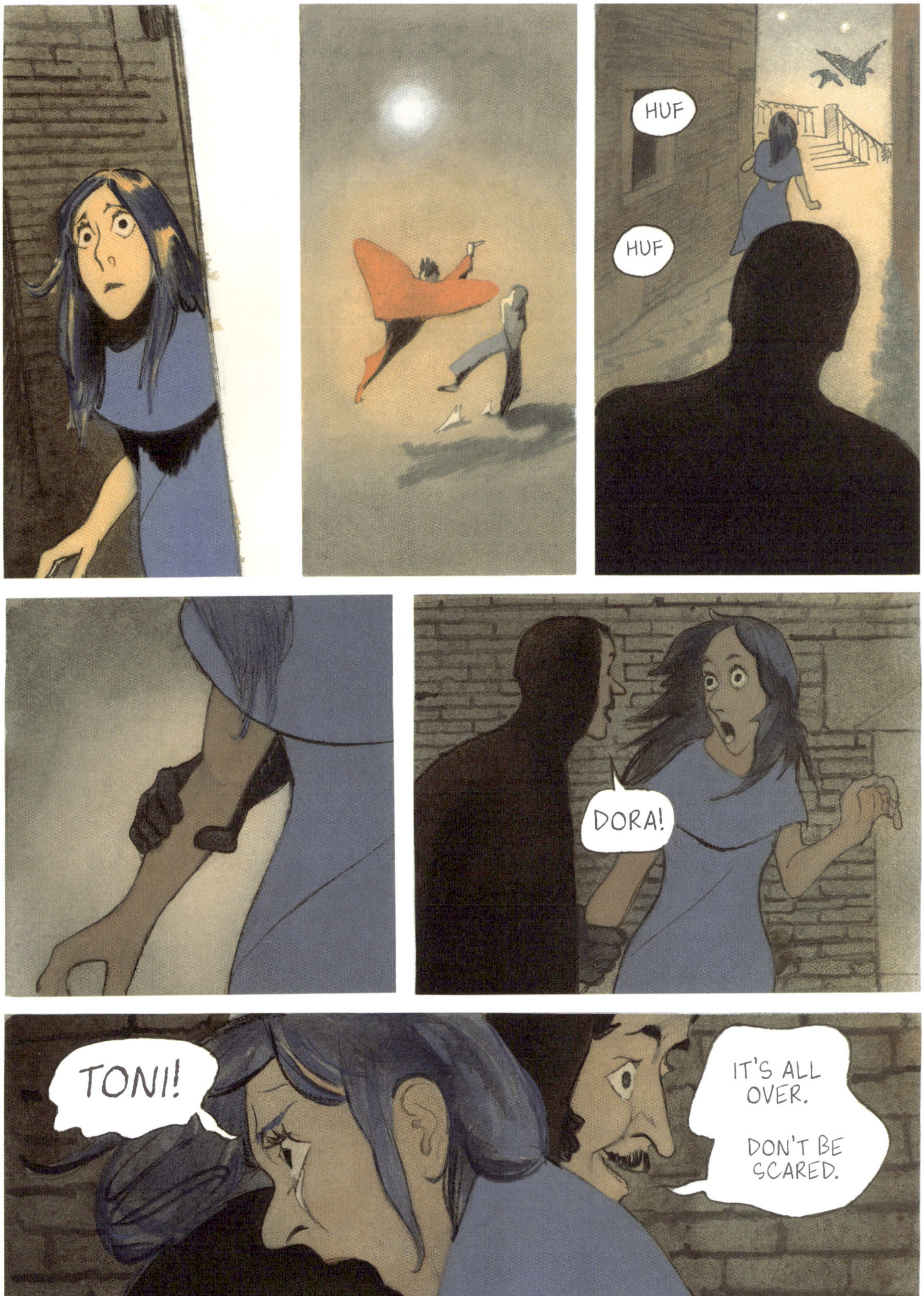
HUF
HUF
DORA!
TONI!
IT'S ALL OVER.
DON'T BE SCARED.

COME ON, WE HAVE TO HURRY.
WAIT.
PIERROT IS ALONE.
THEY'LL KILL HIM.
I KNOW A SHORTCUT...
HE'S OUT-NUMBERED AND...
HE CAN'T COME WITH US
BUT THEY'LL KILL HIM...

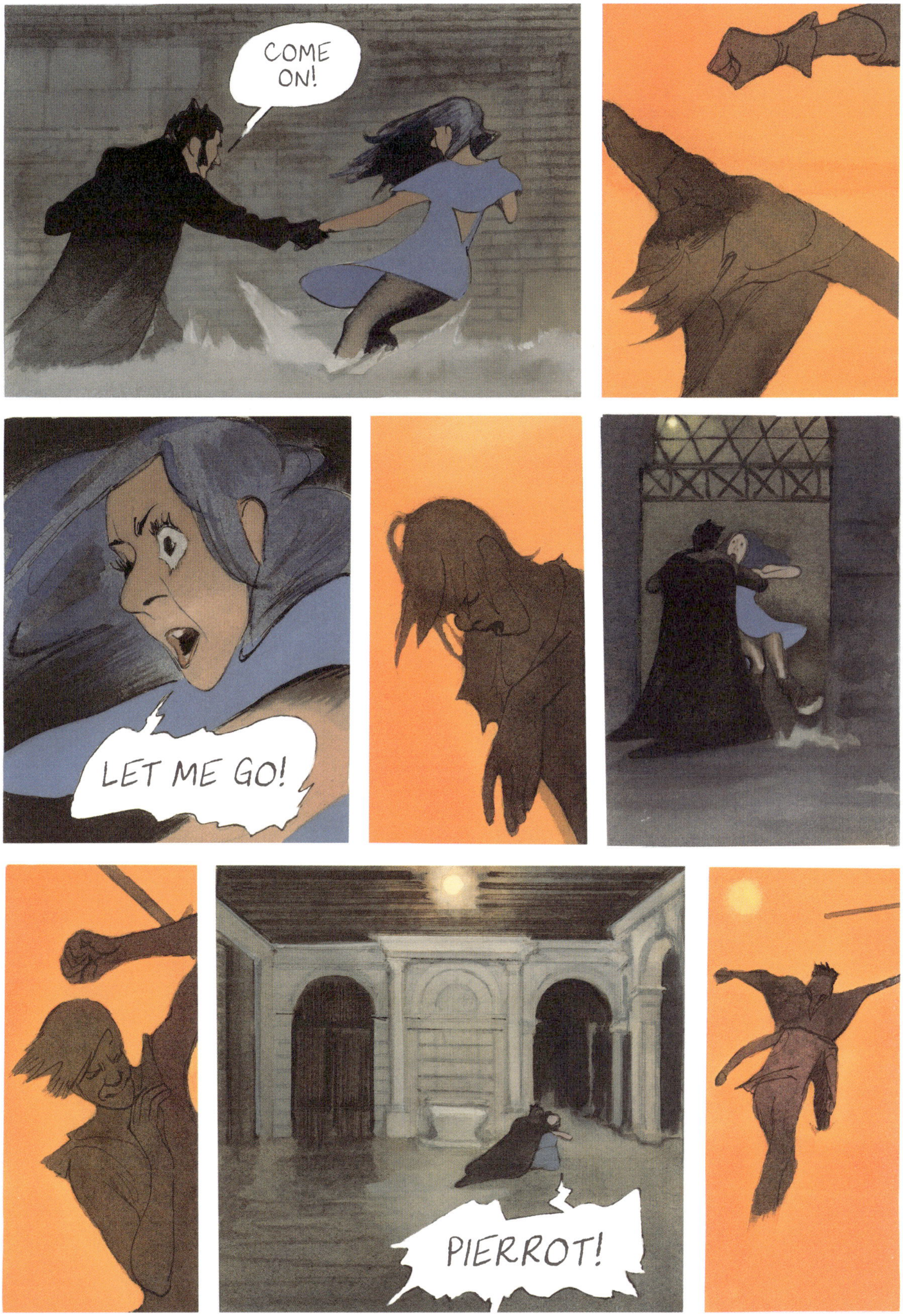
COME ON!
LET ME GO!
PIERROT!

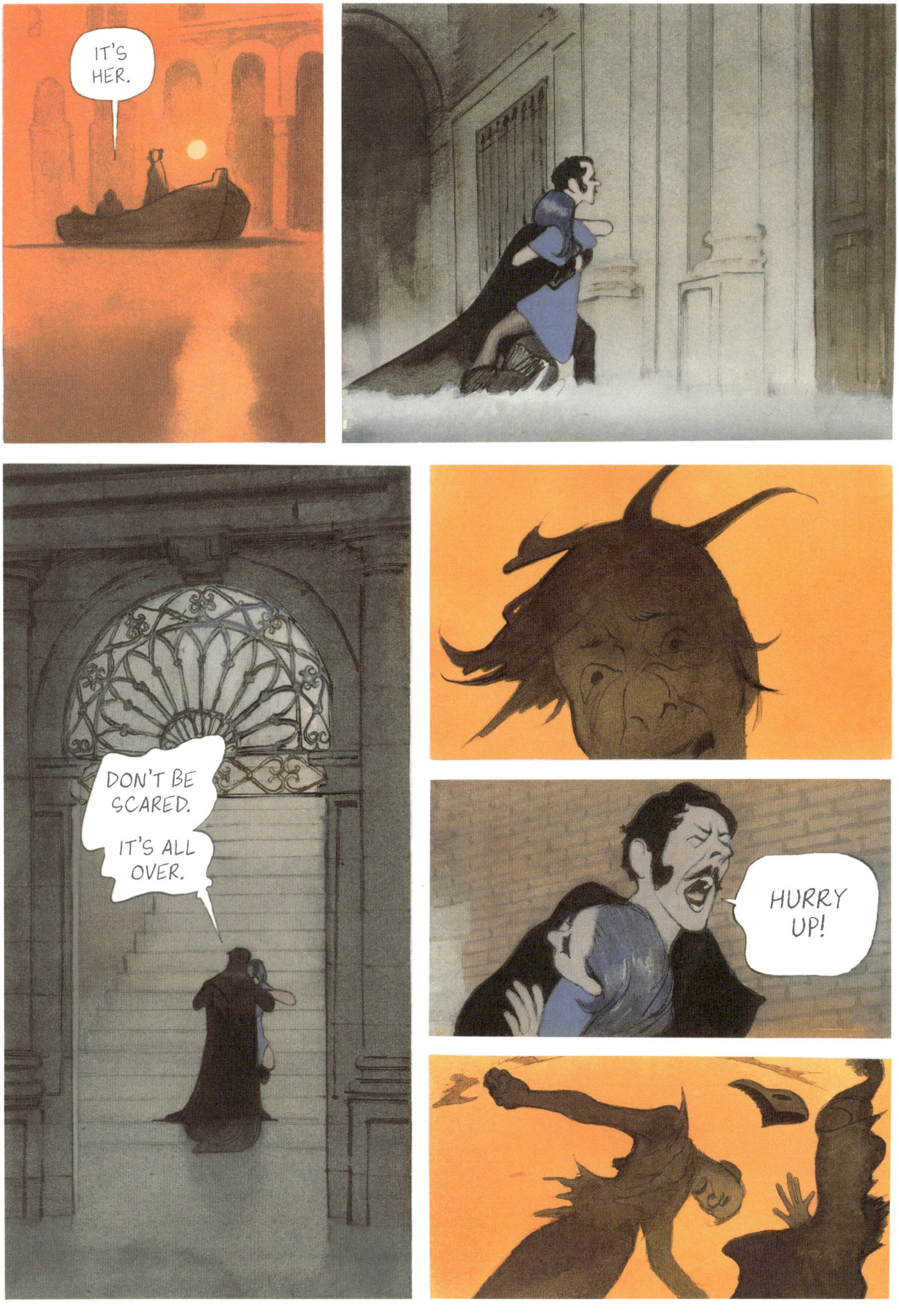
IT'S HER.
DON'T BE SCARED.
IT'S ALL OVER.
HURRY UP!

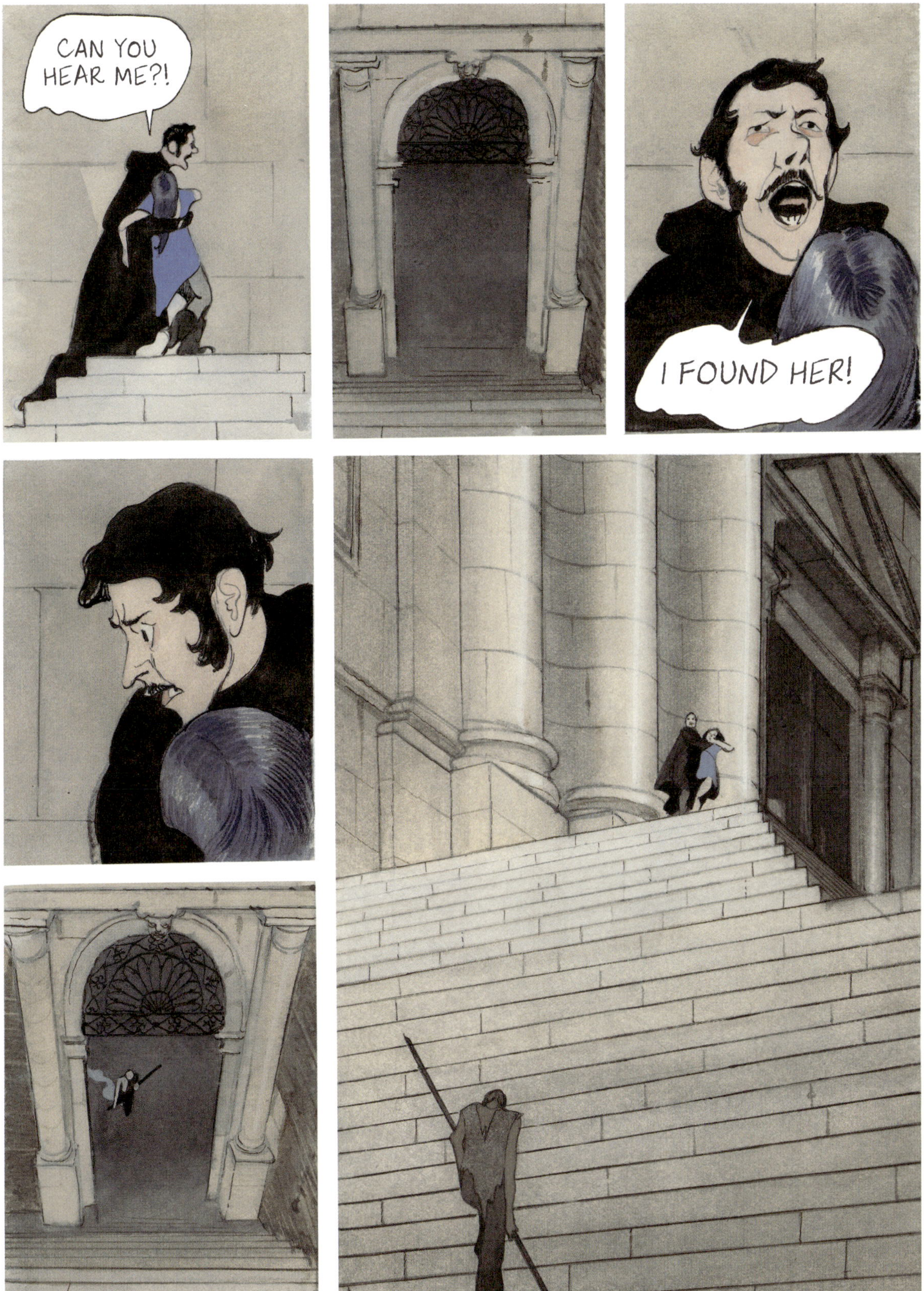
CAN YOU HEAR ME?!
I FOUND HER!

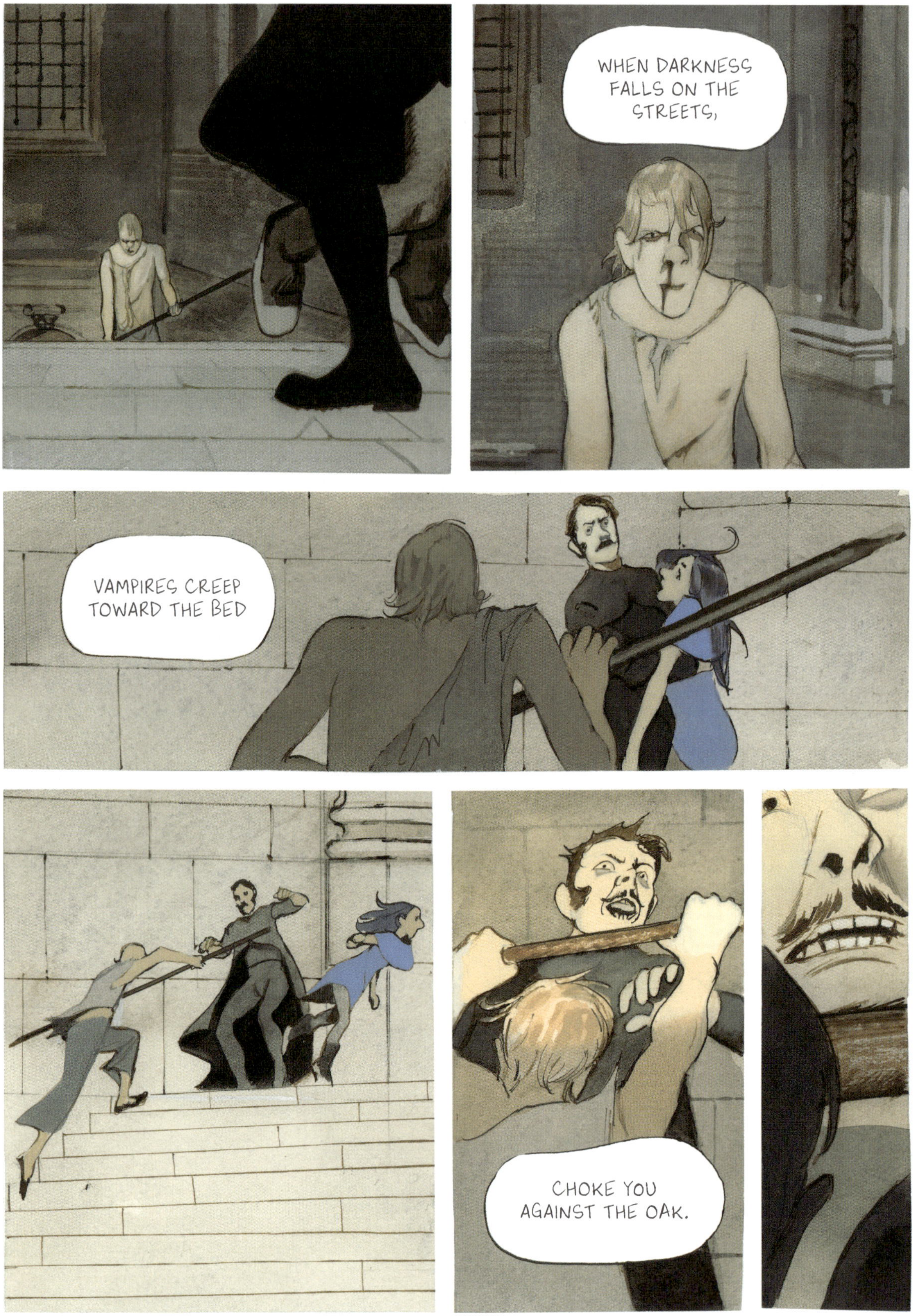
WHEN DARKNESS FALLS ON THE STREETS,
VAMPIRES CREEP TOWARD THE BED
CHOKE YOU AGAINST THE OAK.

IN THE HOUR WHEN THE AIR IS STILL

PIERROT, STOP!

PINNED AGAINST A MARBLE WALL

A WEIGHT ON THE TIGHTROPE OF TIME

A VOICE CRIES OUT FROM THE DEPTHS

BUT I

STOP, PLEASE

DON'T NOTICE THE END

RISE FROM THE WATER UP TO MY VEINS

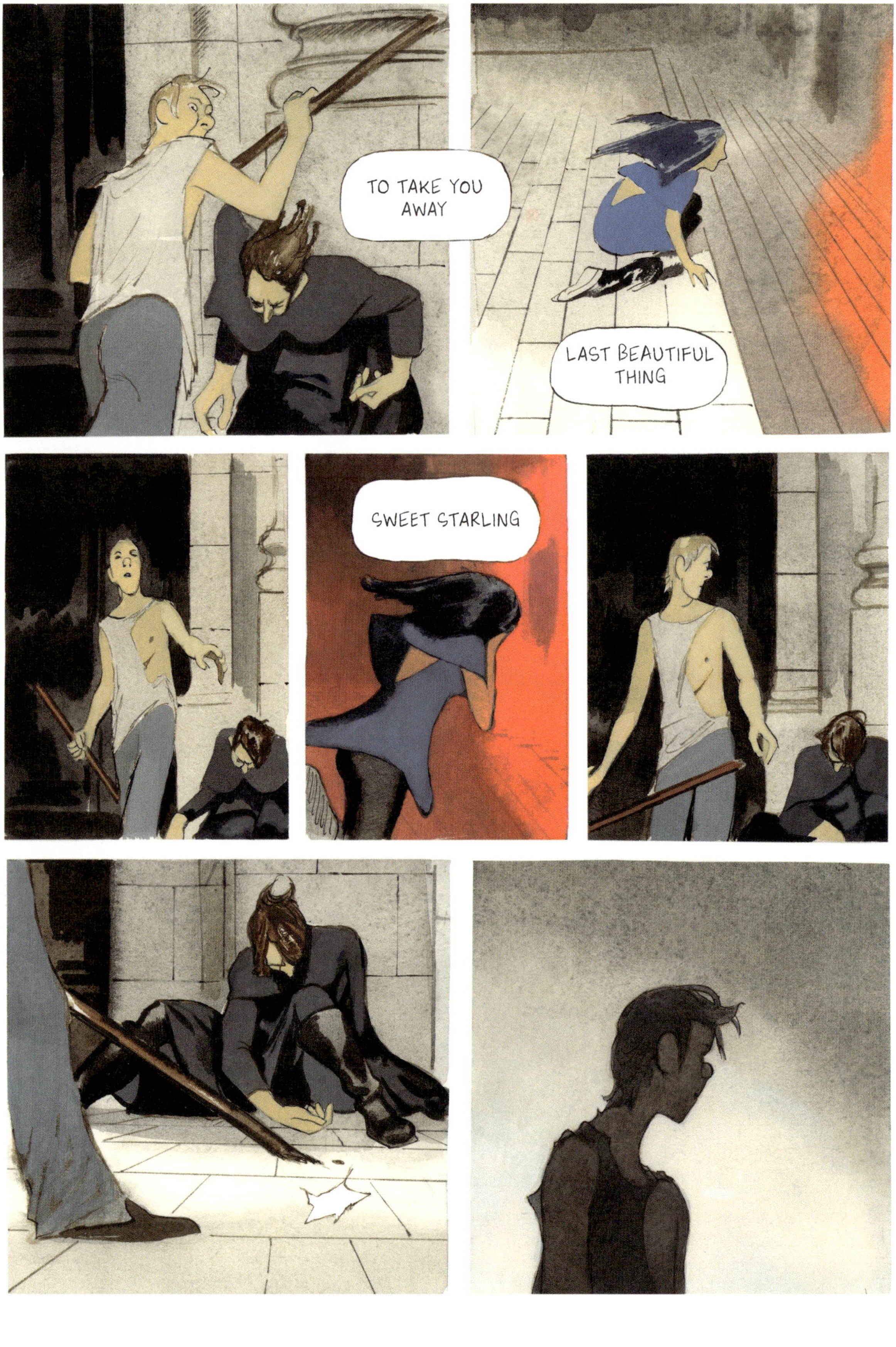
TO TAKE YOU AWAY
LAST BEAUTIFUL THING
SWEET STARLING

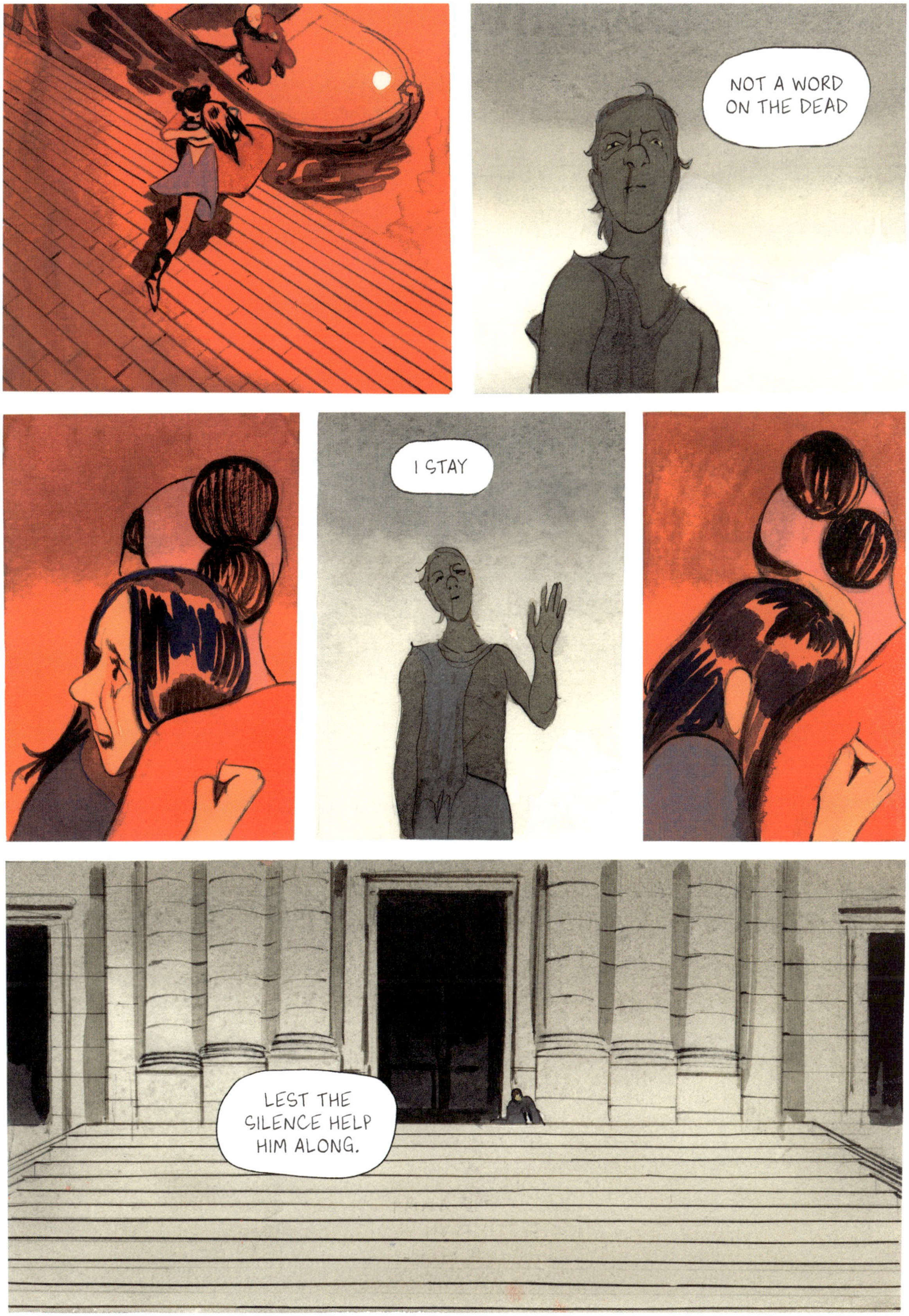
NOT A WORD ON THE DEAD
I STAY
LEST THE SILENCE HELP HIM ALONG.

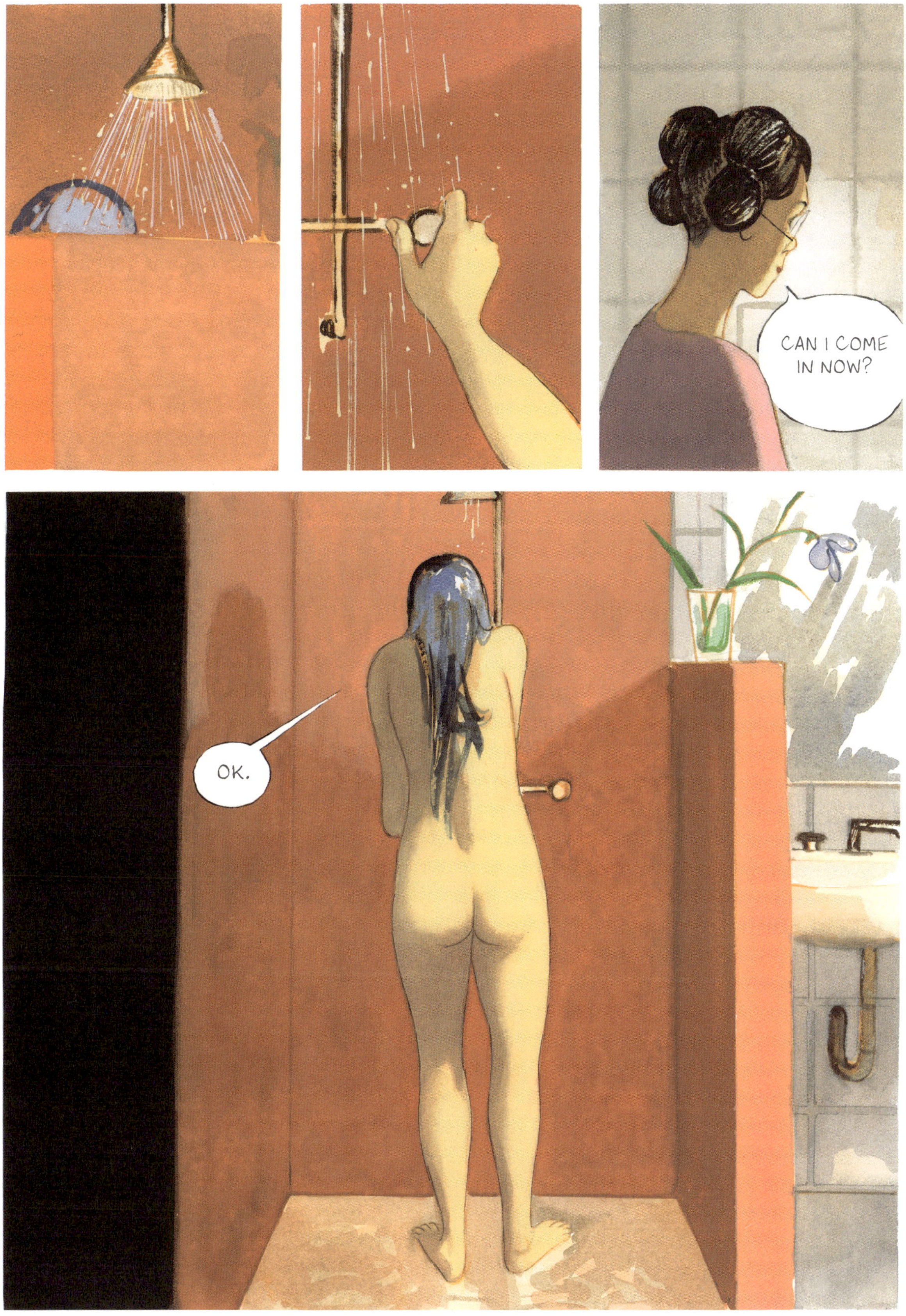
CAN I COME IN NOW?
OK.

"HOW'S THE WEATHER?"

"IT'S WINDY."

"THE TIDE HAS GONE DOWN."

"HOW LONG DID I SLEEP?"

"TWO-AND-A-HALF-DAYS."

I WANT TO GO BACK TO BED.
I'M TIRED.
LOOK.
I BROUGHT YOU SOMETHING.
TRY IT ON, IT DOESN'T FIT ME ANY-MORE.
ME?
I DON'T KNOW IF...
I DON'T THINK THAT...
WELL?

IT'S NICE.
NOW CAN I GO BACK TO SLEEP?
IT FITS YOU LIKE A GLOVE.
NOW WE CAN GO OUT.
IT'S OVER, ROSSELLA.
THE DOCTOR, OUR GROUP.
TELEPATHY.
ENOUGH.
LET'S GO TAKE A WALK.

I HAVEN'T SEEN VIVALDI AROUND.
HE NEVER WENT BACK TO SCHOOL.
I DON'T THINK WE'LL BE SEEING HIM AGAIN.

BETTER THAT WAY.
EVERY MAN FOR HIMSELF.
STARTING WITH ME.
I CAN'T FEEL ANYTHING ANYMORE.
VERY WELL.
I'M NORMAL AGAIN, FINALLY!
WHAT DID VIVALDI USED TO SAY?
"THOUGHT BELONGS TO INDIVIDUALS. TELEPATHY BELONGS TO THE GROUP."

PERFECT!
NO MORE GROUP, NO MORE TELEPATHY!
AND ALSO NO MORE
A BRIDGE...
A FLASH...
AND A BIG EXPLOSION.
WE ALL SAW IT, YOU KNOW.
THROUGH YOUR EYES.
THROUGH PIERROT'S.
THROUGH HIS MOTHER'S.

"YOU'RE RIGHT, THERE IS NO GROUP NOW."

"EVERYTHING IS HAPPENING OUTSIDE OF IT."

"OUTSIDE CELESTIA, ALL OVER THE LAGOON."

"AND EVEN FURTHER. CAN YOU HEAR IT?"

CAMPO DE LA CELESTIA

"THE ECHO OF THOUGHTS IN EVERYONE'S MINDS"

"SCATTERING IN THE WIND"

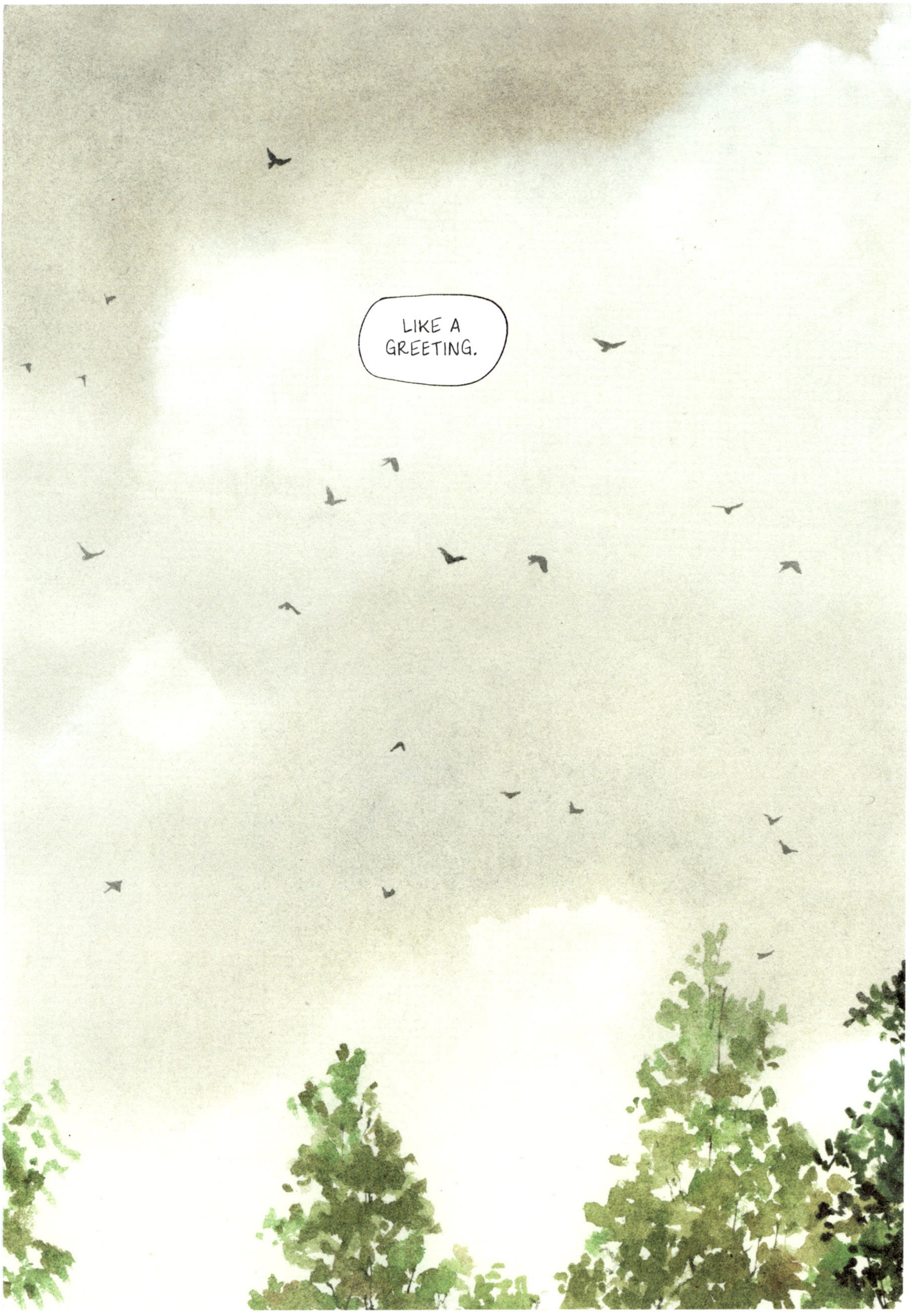
LIKE A GREETING.

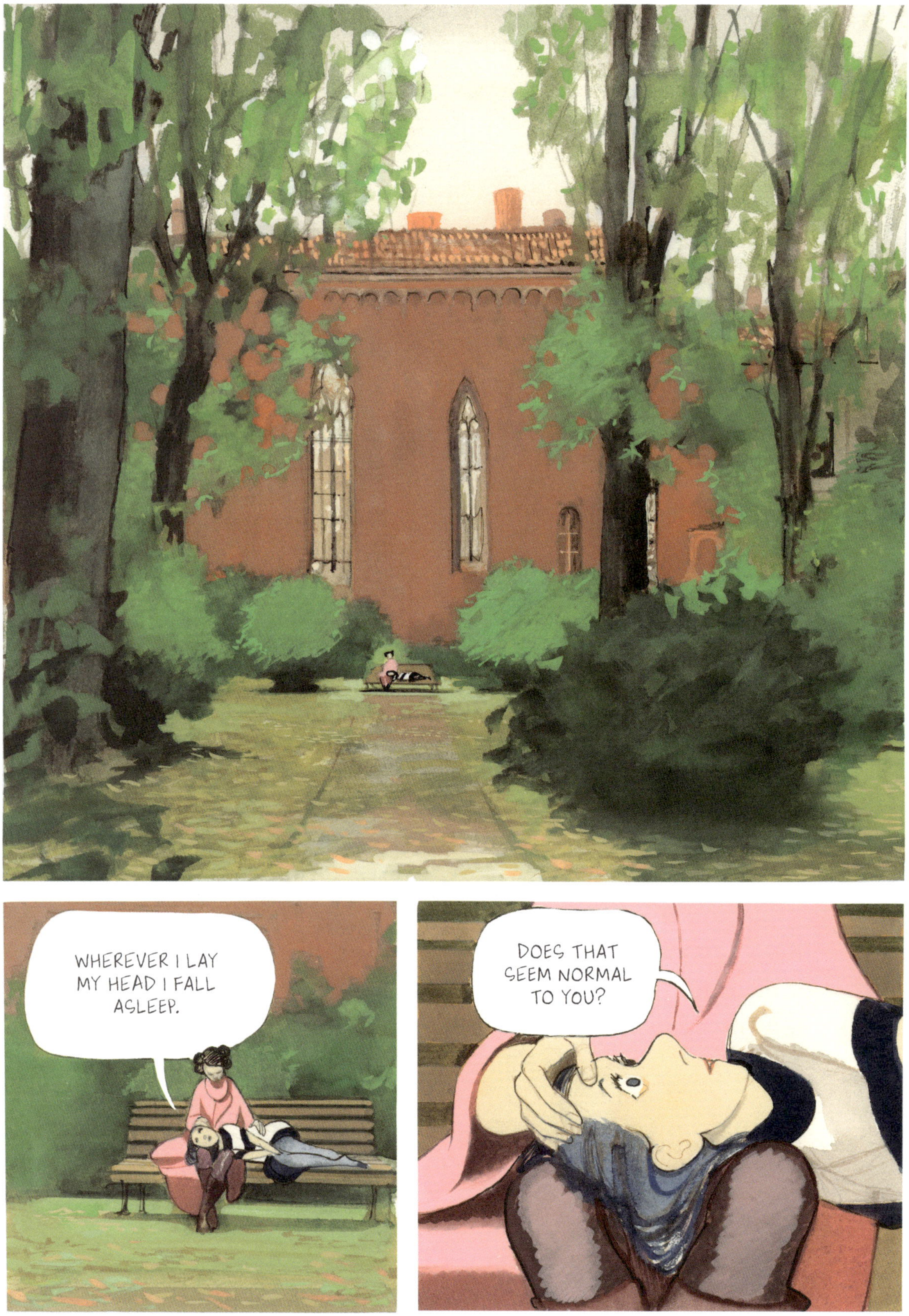
WHEREVER I LAY MY HEAD I FALL ASLEEP.
DOES THAT SEEM NORMAL TO YOU?

"IT'S PRETTY MUCH THE ONLY NORMAL THING IN THIS STORY."

"YOU KNOW, WHEN WE WERE SEARCHING FOR YOU, DURING THOSE DAYS..."

"I KEPT DREAMING ABOUT YOU."

"IT'S MY FAULT."

"I CAN BARELY CONTROL MYSELF ANYMORE."

"AND YOU JUST GO INTO OTHER PEOPLE'S DREAMS?"

"TELL ME WHAT THEY WERE LIKE."

WELL, IN ONE, IT WAS CELESTIA.

IT WAS DARK.

I SAW IT FROM OVERHEAD, LIKE I WAS FLYING.

YOU WERE WRAPPED IN A WOOL BLANKET, TAKING IN THE COOL NIGHT AIR.

IN ANOTHER, THERE WAS A STRANGE HOUSE SHAPED LIKE A TREE.

IT WAS PEAK TIDE.

THE SOUND OF A PIANO BEING PLAYED CAME FROM THE WINDOWS.

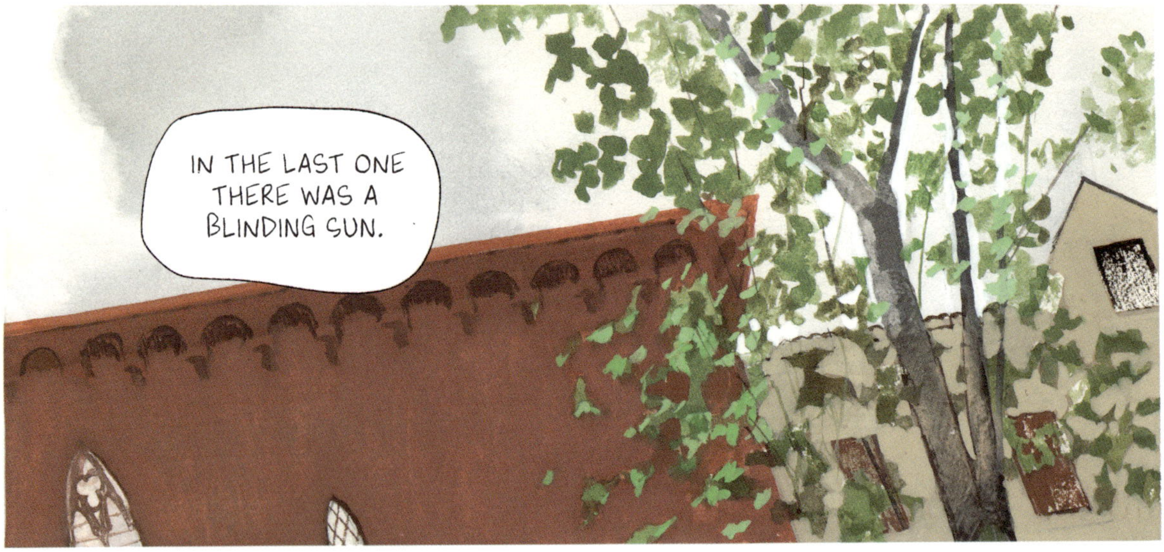
IN THE LAST ONE THERE WAS A BLINDING SUN.

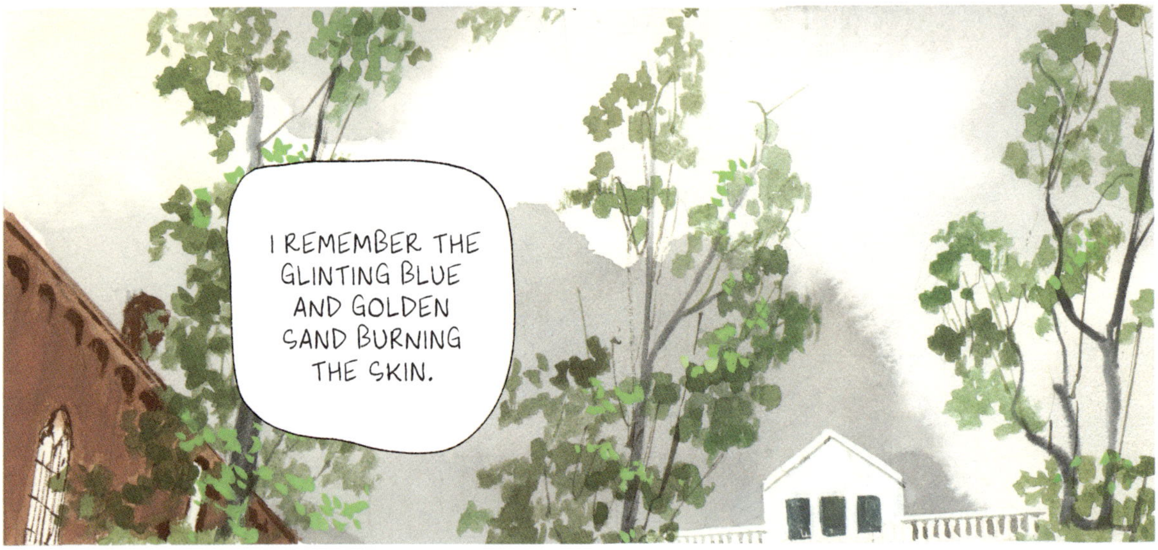
I REMEMBER THE GLINTING BLUE AND GOLDEN SAND BURNING THE SKIN.

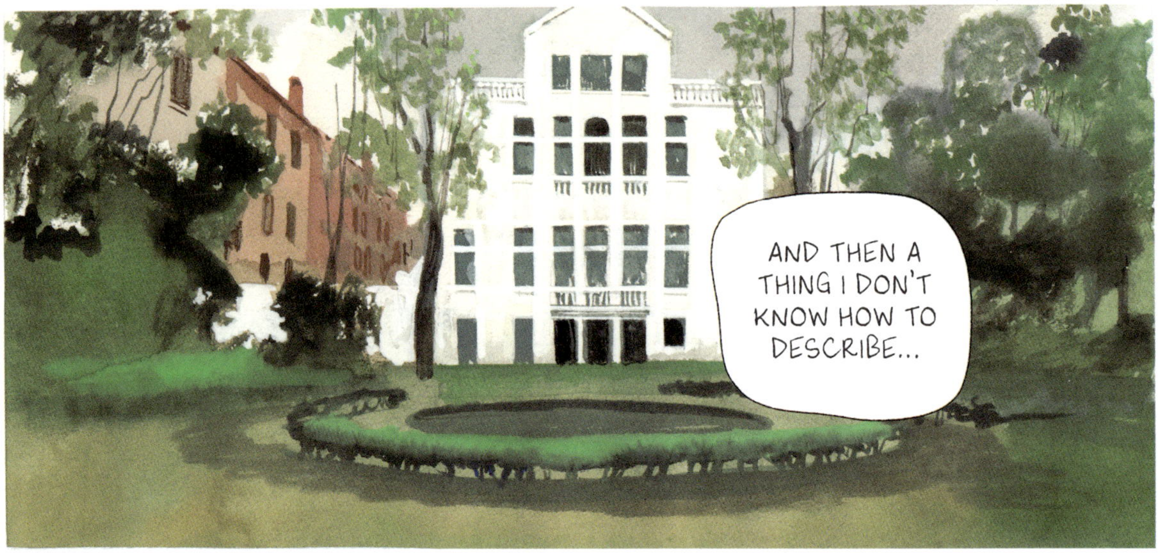
AND THEN A THING I DON'T KNOW HOW TO DESCRIBE...

BECAUSE IT WAS SO SMALL...
PRACTICALLY INVISIBLE.
SO SMALL THAT NOBODY NOTICED IT.
BUT IT WAS INSIDE YOU.
INSIDE ME?

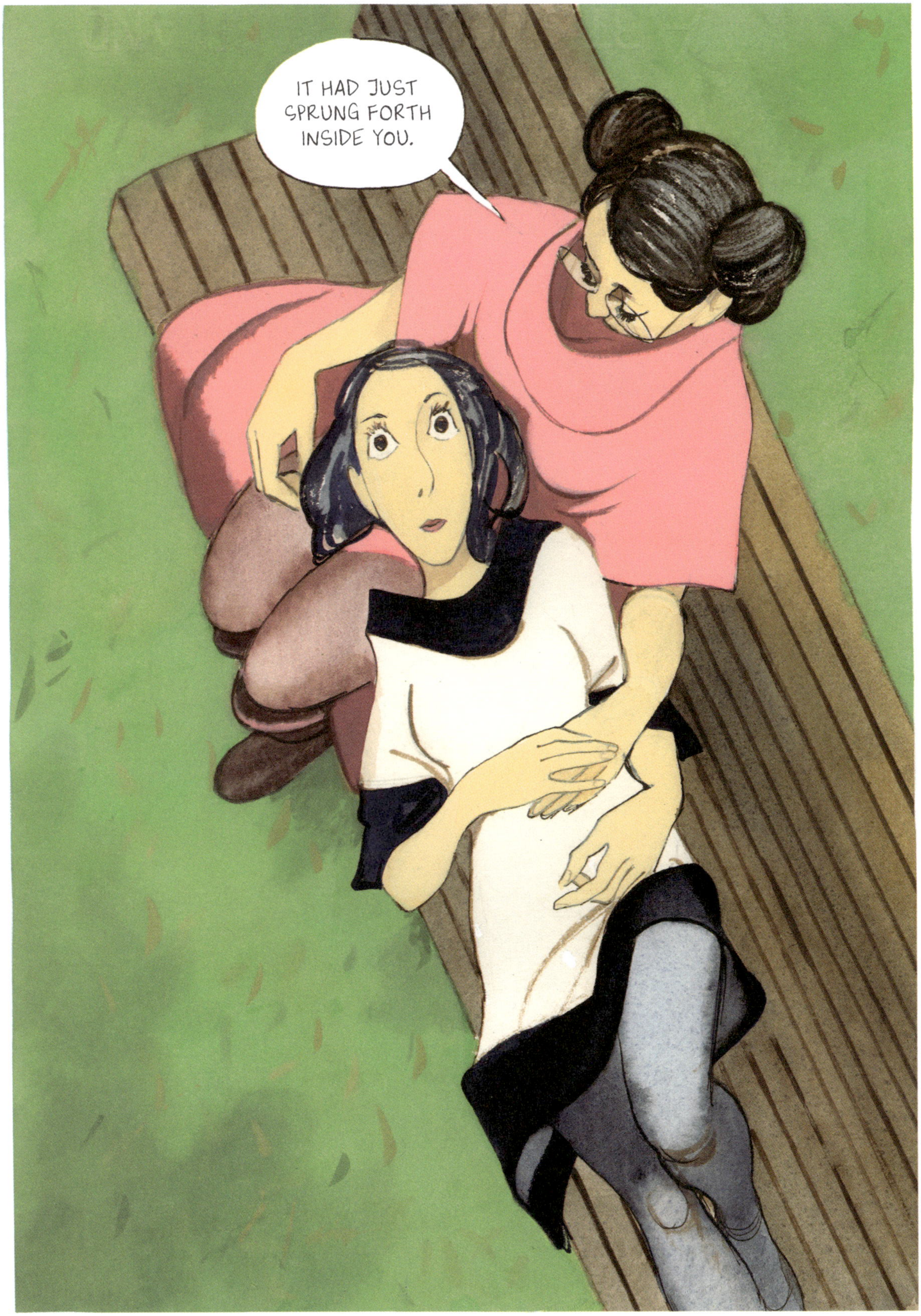
IT HAD JUST SPRUNG FORTH INSIDE YOU.

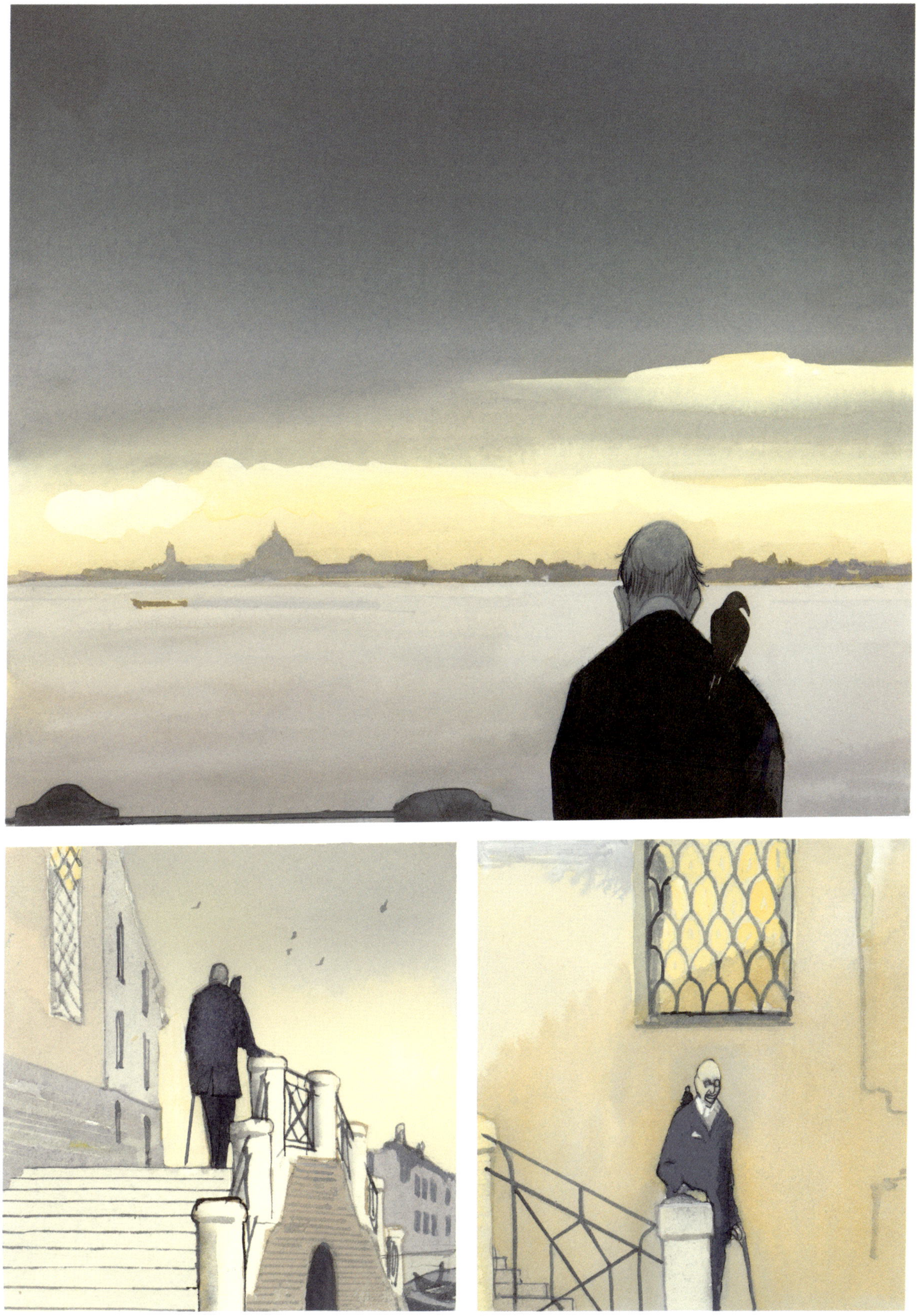

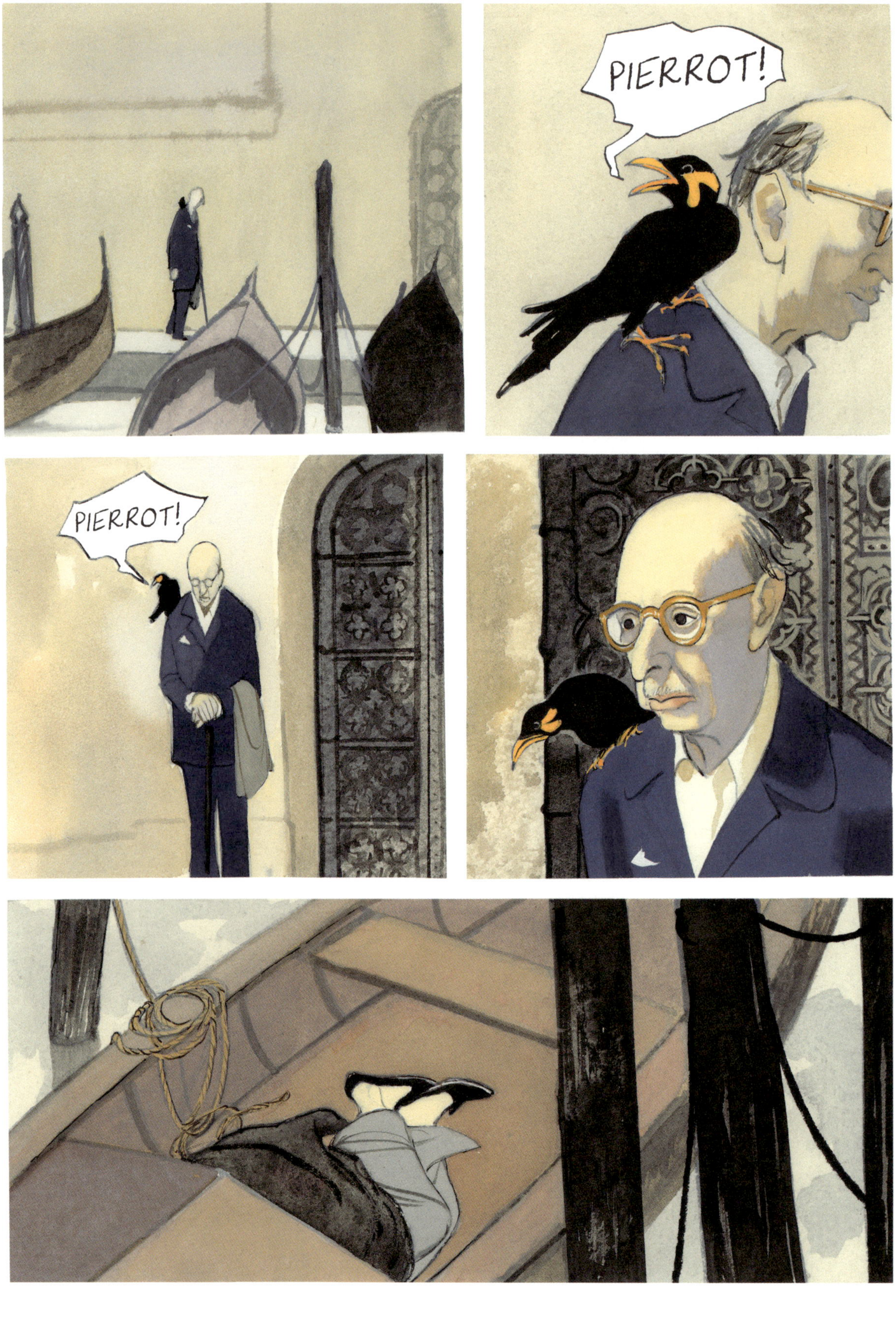
PIERROT!
PIERROT!

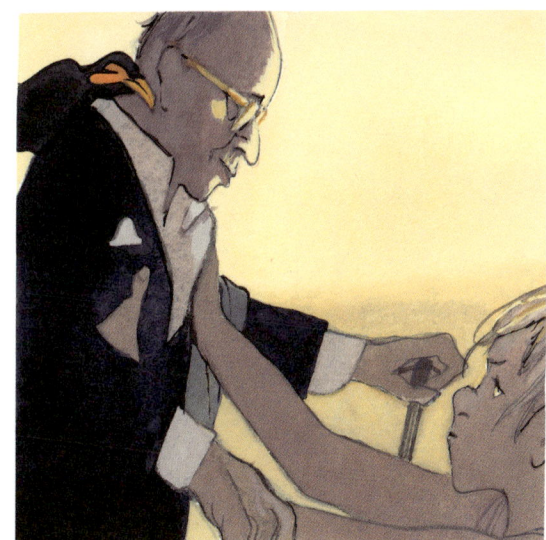

KREEK!

HELP ME, PIERROT.

HERE.

YOUR CLOAK.

THANKS, PAPA.
LET'S GO, PIERROT.
WHERE?
OUT.
I WANT TO SEE WHAT IT'S LIKE.

Thanks to Igort, Orsola Mattioli, Dimitri Moretti,
Daniel Pellegrino, Cristina Piovani, Piero Macola,
Matteo Alemanno, Nicola Andreani, Massimo Colella,
Emilio Varrà, Carlo Zoratti, Luca Baldazzi, Nicolas Grivel,
Clément C. Fabre, Alessandro Tota, Marino Neri.

Thanks to Mamma and Papà, Dani and Delica.

Thanks to Arianna and Milo for their love.

Dedicated to Marco Battistutta,
who shoots arrows at sunsets.

M.F.

OTHER BOOKS BY MANUELE FIOR

5,000 KM PER SECOND (2016)

THE INTERVIEW (2017)

BLACKBIRD DAYS (2018)

RED ULTRAMARINE (2019)

Celestia is copyright © 2021 Manuele Fior.
Rights arraged through Nicolas Grivel Agency.
This edition is copyright © 2021 Fantagraphics Books Inc.
English translation is copyright © 2021 Jamie Richards.
All Permission to reproduce content must be obtained
in writing from the publisher. All rights reserved.

FANTAGRAPHICS BOOKS INC.
7563 Lake City Way NE
Seattle, Washington, 98115
www.fantagraphics.com

Translated from Italian by Jamie Richards
Editor and Associate Publisher: Eric Reynolds
Book Design: Manuele Fior & Justin Allan-Spencer
Production: Paul Baresh
Publisher: Gary Groth
ISBN 978-1-68396-438-4
Library of Congress Control Number 2020949179
First printing: July 2021
Printed in Republic of Korea